INFINITE
PROGRESS

How the Internet and Technology Will End
Ignorance, Disease, Poverty, Hunger, and War

BYRON REESE

GREENLEAF
BOOK GROUP PRESS

Published by Greenleaf Book Group Press
Austin, Texas
www.greenleafbookgroup.com

Distributed by Greenleaf Book Group LLC
For ordering information or special discounts for bulk purchases, please contact Greenleaf Book Group LLC at PO Box 91869, Austin, TX 78709, 512.891.6100.

Design and composition by Greenleaf Book Group LLC
Cover design by Greenleaf Book Group LLC

Publisher's Cataloging-In-Publication Data
(Prepared by The Donohue Group, Inc.)

Reese, Byron.
  Infinite progress : how the internet and technology will end ignorance, disease, poverty, hunger, and war / Byron Reese. — 1st ed.

    p. ; cm.

  Includes bibliographical references and index.
  Issued also as an ebook.
  ISBN: 978-1-60832-404-0 (hardbound)

    1. Internet—Social aspects. 2. Technology—Social aspects. 3. Forecasting.
I. Title.

HM851 .R44 2013
303.483/3   2012951267

Part of the Tree Neutral® program, which offsets the number of trees consumed in the production and printing of this book by taking proactive steps, such as planting trees in direct proportion to the number of trees used:
www.treeneutral.com

Printed in the United States of America on acid-free paper

13 14 15 16   10 9 8 7 6 5 4 3 2 1
First Edition

To my parents, who taught me how to think.
And to my children, who give me a reason to.

CONTENTS

Introduction: The Case for Optimism   1

An Optimist's Reasoning, in Five Easy Premises   9

    Futurists Often Get It Wrong   10

    History Can Help Us Get It Right   12

    Internet Technology + Human Ingenuity =
       Infinite Promise   14

    Accelerating Progress is Inevitable   19

    The New Renaissance Has Begun   22

The End of Ignorance   29

    The High Cost of Ignorance   29

    Your Digital Echo   34

    Surprise! We share.   37

    Data and Knowledge   40

    Wise Decisions   43

    The Jim Haynes Effect   48

    How the Internet and Technology
       Will End Ignorance   53

The End of Disease   55

Disease (and Cure) Defined   56

"Could You Patent the Sun?"   59

Dairymaids, Folklore, and Smallpox   63

A Reason to Hope   67

Disease: A Timeline   68

We May Already Have the Answer   72

The Promise of the Genome   79

Information and Disease   86

How the Internet and Technology
    Will End Disease   91

The End of Poverty   93

How Is Wealth Created?   94

Scarcity   102

Free Trade, Technological Displacement,
    and Outsourcing   108

Chad Gets a Better Job   114

Robots and Nanites and Jobs, Oh My!   117

Wealth and Poverty in History   132

Earning a "Living"   144

Left Behind   147

How the Internet and Technology
    Will End Poverty   155

The End of Hunger   159

A History of the Hungry   160

Nutrition   166

Enough Food Already   170

Why Is There Hunger?   175

Agriculture 1.1   179

The End of the Farmer   186
Genomics   191
Information and Agriculture   200
Food as a Human Right   205
Beyond Hungry to Healthy   212
How the Internet and Technology
    Will End Hunger   213

The End of War   215

War   216
Civilization   217
Must We End War?   225
Is It Possible to End War?   227
The Difficulties of Ending War   232
How the Internet and Technology
    Will End War   235

In Conclusion   279

Do We Lose Our Humanity?   279
What Could Possibly Go Wrong?   283
Optimism, Revisited   291

Acknowledgments   295
Index   297

Introduction

THE CASE FOR OPTIMISM

I'm not sure whether the optimists or the pessimists are right,
but I know this: The optimists are going to get something done.
—J. Craig Venter

There exist two sorts of optimists. There are the people who hope the future will be better. Then there are the people who reason the future will be better.

I am the second variety.

In this book, I maintain the future will be without ignorance, disease, hunger, poverty, and war, and I support those assertions with history, data, and reason. After reading my arguments, you may or may not believe the future I describe is *inevitable*, as I say it is. But I hope you will at least believe it to be possible. And you may even—reasonably, optimistically—think it to be quite likely.

If you happen to live in the United States, as I do, optimism should be coursing through your very veins. America was birthed in optimism. The American Revolution was not the story of the "have nots" overthrowing the "haves" in a bid to increase their place in society. Just the contrary: It was the entrenched social order, those with everything to lose, who decided to fight a war with the most powerful country on the planet against overwhelming odds.

But all along, they believed they would ultimately prevail—and not just win the war, but also do something epic that would change the course of history for all time. They believed they would build a great empire of liberty that would begin a series of revolutions for liberty all around the world. And they did! While America was just a sliver of land on the Eastern Seaboard, these founders foresaw a time when it would fill up the entire continent.

As the nation grew, so did what came to be called the American Dream. It is a simple premise and yet, at the same time, an article of faith—a faith that the future would be better than the past. You may come to America and be poor, but if you work hard, your children will have a better life and a better opportunity. And their children even more. John Adams wrote of it in a letter to his wife in 1780:

> I must study Politicks and War that my sons may have liberty to study Mathematicks and Philosophy. My sons ought to study Mathematicks and Philosophy, Geography, natural History, Naval Architecture, navigation, Commerce and Agriculture, in order to give their Children a right to study Painting, Poetry, Musick, Architecture, Statuary, Tapestry and Porcelaine.

Our national character is centered on optimism. Just as ancient cultures used creation myths to explain their beginnings, we have stories of the "American Experience" that we tell again and again until they acquire mythic status. We were born and raised on these optimistic narratives: The Immigrant Who Arrives with Nothing and Makes a Fortune. The Regular Worker Who Risks It All and Strikes It Rich. The Person Who Dreams Bigger than Anyone Else and Makes It Happen. The Garage Tinkerer Who Invents the Next Big Thing.

By the midpoint of the twentieth century, America's dreamers were preoccupied with the future—and not just any old future, but the great and glorious future that seemed inevitable. Everywhere you turned, people were speculating about, or building models of, the "House of Tomorrow," the "Car of Tomorrow," or the "Workplace of Tomorrow." At expositions and fairs around the globe, exhibits forecast a coming day when everything would be faster, cheaper, cleaner, easier, and just altogether more wonderful. Science would solve everything, prosperity would grow indefinitely, and people would thrive.

In the spirit of that time, the audacity and the unwavering confidence, John F. Kennedy told the world of plans to put a man on the moon by the end of the decade. The speech he gave in September 1962, announcing that goal, spent a good amount of time justifying the expense and explaining the urgency. But nowhere in it was there even a hint that it might not be possible. He said, in part:

> But if I were to say, my fellow citizens, that we shall send to the moon, 240,000 miles away from the control station in Houston, a giant rocket more than 300 feet tall, the length of this football field, made of new metal alloys, some of which have not yet been invented, capable of standing heat and stresses several times more than have ever been experienced, fitted together with a precision better than the finest watch, carrying all the equipment needed for propulsion, guidance, control, communications, food and survival, on an untried mission, to an unknown celestial body, and then return it safely to earth, re-entering the atmosphere at speeds of over 25,000 miles per hour, causing heat about half that of the temperature of the sun—almost as hot as it is here today—and do all this, and do it right, and do it first before this decade is out—then we must be bold.

Think of the optimism! Jet planes were only a few years old. People were still alive who knew the Wright brothers. And this man was saying we were going to the moon in a rocket ship made of metals we hadn't even invented.

And you know what? We did!

As the Jim Lovell character in the movie *Apollo 13* said, "From now on, we live in a world where man has walked on the moon. And it's not a miracle; we just decided to go."

That mindset—"Why don't we decide what kind of world we want to live in and then make it?"—permeated our collective consciousness for a long time. People overwhelmingly believed the future would be better, and they were right! They may have missed on specifics (such as each of us owning a personal jet pack and a flying car) but in general were dead-on. The present *is* better than the past. Not just a little better, but gloriously and fantastically better.

Whether you are rich or poor, live in the developed world or the developing world, life today is better and easier than it was a century ago by virtually any measure. Life expectancy. Infant mortality. Disease. Hours of leisure. Access to education. Equality. Self-rule. Opportunity. Rule of law. Wealth. Comfort. Technology. Access to information. Medical care. And on and on.

I am not saying we live in a utopia. I am not ignoring that the world is full of extreme and unacceptable want and misery. But I am making a simple statement that life is better now than it has ever been. The optimists, thus far, have been right. We have, in fact, envisioned a better world and have made it happen. Why should we expect that to change?

And yet, against all reason, starting in the 1970s our collective optimism faltered. Through some perfect storm of wars, downturns, and disasters, the once-sunny outlook turned dark. The cadence and view of life changed, and people began to think the future was not going to be better than the past. Analysts declared each successive generation might be "the first to have a lower standard of living than their parents." Scarcity was the new watchword as the focus turned to all the problems of the future, not all the possibilities. Energy depletion, pollution, landfills, and overpopulation. Ozone holes, CFCs, and global warming. Mass extinction, deforestation, dead zones in oceans, and on and on and on.

The world indeed has all sorts of challenges ahead. Some will be extremely difficult to overcome. But the present is manifestly better than the past because of all the people who expected it to be so and therefore got up early and worked hard to make it so. "Hey, someone has to discover penicillin—it might as well be me." Someone has to sequence DNA, cure polio, create hybrid seeds to feed the world, and invent the Internet. Such bold achievements are driven by the optimism that is the natural state of humanity, and among the most powerful forces on the planet.

Is optimism rational? Blind optimism is not, to be sure. If you have an unwavering commitment to an idea that all things will be good all the time, then that is irrational. But what about a reasoned belief based on a balanced look at both history and current reality that leads you to be optimistic? Obviously, that is rational. And as I look to the past and the present, I see two phenomena that especially drive my optimism.

I see how human ingenuity and new technologies have eliminated previously insoluble problems once we stand back and let free markets do what they do best: direct the allocation of capital to find a solution. When whale oil got scarce and went up in price, the market made cheap kerosene for lighting. When the light bulb was cheaper and better, we ditched kerosene. And this will go on as long as we have the free enterprise system, where markets reward those who devise solutions for, say, pollution abatement or alternative energy creation.

I also see the pace of problem solving—and change in general—accelerating at an astonishing rate.

If you had been born in Egypt in 2570 BC, during the reign of Khufu, as the Great Pyramid of Giza was being built, you would have turned twenty in 2550 BC. From that vantage point, if you had tried to look fifty years ahead to what the world would be like in the year 2500 BC, you would have expected very little change. And you would have been right. The years passed and almost nothing changed. There is no hieroglyph for the word "progress" because the very idea of progress didn't exist.

If you had been born in 1170 in Paris, you would have turned twenty in 1190. If you had looked ahead fifty years to 1240, you wouldn't have anticipated much change. And you would have been right. The great cathedral Notre Dame de Paris, which was begun before your birth, would not be finished by your death. Very little would change in this seventy-year stretch of life.

However, if you had been born in 1992, turning twenty the year I am writing this, and tried now to imagine life in 2062, you would suppose that everything is going to change. And you would be right.

This book is about that future and what it is going to look like—how it will be a place glorious and spectacular beyond our wildest hopes. And while it may not be perfect, life will be profoundly better for everyone on the planet.

Can you imagine a world without poverty? Disease? Famine? Ignorance? War? Most people haven't even tried because we cannot reasonably imagine a way by which we can be rid of them. But I can see a path. And not just a path, but a well-lit, eight-lane highway. We are already well on our way.

For although these five woes have long plagued humanity, I am confident their days are numbered. Consider this: None of them is necessary or inevitable. There is no reason any of them have to be. They exist simply because we have not had the means to solve them in the past.

But that is changing. They are all about to vanish, courtesy of the Internet and its associated technologies. By that, I am referring to computers, connectivity, GPS, fiber, the cloud, and all things made of, or influenced by, silicon—the entire bundle of technologies relating to computation and communication.

To be perfectly clear, I am not saying the Internet and technology will solve every human ill. It won't cure gluttony, envy, vanity, sloth, pride, or jealousy. In the end, our fundamental challenge is to become better individuals, and technology offers little help on that front; it is up to each one of us to solve that for ourselves. But the five phenomena I chose to tackle in this book are among the great blights on humanity that I believe the Internet and technology will help solve.

I love thinking about the future. I love technology. I earn my living by it. I live it, breathe it, think about it, and am fascinated by all it has to offer us, all it has done for us. I am also a historian with a full understanding of how poverty, disease, ignorance, famine, and war have dominated life on this planet. But it is precisely because I am a historian that I am so optimistic. Because I am a historian, I know that big changes happen in history, and they are brought about by the most unlikely of causes.

Could you have foreseen that the advent of a technology called "air conditioning" in homes would alter the social fabric of the nation? That it would mean people would no longer know their neighbors? Who connected the dots to say that when the inside of the house is cool, people will no longer need to sit outside on their front porch to pass the hot evenings? And because of this, we would therefore lose the inevitable relationships that naturally formed?

Had you been around then, would you have seen the inscrutable lines of cause and effect that connected the new technology Gutenberg pioneered and an unknown monk named Martin Luther? That when printing became affordable, it unleashed a pent-up demand in the general public for books and pamphlets and that this would end the monopoly the church and state had on information? That this democratization of information and opinion would lead to vigorous debate and encourage a young monk to question the church? And that same technology would allow his questions to be spread across Europe, thereby igniting the Protestant Reformation?

How difficult it would have been, at that time, to perceive that the discovery of America would inevitably end the Italian Renaissance and result in the decline of the Mediterranean world and also trigger the rise in influence of Portugal, France, Spain, and England, the west-facing marine powers, who suddenly found themselves to be at the center of the world.

Well, the Internet is bigger than air conditioning. It is bigger than movable type. Bigger than TV and cars and anything that has come before it. So isn't it just possible that it could end ignorance, disease, poverty, hunger, and war?

And wouldn't that be something?

AN OPTIMIST'S REASONING, IN FIVE EASY PREMISES

This book is unusual for two reasons. First, in the magnitude of what it claims, and second, in the degree to which it differs from what pessimists predict.

I make the predictions in this book not to be sensational or controversial. I make them because I believe I can back them up with convincing proofs and arguments. To lay the foundation for those arguments, I offer five simple premises—optimistic yet realistic assertions about the predictive nature of history, the infinite promise of technology, and the power of humanity to wield new technologies to create this world of infinite progress.

Premise One: Futurists Often Get It Wrong

Premise Two: History Can Help Us Get It Right

Premise Three: Internet Technology + Human Ingenuity
= Infinite Promise

Premise Four: Accelerating Progress Is Inevitable

Premise Five: The New Renaissance Has Begun

Futurists Often Get It Wrong

*For I dipped into the future, far as human eye could see, saw
the vision of the world, and all the wonder that would be.*
—Alfred Lord Tennyson

Let's face it: Futurists as a whole have a pretty poor track record. I think it is because they traditionally make one of two fatal errors in their approach to predicting the future.

The first error is to assert that history unfolds in a basically linear fashion, that there is a fundamental continuity between the past, present, and future. This viewpoint seems reasonable because it is largely consistent with our everyday experience of life. But while this approach is fairly reliable across relatively short spans of time, it is almost always spectacularly wrong when used for longer-range predictions. For example:

- In 1894, a writer studying population growth in large cities along with the rising need of horse-drawn conveyances such as taxis and carriages concluded that in fifty years, every street in London would be buried under nine feet of horse manure. He didn't know the car was coming.

- In the 1930s, the resulting decrease in birthrates brought about by the economic malaise of the Great Depression led social commentators to predict an end to the human race, fed by a decrease in procreation. They didn't foresee the baby boom brought about by a new post-war prosperity.

- A wild-eyed, crazed techno-optimist of the nineteenth century concluded that in fifty years there would be a telephone in every town in America. He didn't foresee the consumer demand for the telephone or its massive decline in price.

I don't cite these examples to mock these prognosticators. They were faithful straight liners. I include them to point out that history is discontinuous. It lulls you into thinking that things behave in a straight-line predictable way, and just when it looks like you have it all worked out, along comes an unforeseen, game-changing event, and WHAM!, it hits you upside the head.

The second methodology error that futurists often commit is the exact opposite of the first. This viewpoint acknowledges that history unfolds in a discontinuous manner and so assumes it must be random, arbitrary, and unpredictable. Therefore, any projection about what might happen is deemed legitimate. After all, who knows?

This approach is even more flawed than the first. Bad science fiction plots, speculating on futures which could not really happen, are the worst examples of this. These are easy to spot: They rely on huge conceptual leaps without a framework to support them. Or astounding technological breakthroughs that have no precedent in reality. Or radical shifts in human behavior or human nature, which will never happen. Books based on this "wouldn't-it-be-great-if . . ." approach to the future are works of pure faith or pure fiction, not of reason. While entertaining, they are never, ever correct.

A third way to predict the future that I believe is reliable rejects both the slavish following of the straight line and the purely speculative approach. This third way is based on the principle that it is possible to see the future by accepting discontinuity but not unpredictability.

Imagine if someone had come to you on January 1, 1991, and said, "Before the end of the year, the Soviet Union will vote itself into nonexistence and peacefully break into fifteen republics. The defining political struggle of the world for nearly half a century will end without a shot fired, and Russia itself will reject Communism as a failed system."

You would have thought this was crazy. So would have I. So would have everyone. It seemed as if no one saw that coming because, frankly, no one could conceive of it happening.

But wait! A few people *did* see it coming. In 1970, Andrei Amalrik, a Russian writer and dissident, wrote an essay entitled "Will the Soviet Union Survive Until 1984?" in which he concluded of the USSR that "the logical result will be its death, which will be followed by anarchy." His timeframe was off by a few years, but his prediction was right.

History is full of radical breaks with the past that only seem to have come out of nowhere but were, in fact, predictable.

What if you were a pilot who had met the Wright brothers as a child and someone had come to you in 1944, when every plane you had ever seen had a propeller, and said, "In twenty-five years, we will walk on the moon." You would have said that was crazy. And yet, that happened. As impossible as it must have seemed to most people in the 1940s, a few people in that era in fact foresaw the moon landing. They made their predictions mindful of both the non-linear increases in aircraft speed already being seen and their beliefs about the potential output of the new technology of jet engines.

Discontinuity happens, but it is not unpredictable. I believe we are living at a peculiar time, with many discontinuous breaks about to happen. I further believe the aggregate effect of these breaks will forever change life on this planet and usher in a new Golden Age for humanity.

How will we see these discontinuities coming? By looking, in part, at history.

History Can Help Us Get It Right

*Look back over the past, with its changing empires that rose
and fell, and you can foresee the future, too.
—Marcus Aurelius, Roman Emperor, second century*

I don't use history to predict the future, like some talisman that lets me pick winning lottery numbers (don't I wish). But I do use history to guide my thinking and reasoning and to inform what I imagine of the future.

I don't dispute the cliché, "Those who do not know history are doomed to repeat it." However, I often have thought that a second sentence should follow: "Also, those who *do* know history are doomed to repeat it." This is because history repeats itself—at least, as the great historian Will Durant says, "in outline form."

Why is it that history repeats itself? It repeats itself because it is the record of the choices of people. And because human nature changes either not at all or very slowly, people make the same choices over and over again.

When we look at this record of the choices of people, we see a wide range of behaviors. It shows us at our best and at our cruelest. Noble, wretched, magnanimous, heartless, petty, generous, self-sacrificing, and selfish. It is the record of innumerable conflicts and resolutions and a chronicle of uncounted victories and defeats.

Because history is a record of the choices of people, it generally holds that when we put people in similar circumstances, they will make basically the same choices. In short, it tells us everything about ourselves. It's all there. The historian Will Durant described it remarkably in his 1945 radio broadcast called "Invitation to History." It is well worth listening to, but you can get a sense of it in this transcribed passage:

> It is a mistake to think that the past is dead. Nothing that has ever happened is quite without influence at this moment. The present is merely the past rolled up and concentrated in this second of time. You, too, are your past; often your face is your autobiography; you are what you are because of what you have been; because of your heredity stretching back into forgotten generations; because of every element of environment that has affected you, every man or woman that has met you, every book that you have read, every experience that you have had; all these are accumulated in your memory, your body, your character, your soul. So with a city, a country, a race; it is its past, and cannot be understood without it. It is the present, not the past, that dies; this present moment, to which we give so much attention,

is forever flitting from our eyes and fingers into that pedestal
and matrix of our lives which we call the past. It is only the
past that lives.

Therefore I feel that we of this generation give too
much time to news about the transient present, too little
to the living past. We are choked with news, and starved
of history . . .[1]

Examining history is not like gazing into some fantasy crystal ball, where
what we see is prophetic in detail. But history does give us plenty of patterns
of behavior and examples of cause and effect, and in those patterns and
examples we usually can find ones that approximate our circumstances. I
refer to history extensively in these pages because I believe historical people
are *exactly* like us, only in different circumstances. Thus their actions, when
placed in situations like ours, show what we would do. At the very least, history can clearly show the range of outcomes that are likely.

This will be extremely useful, because the game, as they say, has just
changed completely.

Internet Technology + Human Ingenuity = Infinite Promise

The beginning of wisdom lies in calling things
by their right name.
—Chinese proverb

According to Dictionary.com, the Internet is "a vast computer network link-
ing smaller computer networks worldwide."

It is an interesting definition, for in it there is no clue as to what this
device is for—what the Internet actually *does*. Contrast it to the definition

---

1. From radio broadcast "Invitation to History: The Map of Human Character" by Will Durant. Copyright ©
1945, 2006 by John Little and the Estate of Will Durant.

of another piece of similar, albeit older, technology—namely, the telegraph, which Dictionary.com defines (in part) as "an apparatus . . . for transmitting messages or signals to a distant place."

Do you see the difference? Bound up in the very definition of the telegraph is its purpose.

Why is the Internet so sterilely defined? Why is it only described as a mechanical device divorced from any purpose? It would be tempting to say this is an effect of the relative newness of the Internet, reflecting a time not long ago when we literally had to explain to less digital friends exactly what it was.

But this is not really a satisfying answer. The consumer Internet is roughly two decades old. If we go back and look at definitions of the telegraph when it was a similar age, we discover that Noah Webster's 1828 American Dictionary defined it as "an apparatus . . . for communicating intelligence rapidly between distant points." So, what the telegraph does is in its definition even at its early age.

I submit that the Internet is not defined in that way because it is a technology without an implicit purpose. Its purpose is neither evident nor predetermined; its purpose must be imputed to it. A telegraph exists only to transmit messages—in short, it *is what it does*. The Internet *is whatever we make it to be*.

When new technology comes out, we generally understand it in terms of what it displaces. This is not a shortcoming of our imaginations but rather a simple reality. When contemplating the future, our only point of reference is present reality. Whether things in the future stay the same as they are today or change from what they are today, both are understood in terms of the current reality.

Thus, when television first came out, people said it was "radio with pictures." The first cars were called "horseless carriages." Telephones, when they first appeared, were called "talking telegraphs." Then when telephones became untethered, they were "wireless telephones." ATMs replaced human bank tellers, so they are called "Automated Teller Machines." E-mail is electronic mail. The list is long.

Sometimes the new technology so overwhelms the old that when looking back, we explain the old technology in terms of the new. Diapers weren't called "cloth diapers" until disposable ones came out. All corn used to be "corn on the cob" until canned corn came along. And the U.S. Postal Service delivered mail until the electronic age demoted it to "snail mail."

When we only understand the new technology in terms of the old, how we use the new technology is also solely an extension of how we used the old technology. Because television was radio with pictures, the first television shows were simply men in suits standing in front of microphones reading the news. It took a decade or two for the new medium to be seen in light of itself, not just in terms of what it displaced.

Even most futurists have fallen into this trap. The 1920s to 1950s renderings of what people thought the future would look like are full of things like personal jetpacks and flying cars. Because the major technological advances occurring in those eras were related to transportation, that's what they thought of when pondering technological advance. And I think that helps explain why no one quite foresaw the rise of the Internet: *because it doesn't have an offline corollary of its own.* The future of cars? Flying cars, faster cars, more features in cars, we all get that. But what could you have seen in the 1950s from which you could deduce the Internet?

This tendency to only be able to see new technology as an extension of the old is exactly the phenomena we have seen with the Internet. Because its meaning has to be imputed, we have tended to describe it in terms of prior technologies—which, in many cases, understates its potential by many orders of magnitude.

So when we say, "The Internet is an electronic library," this is true. But it is an electronic library bigger and better than any other library that has ever existed or even been contemplated by humans. (In this allegorical understanding of the Internet, we could say Google is the card catalog—although as I write this, it dawns on me that not too many years hence, the average reader won't ever have seen a card catalog and probably won't even know the term.)

And when we say, "The Internet is an electronic store," this is true. But it is the biggest, best store ever, where you can buy anything from anywhere, based on reviews by other buyers, at a discount, and have it gift wrapped, engraved, altered, drop-shipped, and probably delivered by tomorrow.

And if the Internet is an electronic debate, it is a more robust forum for debate than has ever before arisen on the planet, where you can find people expressing any viewpoint on any topic. And if the Internet is an electronic cocktail party, it is more like a hundred million cocktail parties going on at once, with friends connecting, professionals networking, competitors playing games, and groups coalescing around every sort of interest. What's more, the Internet can be a fact checker, post office, Rolodex, Yellow Pages, White Pages, game board, garage sale, university, movie theater, jukebox, matchmaking service, travel agent, photo album, bank, support group . . .

My point is: While the Internet does all those things, it is not accurate to say the Internet *is only* any one of them.

This is not merely a linguistic distinction. It is like my car. My car has a CD player. It has GPS navigation. It has an air conditioner. But my car is not a CD player, GPS navigation system, or air conditioner. The essence of my car is that it takes me places I want to go.

The Internet does not, like the car, have a single essence. It has many. And to the extent that our minds still perceive the Internet as an extension of offline things, we will fail to see its most revolutionary possibilities.

Until we see how the Internet changes us and allows us to do things we never even thought about doing—never imagined we would want to do—we will miss the enormous impact it can have.

We are getting there, though. We are at the point, finally, where we are seeing uses of the Internet that have no offline corollary. Think, for example, of Twitter. Nothing exists that even remotely looks like Twitter before the Internet. The mark of these technologies is that they are greeted with universal skepticism at first. That is because they seem so far out of the daily experience of most people that they cannot conceive of how or why they would use them.

I mention Twitter as an example, but there are hundreds more, most of which are presently obscure. These, to me, are the most exciting companies to look at. To paraphrase the old saying about the thin line separating genius from insanity: Online, there often is a thin line between "brilliant new idea" and "utter lunacy." But sometimes it is hard to tell them apart when we don't have an offline frame of reference. When you hear about a new company and your response is, "Why in the world would anyone want to do that?" it will be because there is no offline corollary. Will people like it? Will they do it? Only time will tell.

And that leads us to a critical question: *Who decides what we will make the Internet do?* Who decides what the Internet will become?

All of us, through the choices we make.

The Internet has no central planning agency deciding what new, cool websites should be made. New products are driven not by some central authority but by the free market. When it comes to starting a new business, nothing that previously existed can rival the Internet in terms of both ease of entry and breadth of potential. It's the ultimate environment for an entrepreneur who, as Peter Drucker noted, "Always searches for change, responds to it, and exploits it as an opportunity."

Let's run through a scenario with a fictional entrepreneur: Linda, a single mom living in Portland, Oregon. Let's say Linda has come up with a pretty interesting idea: a social network for couples. She reasons: "When we think of social networks, we are individualistic in our approach. I have a page about me. That is the basic unit—me. I may be connected to other people, but still it is all about me. What if we thought differently? What if the basic unit was a couple, a relationship, and what if that relationship had an identity? It would have sections called 'How we met,' 'Our first quarrel,' 'How we make it work,' and so on. We post pictures, the progress of our relationship, and people can follow our "us" page."

Good idea? Who knows? I can't think of anything offline to compare it to.

But Linda decides to give it a try. She hires a contract programmer in Russia for $3,000 to code it and advertises on Craigslist for a designer who will work for some stock. She gets web hosting set up for the princely sum of $30 a month. She registers the name Hizznherz.com because the online trademark search she did (for free) turned up no matches. (Awful name, Linda!)

She wants to do business as a limited liability company, so she creates an

LLC online for $200. She researches credit card processors and decides to go with PayPal for now. She creates premium services on her site that cost just $9.95 a year that include a number of additional features and virtual goods. A friend of hers who is a florist asks if she can advertise on the site. Linda thinks about this and decides she wants to keep it ad-free for now.

Linda gets the idea to call Facebook and see if she can advertise to people who change their status to "In a relationship." Facebook doesn't return her call. She drops $300 on Google ads before realizing it might not be a great fit. She e-mails all her friends and asks them to set up relationship pages. One friend suggests she advertise on dating sites. This makes sense, so she spends her last $2,000 in savings to buy ads. Another friend tells her either member of the couple should be able to instantly remove the couple page when the relationship goes sour. This makes sense to Linda, so she gets Dmitri (the Russian developer) to make this small change.

Does it catch on? Does Linda morph it into something else? Does Linda eventually give up? The answers to those questions are what define the Internet. In the past, success relied heavily on whether an entrepreneur could move an offline experience online better than someone else. Today, success still requires good execution, but the larger question is: "Can you discover and fulfill a hitherto-unknown, latent desire in people that the Internet enables?"

That's when it gets interesting. The choices we make to test options never before contemplated will tell us all kinds of new things about ourselves.

Plus, it's all about to speed way, way up.

Accelerating Progress Is Inevitable

After growing wildly for years, the field of computing appears to be reaching its infancy.
—John Pierce

In 1965, Gordon Moore, cofounder of Intel, described a phenomenon and made a projection. He noted that the number of transistors that could be cheaply placed on an integrated circuit had doubled every year for some time, and predicted it was likely to continue to do so.

Time has borne out the accuracy of this observation and even bestowed upon it the lofty title Moore's Law. It has endured far longer than most people—probably even Moore himself—ever imagined it could. Meanwhile, the capabilities of many more digital devices seem to be following similar trajectories. Any regular purchaser of computer equipment has noticed the growth—in hard drive size, megapixels on digital cameras, processor speed, and so on. It is expected to continue into the foreseeable future.

Inventor, author, and futurist Ray Kurzweil makes the case that the dynamics underlying Moore's Law have been operating since well before Moore mentioned it, for at least a century. Obviously in that time, the underlying technology kept shifting—computers went from electromechanical to relays to vacuum tubes to transistors and then to integrated circuits—and the abstraction, the calculations per second, kept doubling. So the physical mechanisms have been serially transformed, yet the law has never hiccupped. The abstraction keeps moving forward, and the technology races to keep up.

What is the significance of this? *It means progress at an ever-increasing pace is inevitable.* Think about it this way: All the technology accumulated from the dawn of time to today has given us a certain amount of processing power. In just eighteen months from now, we will have duplicated that again and effectively doubled our computation power. Then, in eighteen more months, it will double again. And again, and again. It is just as engineer and communication technology pioneer John Pierce said, in the quote I offered earlier: "After growing wildly for years, the field of computing appears to be reaching its infancy."

As the pace of Internet technology's advance keeps quickening, it will not only reveal (and answer) latent desires we never knew we had, but it also will increasingly mean tasks that have been technically impossible will become possible. And after they become possible, they will become very inexpensive.

Where does that all end? I am not prepared to make predictions as dramatic as Ray Kurzweil's in *The Age of Spiritual Machines*. But I do think we will see an end to any effective constraints relating to computers' ability to process data and transfer information. This is going to have profound effects.

Everyone who has been in technology for any length of time realizes the speed of the machines and the speed at which we move data around is growing faster than the tasks we give computers and the information that we move. I spend much less time downloading a file now than I did back in the days of my 28.8 modem, even though the files I am downloading are vastly larger. I spend less time waiting for Excel to do a recalculation of my formulas today than I did on my 386 in the 1990s, even though my spreadsheets are thousands of times more complex.

I doubt you need me to prove these assertions—they are probably part of your daily experience. But a single example will suffice to illustrate the whole: In the early days of computer animation, it would take days to render a single frame. Now kids are making animated movies on handheld tablets. Filmmakers such as James Cameron and George Lucas used to talk about putting off film projects to wait for the computer technology to catch up to their visions. Those films are being made now.

Eventually we reach the point where the technology does everything we need it to do. It used to be, for instance, that digital cameras competed on how many megapixels they had. But at a certain point, you don't need any more, and the technology is mature.

We often see other technologies race toward a point and then stop growing along that axis. Early cars tried to be faster and faster, to break the 60 mph barrier. But once cars improved enough, for all intents and purposes we stopped increasing their top speed. Could we make a car that can go 300 mph? Sure, but we don't need that from the technology.

If I had an even faster computer than I have today, I could come up with really interesting questions to ask it. But that situation has an end: Once I have a computer doing everything I can imagine (and some more after that), I don't need it to be any faster. We don't need our computers to be infinitely fast, just a whole lot faster than they are today. We don't need bandwidth to be instant, just nearly instant. We don't need miniaturization to go to infinitely small, just really, really small.

And what seems clear is that, sooner or later, we will get there. Our ability to process data, move information, and make things small will progress to a point where they will not be gating factors ever again. It is inevitable.

The New Renaissance Has Begun

I saw the angel in the marble and carved until I set him free.
—Michelangelo

At this point, if you follow my reasoning, we have established at least the possibility of a bright future. But I would take that further: I see the Internet and technology ushering in nothing less than a New Renaissance—and I say we already have entered it.

In European history, the Renaissance (from the French word for "rebirth") was a period of renewed interest in the Classical Greek and Roman civilizations and their art, music, writing, and philosophy. From this period came some of humanity's greatest masterpieces, including St. Peter's Basilica, Da Vinci's Last Supper, Michelangelo's Pietà, and hundreds of other instantly recognizable artistic treasures.

Though it isn't so much a time as a state of mind, historians plot the Renaissance as moving around Europe for a couple of centuries. It is thought to have had its apex in Italy—in Venice, Florence, and Rome. It is generally regarded to have ended in 1564, the year in which Michelangelo died and Shakespeare was born, ushering in the modern age.

The Renaissance was triggered, in part, by the fall of the Byzantine Empire, centered in Constantinople (the city known today as Istanbul, Turkey). When the conquest of the city seemed inevitable, a great "brain drain" of scholars, artists, teachers, theologians, and the wealthy emigrated to Western Europe, especially to Italy. As they fled the falling empire, they brought with them large numbers of Classical works not seen in the West for a thousand years and long thought by Europeans to have been lost. The arrival of these texts—as well as Byzantium's own architecture, science, and art—triggered a sensory and intellectual explosion, which became the cultural movement we now call the Renaissance.

But that movement was, by its nature, backward looking. Its reawakening of the arts derived chiefly from seeking to recapture something thought lost from a past Golden Age. Renaissance thinkers were so focused on the Classical Era that when cheap printing came along, thanks to Gutenberg, much that was printed (aside from theological works) was either Greek or Roman classics, commentaries on Greek or Roman classics, or imitations of Greek and Roman classics. Only after the public grew weary of this did printers go off in search of completely new books, called *novels* to mark their newness.

Unquestionably, an extraordinary amount of talent was present during the Renaissance. The wealthy and influential, trying to distinguish themselves by being patrons of the arts, invested massively in all forms of art, creating a widespread appreciation of it in all the social classes. It must have been quite an exciting time to be alive. It was, however—and this is sure to earn me the wrath of many humanities professors—a time of surprisingly little originality.

I say that to contrast it to the Internet Renaissance we are in right now, in which original art is being created everywhere, and even entirely new art forms are springing up. We have put the Italian Renaissance on such a pedestal that it never occurs to us that our age could measure up to such a lofty time. But the Internet Renaissance dwarfs by a hundredfold, a thousandfold, the Renaissance of Europe. In the Italian Renaissance, only a thin veneer of society's elites participated in the creation or ownership of the frescos, music, statues, and paintings; most were only passive observers. On the Internet are far fewer passive observers. Almost everyone creates, in one form or another. In these early days of the Internet Renaissance, the number of great masters is in the tens of thousands, not the hundreds. And great masters aside, the number of people who create things online—our equivalent to painters, sculptors, composers, authors, and philosophers—is in the hundreds of millions. Almost everyone participates.

Take just one artistic expression, writing, and consider how the Internet has caused it to explode. In a masterful essay in *Wired* magazine, Clive Thompson addresses the effect that the Internet and mobile devices (with SMS, or text messaging) have had on writing. While many people think new technology is having an adverse effect on writing, he says,

> Andrea Lunsford isn't so sure. Lunsford is a professor of writing and rhetoric at Stanford University, where she has organized a mammoth project called the Stanford Study of

Writing to scrutinize college students' prose. From 2001 to 2006, she collected 14,672 student writing samples—everything from in-class assignments, formal essays, and journal entries to emails, blog posts, and chat sessions. Her conclusions are stirring.

"I think we're in the midst of a literacy revolution the likes of which we haven't seen since Greek civilization," she says. For Lunsford, technology isn't killing our ability to write. It's reviving it—and pushing our literacy in bold new directions.

The first thing she found is that young people today write far more than any generation before them. That's because so much socializing takes place online, and it almost always involves text. Of all the writing that the Stanford students did, a stunning 38 percent of it took place out of the classroom—life writing, as Lunsford calls it. Those Twitter updates and lists of 25 things about yourself add up.

It's almost hard to remember how big a paradigm shift this is. Before the Internet came along, most Americans never wrote anything, ever, that wasn't a school assignment. Unless they got a job that required producing text (like in law, advertising, or media), they'd leave school and virtually never construct a paragraph again.[2]

The amount of writing we are talking about is staggering. In 2007, Google researchers estimated there were one hundred trillion words on the Internet. There must be several times that by now. Google CEO Eric Schmidt famously asserted in 2010 that we create more content every two days than in the history of civilization up to 2003. As I write this, something like fifty million blogs and billions of blog posts are online. Fifty million Tweets a day. More than that in Facebook status updates every day. Millions comment on

---

2. From "Clive Thompson on the New Literacy" from *Wired* magazine, Issue 17.09. Copyright © 2009 by Clive Thompson. Reproduced by permission of **Featurewell.com**.

movies, millions write reviews of products. Uncounted millions more post questions in forums, and millions of answers are posted in response.

All forms of online media are exploding in a similar fashion. In 2010, people were uploading one hundred million photos on Facebook every single *day*. At least a hundred million websites are out there. Over a hundred million videos on YouTube. The Internet has made distributing music easy and has unleashed an astonishing amount of new material.

It turns out we all have a desire to be artists or philosophers or singers or photographers or commentators or reviewers. We all desire to leave our stamp on the world. We just lacked these means to do it before.

We are creating at a rate exponentially more than our most recent ancestors. This begs the question, "Is any of it any good, really?"

My answer: yes. Astonishingly great. Better than anything the world has ever seen.

Yes, there is art on YouTube. There, I said it. Now I will try to persuade you.

Let's start with a definition. By art, I am referring to creative expressions that are still relevant to future generations, something people still will consume in fifty or one hundred years. It's hard to know what later generations will deem to be art. In his day, Shakespeare was low-brow entertainment for the common class. It was not at all clear at the time that his work would transcend the ages. In fact, it's likelier that kids of that day were forbidden by proper parents from hanging out at the Globe Theater.

Charlie Chaplin wasn't initially considered art, but a century later, he still makes me laugh, and his work is hailed as groundbreaking. (I almost agree with Orson Welles' judgment that Chaplin's *City Lights* is the best movie ever made.) A. A. Milne's *Winnie the Pooh* series wasn't considered art when it came out, but nearly a century later, I reach for those books to read to my kids at night, and they enjoy them as much as children from 1926. P.G. Wodehouse's *Jeeves and Wooster* books are art, which I think will be read for the next two centuries. The Beatles made art. F. Scott Fitzgerald made art, as did Ernest Hemingway. Daniel Day-Lewis and Joaquin Phoenix and Ralph Fiennes are artists. I think *Phineas and Ferb* is likely to be art and that *Hank the Cowdog* almost certainly is. But only time will tell on that.

I don't play video games much, but I have certainly seen some that I think might survive the artistic test of time. I think the backgrounds in *Myst* from two decades ago are astonishingly good and that Rand and Robyn Miller are masters. I even bought a framed print from the sequel, Riven, which hangs over my desk. I think John Fiorella's Untamed Cinema's trailer for *Grayson* is art (and art done on a budget as well). I think Commoncraft makes things that might be art. I think the social commentary in JibJab's work is art.

We can be sure of one thing: Cartoonist Bill Watterson is a Michelangelo. *Calvin and Hobbes* is art.

So when doubters scoff—*There's art on YouTube?*—I say yes. I can't tell you which clips will be watched in a century, but I'm certain that some will be. (Actually, I could make guesses, but they might well be spectacularly wrong and a guy doesn't want that haunting him ten years from now. I can just see myself getting introduced as "the man who thought 'The Evolution of Dance' was art . . ." I don't need that in my life.)

Now, of course, much of what is on YouTube is not art. It can hardly even be called coherent. But in some ways, it's like antique furniture. We look at antique furniture today and say, "Man, they sure don't make stuff as good as they used to." But the truth is that almost all furniture back in the day was cheaply made junk and only a very few high-quality pieces survived. Those are the ones we call antiques today. The rest was reduced to firewood long ago.

Let's also remember that the Italian Renaissance was not just a flowering of the arts, but of commerce, technology, science, and trade. And in our Internet Renaissance, aren't we seeing an explosion of these same things at a spectacularly more massive scale?

Who could argue there was ever a better time to start a business any time in the world? When has starting a business been so easy? The opportunity so large? The choices so wide? Has there ever before been a time when business opportunity was more blind to color, gender, or creed? When have we seen so many fortunes made by so many so quickly?

And technology? Do I need to prove we have an explosion of technological progress dwarfing the wildest dreams of any age? We are suitably impressed that Da Vinci sketched a design for a submarine and a flying machine. But the inventors of our age have put a billion transistors on an area the size of a postage stamp. Do those two things even compare?

And science? Recent advances in science are mind-boggling: We have mapped the genome, looked into distant galaxies, and produced the iPad, a device that seems more at home in the movie *Minority Report* than on my bedside table.

And trade? My home is full of items from every continent on Earth (well, except Antarctica). The world has become a seamless market where moving items around is so cheap and easy that we make things that cost a dollar (or a dime, or a penny) in distant lands and transport them to where they are wanted.

And philanthropy? In the Italian Renaissance, people of wealth distinguished themselves by their altruistic endeavors. Today, that is vastly more true and widespread. On top of the common-good projects supported with our tax dollars, almost all of us—certainly not just the wealthy—have causes we support. The Internet has allowed for the creation of thousands of new ways to give, both time and money. That is true from one end of the spectrum, with Bill Gates and Warren Buffet calling on the wealthy to give away half of all of their wealth, to the success of initiatives like "Tom's Shoes," where a pair of shoes is donated in the developing world for each pair you buy. And on top of all that, consider the open source movement and licensing mechanisms such as Creative Commons whereby people donate their intellectual ability and time to the greater good.

So truly, I think we have entered an Internet Renaissance that dwarfs anything the Medicis ever saw. I think it is bigger by "twenty hundred thousand times" (my favorite number used by Shakespeare.) This is not to the sixteenth-century Europeans' discredit or even to our credit. It simply has been enabled by technology combined with prosperity compounded over time. People have always had the drive and the ability to build, create, discover, and explore. We have a natural desire to make beautiful things and a bone-deep need to understand the world we live in and our place in it.

Before technology and prosperity, virtually everyone spent long hard days scraping together enough calories for themselves and their family to survive. A very, very few people, however, were freed from this sustenance lifestyle, either by their fortuitous birth or outstanding ability. These few were given the tools to achieve their maximum potential, to live that dream.

Now a billion or more can achieve that dream, and I foresee a time not far off when everyone on the planet can. Today, there are modern-day Da Vincis living in parts of the world where just surviving is a full-time occupation, powerless to develop the gifts they could offer the wider world. But all that is about to change.

The Renaissance artists and thinkers had very few tools: pen and paper, paint and canvas, marble and chisel, and a few more. Today we have the Internet and all its associated technologies, vastly more versatile, almost infinite in possibility.

Imagine a world where everyone on the planet has access to this expanded canvas of human expression that technology has created. Where everyone can live up to his or her maximum potential. Where every Da Vinci can paint his Mona Lisa and every Dante can write his *Inferno*. Imagine a thousand new arts, none of which are even invented yet, each with a thousand new great masters.

It will be a glorious time to be alive, and I believe my children will see it happen.

THE END OF IGNORANCE

- The High Cost of Ignorance
- Your Digital Echo
- Surprise! We share.
- Data and Knowledge
- Wise Decisions
- The Jim Haynes Effect
- How the Internet and Technology Will End Ignorance

The High Cost of Ignorance

Nothing is more terrible than to see ignorance in action.
—Johann Wolfgang von Goethe

On the morning of June 28, 1914, Archduke Franz Ferdinand of Austria and his wife Sophie, Duchess of Hohenberg, were shot dead in Sarajevo by nineteen-year-old assassin Gavrilo Princip. This launched a series of events that led to World War I, in which more than sixteen million people died.

The war helped bring about the Great Depression, which was especially bad in Germany because it had the additional burden of paying war reparations to the winning powers. Financial hardship, coupled with the "humiliation of Versailles" (the treaty that Germany signed to end the war), led to the rise in German nationalism.

That movement helped a former lieutenant named Adolf Hitler come to power. Once again, war raged in Europe and around the world and this time left sixty million people dead.

World War II ushered in the age of nuclear weapons. Its end led directly to the Cold War, which consumed inconceivable amounts of money and almost pushed the world to the brink of nuclear devastation.

What set this in motion?

Although Gavrilo Princip was part of a plot to assassinate Franz Ferdinand that day, when the plot began to unravel, he gave up and went to a café to have a sandwich. But then something totally unexpected happened. Archduke Franz Ferdinand's driver, Leopold Loyka, made a wrong turn. He turned onto Franz Josef Street, where he was not supposed to have been, and drove right in front of a surprised Princip. One can almost picture him, sandwich in hand, slack-jawed in surprise. When Loyka realized his mistake and slammed on the brakes, the archduke and his wife were sitting ducks. Princip seized the opportunity and fired into the open car at a range of five feet, killing them both.

War, poverty, misery, and nearly one hundred million people dead came from what essentially was a single wrong turn. A single bad bit of data. A tiny piece of ignorance.

Maybe World War I would have happened anyway. Maybe it was inevitable at that point that some spark would set off the powder keg of Europe. But maybe not. Maybe a bad piece of information did lead to the deaths of millions. It would not be the first time, or the last, that ignorance in the world exacted a high price.

Dictionary.com defines "ignorance" as "lack of knowledge, learning, information." In a strict sense, I could claim that the Internet will end ignorance because, to the extent someone has access to it, they can obtain any knowledge they need. I could make the case that all knowledge is making its way online and as such, you can know anything. Thus the end of ignorance. Let's call it a day and go home.

If my reasoning stopped there, you would probably start fishing around for the receipt for this book and read up on your bookseller's return policy. While such an argument may be technically correct, I mean a good deal more by "end of ignorance" than just access to information.

The Internet is not unique in solving for this access to information. It does so in orders of magnitude better than what came before it—libraries—but only better, not differently. In 1976, if you wanted to know the middle names of all the signers of the Declaration of Independence, you could find out. It would just take several hours as opposed to a few minutes.

At issue here is what I call "The Truth Is Out There Problem." To understand this problem, consider our relationship with knowledge over the centuries.

Long ago, before Gutenberg, if you wanted to know something, you had to memorize it. That was the only way you could know something—and when the "Knower" died, the knowledge was gone, unless it had been shared with (and memorized by) someone else.

Even if Knower #1 taught someone the fact, story, etc., what if Knower #2 didn't remember it? Or changed it? Or what if Knower #2 died without teaching another? Thus knowledge was fragile; it was difficult to preserve over time because it had to be passed from person to person in an unbroken chain. It was like the Olympic torch in antiquity: All it took was one guy carrying the torch to slip in the mud and the entire chain was broken.

Not only was the extent of your knowledge whatever your own mind held, but as far as you were concerned, the sum total of all human knowledge was the aggregate of what was known by the three or four hundred people in your village. If somebody outside your village knew something, it did not matter; for you, it did not exist.

Then something wonderful happened: the invention of the modern codex, the book, in the form we know it today. And not just its invention, but its production as an affordable item, available to the middle class.

Now all of a sudden, ideas were persistent. The author could die, but the book survived. In fact, the book could survive for centuries, as could new perfect copies of the book, and thus the ideas could be distributed.

Via books, ideas became mobile—or as we would say today, went viral— spreading to other villages and other countries and to multiple places around the world simultaneously. This facilitated progress in science, the arts, theology, mathematics, and virtually every discipline in which human curiosity expressed itself.

This led to the creation of large libraries all around the world—and this was a problem. Why? Because if you come into this library and know with certainty the piece of information you need is in there yet can't find it, then for all intents and purposes, it does not exist. It's irrelevant.

I call this "The Truth Is Out There Problem": Even if you have an intellectual understanding that the truth is out there, if you cannot find it, it's as if it doesn't exist. So the simple fact that all the information in the world may soon be available to everyone via the Internet does not end ignorance, just as the existence of a library in your city doesn't end ignorance.

Search engines such as Google exist to solve this problem. They try to connect the person who wants to know something to the thing that person wants to know. Search engines have done a fabulous job tackling this problem, even given the vast, vast, amounts of information added to the Internet every day. However, even if this problem were solved perfectly, it doesn't really end ignorance. Even if we all had a robot that went with us everywhere and answered every question anyone put to us, there would still be ignorance in the world. The reason for this is what I call "The You Don't Know What to Ask Problem."

Let me illustrate this one from my own life. I enjoy traveling, especially to very different places. When I go to far-flung places, I often know little of local customs and, through ignorance, I have committed more than one faux pas. But even if I had a robot that knew everything, I couldn't really say, "Tell me every custom they have here," and be fully informed. I would need the robot to be able to proactively offer suggestions.

That's part of what I mean by the end of ignorance: having perfect information proactively delivered to you. But even that is not enough.

OF KNOWLEDGE, WISDOM, AND KINGS

To understand the distinction between wisdom and knowledge, consider the story of King Croesus, who ruled Lydia (near present-day Turkey) around 550 BC.

In the ancient world, different cities or regions would have an oracle to whom people could go and ask a question. The most famous of these was the Oracle at Delphi. King Croesus was very intrigued by all these oracles around the world. So he commissioned seven emissaries to go out to seven certain oracles around the world and on a predetermined day, let's say July 12, at a predetermined time, say 3:00 p.m. Lydian time, they were to ask their respective oracle a question: "What is King Croesus doing right now?"

The emissaries, who themselves did not know the correct answer, were to bring the replies of the oracles back to the king.

The Oracle at Delphi actually got it right. She said, "At this very moment King Croesus is making turtle and goat soup." He was, in fact, making this soup, his favorite dish. And Croesus was so amazed that he endowed the Oracle at Delphi with all kinds of gifts and planned to run all-important questions by this oracle. Wouldn't you?

Now, the problem with this is that the answers the oracles gave were somewhat vague or odd sounding. Scholars today are pretty sure that in the case of Delphi, the oracle was inadvertently breathing gases that rose from the cave in which she sat. These gases pretty much made the oracle loopy, like the famous "David after Dentist" video on YouTube. This accounted for the odd answers.

In any event, King Croesus had it in his mind to wage war against the Persians, so he asked the oracle: "Should I attack the Persians?" The oracle responded that if he crossed the river Halys and invaded Persia, a mighty empire would fall. Croesus heard what he wanted to hear and interpreted this as a good sign, but it turns out the oracle meant King Croesus's empire would fall. Croesus attacked, was defeated, and was killed.

I tell this story to make a comparison between modern times and the past. In the ancient world, man wanted guidance from the gods on what he *should* do. He wanted the wisdom of the gods. It is wisdom that King Solomon asked God for, not intelligence. In the modern era, we don't really turn to machines for their wisdom but instead turn to them for information. Think of how the computer in the Star Trek universe was a purely factual machine. Its purpose was to answer factual questions ("Computer, what is the closest planet with dilithium crystals?"), not wisdom questions ("Computer, should we go there?").

I think this is, in part, because we are only now reaching the point where machines can suggest what we should do, and for the first time, we are beginning to see how it will be technically possible to build wise machines. Wise machines are dramatically more valuable than machines that just store and retrieve information.

We will finally be able to build an oracle, and we will use that tool, that collection of life experiences, to optimize our own lives.

"If only I had known," we often lament, in the widespread belief that to know everything would mean we would never make mistakes. But knowing isn't enough. You can know everything in the world and still make bad decisions. You have to have something more: wisdom. I define wisdom as deriving a course of action from applying a value system to a situation.

Knowledge is cold facts. Knowledge is a statement like, "The interest rate on this credit card is 29.9 percent." Wisdom looks at that piece of knowledge and applies a value to it—such as, "I don't want to be in debt." And wisdom probably concludes, "I should not apply for this credit card."

So there is truth in the expression "knowledge is power," because knowledge can lay the foundation for good decisions. But it requires wisdom to put knowledge into action. It requires knowing what you should do in a given situation. So really, wisdom is power.

And I think that is what the Internet will deliver. It will make us all profoundly wise, wiser than the wisest person who has ever lived.

So let's raise the bar to this lofty level. By "the end of ignorance," I mean a world where everyone everywhere will be able to go through life making wise decisions based on near-perfect information. Or at least they will know the wise choice to make; whether they will choose it is another matter.

Now, let's see how this might come about.

Your Digital Echo

To photograph truthfully and effectively is to see beneath the surfaces and record the qualities of nature and humanity which live or are latent in all things.
—Ansel Adams

As you pass through modern life, you leave a Digital Echo, a picture of who you are and what you are doing. More and more of your everyday life leaves such an echo.

When you swipe a credit card to fill up your car with gas at the corner of sixth and Congress on January 21 at 11:38 p.m., your location and activity are digitally recorded, presumably for all time. Your credit card statement captures an accurate, albeit extremely abbreviated, record of your comings and goings.

Pushing this to its logical extreme: What if everything you did was digitally remembered? To avoid privacy issues at this point, let's stipulate that everything is recorded only for your future reference. Just for you.

Imagine that every word you said was recorded by your personal recorder and automatically transcribed. This would be very useful: No more struggling to remember what you promised the client you would deliver by Friday; you just look up the transcript.

Then imagine GPS is layered in—very accurate GPS that tracks your every move, even in your own home. No more trying to retrace your steps to find your car keys; you can see where you left them by checking your GPS system records.

Next, imagine everything you do is remembered in detail. Not just that you went to a certain address but that the address was a movie theater and—based on where you sat and that you ordered tickets online—you saw Episode VII of *Star Wars*. Or: You are watching TV, flipping through the channels—and every channel you pause on, every channel you watch, every channel you come back to, are all perfectly logged.

Why would you want a record of this? Bear with me a little longer.

Now, think about everything being recorded. Everything you buy. Every meal you order. Every restaurant you visit. Every word you type. Every book you read. The time you have set for your lawn sprinkler to turn on. Every phone call you make. When you last went to the dentist. Everything you saw, that your eyeballs tracked to, how long you looked at it—and not just everything you ever looked at, but your physiological response. Did your eyes dilate? Your pulse increase? Your muscles tighten? Did you smile?

All your medical records. All your tax records. Every song you download and how many times you play it. Every person you meet (we all have GPS). Everything your body does. Every heartbeat. Every bite you eat, every step you take. Every breath you breathe.

Imagine it is all recorded. A complete Digital Echo of your life.

Isn't this the direction technology inevitably is heading? Whether you love it or hate it, do you doubt it will happen?

But let's not stop there.

The always-entertaining Jesse Schell, a computer-game designer and author, gives a talk about a future in which sensors are recording your every action passively. He says, in part:

> Technology keeps getting cheaper and cheaper and cheaper. And there's gonna be sensors everywhere, detecting so many things in your life. . . . So, we're moving on a road towards disposable technology. If anyone here ever bought a Furby, right, a Furby cost $20 or $30. It has more technology in it than they used to put a man on the moon. And many people have now thrown out their Furbys, because it's like "it's kinda dumb" and they throw it out. It's disposable technology. We are, before too long, gonna get to the point where every soda can, every cereal box is gonna be able to have a CPU, a screen, and a camera on board it, and a Wi-Fi connector, so that it can be connected to the Internet.
>
> And what will that world be like? Well, I think it will be like this. You'll get up in the morning to brush your teeth. And the toothbrush can sense that you're brushing your teeth and so, hey, good job for you. Ten points for brushing your teeth. And it can measure how long, and you're supposed to brush them for three minutes and you did. Good job, you brushed your teeth for three minutes. And so you get a bonus for that. And hey, you brushed your teeth every day this week, another bonus. Who cares? The toothpaste company, the toothbrush company. The more you brush, the more toothpaste you use. They have a vested financial interest.[3]

Schell regards sensors largely in terms of gameplay—but for our purposes, think of them passively logging your life. Most of the time, the logging of your life, your Digital Echo, will simply be a by-product of some

---

3. From Professor Jesse Schell's "Design Outside the Box" presentation made at the D.I.C.E. Summit, Feb 2010. Copyright © 2010 by **Jesse Schell**. Reprinted by permission of the author.

action, much like your credit card statement is today. The statement is not there because you want the log per se but because the logging of the actions is what documents how much you need to pay.

A contest awhile back called for people to speculate what would be the best device to hook up to the Internet. I can't really remember what won, though at the time, I thought it all very forward looking and exciting. Now my expectations have changed so much that I'm annoyed everything isn't already connected to the Internet. Everything. My car, refrigerator, lawn-mower, sprinkler system, smoke alarms, locks, and even my clothes.

Remember the notion that the Internet wouldn't turn out to be only for one purpose—that while my car is clearly for taking me places, the Internet won't be for doing one single task, but many? That said, if I had to pick one function I think the Internet will turn out to "be," it is this: The Internet will become a repository and a set of applications for storing the sum total of all life experiences of all people on Earth. It will be the collective memory and experience of the planet.

Before we take that further, let's consider something the Internet has taught us about ourselves.

Surprise! We share.

The miracle is this: The more we share, the more we have.
—Leonard Nimoy

I am intrigued by what we have built the Internet to do that has no offline corollary. These tell us something about ourselves we didn't know before.

I already knew people wanted to sell the stuff in their attic or send money to other people before eBay or PayPal came along, because the offline world had already invented garage sales and Western Union. But Twitter? Well, that tells us something new about ourselves—in fact, a lot of things: the kinds of information we want to share, the kinds of information we want to consume, and the immediacy with which we want it all to occur.

Overall, I am really proud of what we are building the Internet to do. It reflects well on us. We are building the Internet to connect with each other better, to share information, to collaborate, to offer mutual support, and so on. I know the list of nefarious uses of the Internet—but on balance, we are building it for good purposes.

One aspect of Internet use that has surprised me is how willing we are to expend time and energy for strangers with no hope of anything in return—no money, no fame, no glory, no nothing. You see it all over the Internet. You post some problem that you have—personal, technical, culinary, whatever—and people will give you advice. They will take time to write a great big forum post just for you, a total stranger they will never meet.

The Internet is full of sites that offer good to humanity and yield no profit for the people working on them. The Open Directory Project—where fifty thousand editors try to organize the web into a directory of sites for no reward at all—comes instantly to mind. Of course, Wikipedia is another textbook example where people toil for no payment, and anonymously as well. All they gain is a sense of contributing.

But as I watch how we are building and using the Internet, the one-on-one encounters impress me most. People who take time out of their schedule to do something that helps just one person. That isn't some "I want to contribute to the greater good of humanity" kind of sacrifice, but a highly personal one. I guarantee that if I post to a forum, "I am going to Seattle this weekend with my family; what are some things we should do?" people will post answers.

It's nice, isn't it? We have a natural desire to want to help others. The open source movement and Creative Commons licensing are examples of people willing to share their intellectual labor to help others. Other examples include Ruby on Rails and Project Gutenberg to Freecycle and the entire concept of freeware. Online, people are constantly thinking up new ways to share with others.

Given that, I consider it highly likely that people will share their Digital Echo. Probably anonymously, probably with certain controls—but I believe they will share it.

Would you? Consider what you would do in the following situations.

You buy a movie ticket online, go to the theater at the appointed time—and an hour into the movie, you get up and leave. Certainly, you don't want the whole world to know where you were last night. But would you anonymously let the simple fact that a person with your demographics got up and left be used to compute a "percentage of people that got up and left" measurement that will become a factor in movie recommendation engines? Granted, you may have gotten up and left simply because you received an urgent phone call or text instead of dislike for the movie, so would you let the system check your reason for departure by looking at your incoming call and text records before your "I got up and left the movie" vote was cast?

Again, we aren't talking about anyone knowing anything about you personally. We are talking about a setting to your Digital Echo file that says, "Information that isn't tied to me personally can be contributed to pools of rolled-up data."

Furthermore, would you allow this "I got up and left" vote to include other information about you that cannot be tied to you personally—such as all the movies you rented, went to, and so on—so that this information can be used to help inform the kind of person who gets up and leaves this type of movie?

I think most people would. I think to the extent the data is not identifiable to a person and is only used to make suggestions to others, people will participate.

Let's try another one. You probably have a device, such as a smart phone, that has an Internet connection and a GPS. That device can track where you are at any time. Individuals understandably have concerns about the use of this information. But let's say everyone had their device set to "broadcast my location but not my identity" constantly. What can you do with that?

For one thing, you can have a completely fluid, fully dynamic, real-time map of traffic patterns in your city. Armed with everyone's locations, your navigation system could know the fastest route, and traffic could be evenly distributed across the entire grid. Would you contribute your anonymous location to a traffic-speed-optimization engine? I think most people would.

How about people with incurable diseases: Would they pool medical and demographic information in the hopes a cure could be found? Countless people already do.

Of course, privacy protection will be key. People will only contribute to the extent that their most personal information is protected. But over time, as people have more and more experiences where they benefit from certain data being shared (like the traffic example), they will become more inclined to add their information to the pool. They will contribute to the greater good. They will become part of the solution.

Over time, people will see they will be contributing to the construction of a knowledge base which really is the complete recording of every action of every member of humanity. And they will see how this information will be used to better the lives of other people in very real ways.

Data and Knowledge

All men by nature desire knowledge.
—Aristotle

Let's review. When I use the word "data," I am referring to observational or demonstrable facts (for example, the average high temperature in Austin, Texas, in August for the past one hundred years—a simple, measurable fact).

When I use the word "knowledge," I am referring to a conclusion logically drawn from facts, such as, "It is usually very hot in August in Austin." Knowledge often consists of the rolled-up conclusions from many pieces of data.

Finally, when I use the word "wisdom," I am talking about applying a value system to knowledge to suggest a course of action. For instance, my value may be "I don't like being hot." Therefore, the wise decision is to avoid Austin in August.

With these terms in mind, consider this observation: For the better part of human history, as people have sought to understand their world, an extensive amount of their time has been spent collecting or retrieving data.

Think about notable astronomers of centuries past, who collected their own data through years of careful observation. Or social scientists who spent vast amounts of time poring over millions of pages of census records. Or early climatologists who made their own daily observations of precipitation and barometric pressure, interpreting as well as collecting readings.

Even today, the scientific method involves experimentation that almost always necessitates some amount of data collection. But more and more, human progress is about gleaning knowledge from the incomprehensible amounts of data that already have been collected over the course of human history.

Remember Eric Schmidt's statement that more information is created every two days than in all of human history prior to 2003? Statistics like this are generally not rigorously calculated. But as a meme it captures something we all know instinctively—more data, more raw information, is available now than anyone presently can process or understand.

So we've reached an unprecedented situation in the course of human learning, which is this: The amount of data we have available has outstripped our ability to process it and turn it into knowledge. In our modern age, people disagree not just in terms of values they apply to knowledge, but they disagree on actual pieces of knowledge. Does human activity cause the planet to warm? Does eating eggs raise a person's cholesterol? Does illegal immigration take jobs from citizens? These are not differences of values but disagreements in terms of knowledge. These are all knowable things, and yet there is no universal agreement on them.

This unique phenomenon will pass as we learn to cope with vast amounts of data. More precisely, we will probably teach machines to teach themselves how to process it for us and surface findings to us. We will be completely insulated from the collecting and researching of data so that we can focus entirely on turning data into knowledge.

This technological shift will have profound effects on the course of human history. Science's progress over the past few hundred years has been determined mainly by the relatively slow speed at which we were able to collect data. Although the pace of technological change has quickened, in the future it will become astonishingly faster because the amount of data we can access and our ability to transform data into knowledge will catch up with each other. This will turbocharge science, which will no longer rely exclusively on slow observations in real time. Instead of science proceeding at the slow speed of time, the only limit on its progress will be processor speed—and those two speeds hardly can be compared. Just as an example: Imagine how much astronomy will progress when, instead of once a day, observations can be made up to one billion times a second.

A website called Wolfram Alpha is amazing to me, especially in its aspirations. It is an answer engine, but one that attempts to answer questions that have never before been asked. You could ask it, "What is the number of presidents of the United States born on Friday who have older sisters, multiplied by the number of wars lost by Bolivia?" and it could instantly give you an answer. I say "could" because I doubt they have all those databases loaded yet, but you get the idea. It is a safe bet that no one has ever asked that question before, and yet this system is designed to answer it.

Up until now, we have thought of the Internet as a place to store information, and we have depended upon search engines to help us find it. But this arrangement is of little use if the question has never before been asked.

Imagine not only that you could get instant answers to questions that have never been asked but also that the (anonymous) combined experiential data of everything every person ever did was the data that powered it. You could start looking around for lines that connect things we didn't previously think were connected.

But take it a step further. The machine should start looking for correlations we would not expect. What if it surfaced that people who drink a certain kind of coffee have, on average, higher incomes and, further, that people who switch to this coffee subsequently make more money? Or that a certain group of people who do a seemingly unrelated set of a dozen activities report levels of happiness higher than average?

Or to continue with fictional cases: Why does gasoline made from oil refined at one refinery burn more efficiently? Why is the population of some endangered animal declining everywhere but in one location? Why are there fewer traffic jams in one certain city than in any other of its size? Why are dropout rates in some schools lower than demographically matched schools anywhere else in the world?

Imagine what can be culled from this data. In the past, a scientist began with a surmise or hunch and began gathering data to prove or disprove it. Or, through serendipity, scientists stumbled into things—with those "your chocolate is in my peanut butter" moments. It really is embarrassing how many scientific advancements resulted from accidents, including Alexander Fleming's 1928 discovery of penicillin, Louis Pasteur's 1879 discovery of the principle of vaccination, and Wilhelm Roentgen's accidental discovery of X-rays, for which he earned a Nobel Prize.

What if the capability to see connections and even to have them detected was all there for us?

The ability of science and technology to improve human life is known to us. Simple measures of GNP and prosperity vastly underreport this. Quantitative measures don't reflect qualitative improvements. It is true that I own a car just like my grandfather did, but my car is more reliable, allows me to travel in more comfort, tells me how to get where I am going, and is vastly safer than his. And yet, by the coarse measures we use, in a sense we have the same level of prosperity because we both have cars. My grandfather had a local Carnegie Library. I have the Internet. GNP and "standard of living" measurements don't capture this.

I will return to this topic in the disease chapter, but for now I needed to provide an argument to tackle the "ignorance" challenge.

Wise Decisions

To make no mistakes is not in the power of man;
but from their errors and mistakes the wise and good
learn wisdom for the future.
—Plutarch

To make my case that machines will bring about the end of ignorance, I begin with a company I admire: Amazon.com, the world's largest online retailer.

Since it debuted selling books in 1995, Amazon has expanded to sell all kinds of products. When you look at a product on one of its web pages, Amazon suggests other products you might like as well. On the same page,

Amazon says "Frequently Bought Together" and then lists a few other products. For instance, I just searched Amazon for "Apple TV," and it suggested an HDMI cable and a digital audio optical cable. These are good suggestions! They show complementary products to the one you are considering.

Additionally, right below that is a section called, "What Do Customers Ultimately Buy After Viewing This Item?" (I am not entirely sure why they capitalize the first letter of each of the words, but they probably have a good reason.) This section shows not complementary products but, essentially, competitive products. Most people buy Apple TV, but a few buy the Roku XDS Streaming Player. Amazon even tells you what percentage of people buys each one.

Both of these sections offer tremendous value to the shopper. I daresay if you have purchased anything on Amazon, you have almost certainly, at some point, purchased an additional item Amazon suggested.

How do these features work so well? Well, obviously, Amazon is able to collect this data as they make sales. These features weren't on the site when it was first launched because the necessary data did not yet exist. Over time, Amazon has achieved such scale and thus has collected so much data that their suggestions are really useful. This compounds because every time they make a sale, they get a new piece of data, which makes making the next sale easier. And every day, their product gets better because it is being fed more data.

Does this behavior have an offline corollary? Absolutely. Picture yourself in a men's clothing store. You are being helped by an excellent salesperson who has been working there for twenty-five years. You have picked out a suit, a sharp grey one with barely detectable pinstripes. Now you need shoes—but which ones? The salesperson offers, "I find that my customers who buy this suit almost always get wingtips."

After a few minutes more, you decide this really isn't the suit for you. It's wool and is a bit scratchy. So the salesperson says, "If you like that suit, then come over here and try this one from Ralph Lauren."

This scene, in one form or another, should seem familiar. In general, when you have such a salesperson, the information is useful. The twenty-five years of experience really does make a difference.

That said, the suggestions of the twenty-five-year sales veteran wouldn't stand a chance against Amazon. Even an exceptional salesperson has an imperfect memory. Of the twenty thousand sales he has made in his career, he probably remembers a few hundred distinctly and a few thousand vaguely. Amazon remembers millions of transactions perfectly.

Any time you can move data collection from humans to computers, you get vast improvements in efficiency. Any time you can move data storage from brains to hard drives, you get vast improvements in efficiency. Any time you can move data processing from intellects to CPUs, you get vast improvements in efficiency. Not by a factor of 50 percent or 70 percent, but by millions of times.

A great example of this is the calculation of the mathematical constant pi, or π. In 1400, Mādhava of Sangamāgrama calculated pi to thirteen decimal places, that is, 3.1415926535897. Two hundred years later, Ludolph van Ceulen calculated it to thirty-five digits. It took him most of his life to do this, and the value was engraved on his tombstone. Two hundred years later, William Rutherford thought he had calculated it to 208 digits but only got the first 152 correct, so we will give him credit that far.

A century later, machines entered the scene. Using a desk calculator in 1949, D. F. Ferguson calculated it correctly to more than one thousand digits. Ten years later, in 1959, Francois Genuys used an IBM 704 and calculated pi to more than fifteen thousand digits in just four hours. By 1973 it was calculated to more than a million digits, in 1983 more than ten million digits, in 1987 more than one hundred million digits, in 1989 more than one billion digits, and in 1997 more than fifty billion digits. In 2009, pi was calculated to more than two trillion digits—in less than thirty hours.

Now, don't get me wrong. When I watch a *Terminator* movie, I am rooting for the people, not the machines. Machines can actually do a very limited palette of things. But give credit where credit is due: For certain tasks, machines perform vastly better than humans.

Returning to our twenty-five-year-veteran salesperson, let's say he has been replaced by a robot powered by a version of Amazon's suggestion engine. So now that the task of remembering past purchases and using that information to suggest future purchases is completely transitioned to machines, it operates on a whole different scale. CPU cycles have replaced the passing of time. Four things will then happen that will make the suggestion engine get vastly better over time:

1. The database of associations will grow forever. Every sale from the point the robot was turned on to when the sun finally burns out will be perfectly remembered. By contrast, when our veteran salesperson retired, he could have been replaced by a new kid, who would have had to start from scratch.

2. Self-teaching algorithms will get better and better at making suggestions. For instance, they will learn subtleties such as suggesting beach gear if a person buys a cooler in July and tailgating gear if the same purchase is made in October. The machine will figure this out as it collects more data and incorporates more variables, and then experiments on people to see which combinations of factors work the best. This will allow the algorithms to get progressively better until the end of time.

3. More and more data about each customer will be available. That includes data you voluntarily provide so that machines make better suggestions, data it learns about you based on its prior interactions with you, and public data taken from the Internet (your age, for instance). Armed with this data, it will suggest different products to me than to you. Because I am a forty-two-year-old man and I pay with an American Express and was born on a Friday, part my hair on the left, and have a thirty-four-inch waist, the machine suggests what I should buy. When all possible data becomes available, the most unimaginable and arcane associations can be tested.

4. Because of Moore's Law, computers will get faster and storage will be cheaper. More data will be saved and more algorithms tested, more obscure data scrubbed in a never-ending search for patterns. In other words, the rate at which it learns will increase indefinitely.

As time passes, the suggestions will become astonishingly on-target—and no human will have programmed that. Once we get the problem off our "to-do list" and stick it onto the computer's, we largely will be done. We will just sit back and let the machines sort it all out.

Once that is achieved, the sort of event that will happen is: You will be online to order, say, a replacement water filter, and the suggestion engine will propose that along with the filter, you might like to buy . . . a pogo stick. If you were to ask to see the basis for that suggestion, the output would be tens of thousands of pages of analysis, correlations, tests, demographics, and so forth. A person could dedicate his life to understanding just one suggestion and never even get close. But it would be eerily, astonishingly, mind-blowingly accurate. You will find that you probably really *did* want a pogo stick. No human could ever do this, for in these purely computational matters, machines are vastly superior to us, and always will be.

Humans should not feel threatened in any way by this, and yet it still makes some people defensive and uncomfortable. They might balk at getting on an airline flight flown by a computer and prefer having a pilot on board to take over if he "feels in his gut" that something is wrong (even if that feeling is the airport burrito he had for lunch). They feel validated by stories in which a human believed a computer was wrong, ignored the computer's advice, turned out to be right—and got a happy ending instead of the ominous "what if . . ." of heeding the computer.

To me, those stories feel a bit desperate. They're like the fable of John Henry, who hammered in railroad spikes and worked himself literally to death in a frenzied effort to prove he could outperform the newfangled steam drill. He should have just become a steam drill operator! Because even if computers are not 100 percent right 100 percent of the time, here are two statements I believe are absolutely true:

1. A computer can do some tasks better than a person can.

2. Any task a computer can do better than a person is, by definition, a task requiring no human creativity or ingenuity. If it required those things, the computer couldn't do it.

Machines will never, in my opinion, be able to be creative. That is what we humans do. And that is why, if we are to use the Internet and technology to end ignorance, we still need people like Jim Haynes. Let me introduce you to him.

The Jim Haynes Effect

What we do in life echoes in eternity.
—Maximus, in the movie Gladiator

An American originally from New Orleans, Jim Haynes lives in Paris. He is well known because of an extraordinary practice. Almost every Sunday for the past thirty-four years (except during summer vacations), he has hosted a dinner party. For each dinner, sixty or more people show up. The same people seldom show up twice. And Jim never has met any of his dinner guests beforehand. They are people who heard of his gatherings, contacted him, and said, "I want to come to your dinner party." And he said, "Okay."

Once Jim extends the invitation, he memorizes all the individuals' names, where they are from, what they do for a living, information about their families, and so forth. So when I knocked on the door of Jim's atelier and said, "Hey, I'm Byron Reese," he said, "Oh, Byron, come over here, I want you to meet this guy. He is also from Austin, and he's in Internet publishing, too." Jim Haynes has had well over 100,000 people come over for dinner.

Years ago, Jim published a series of guidebooks for foreign destinations that aren't about what you should see or what the monetary system is or how public transit works or how you ask "where is the bathroom" in the local language. These guidebooks are lists of people who live in that area who would be willing to meet you for coffee. To him that is what seeing the world is about.

He once said he does all this because he wants to introduce everyone in the world to everyone else.

I like this goal, and I would like to do it as well, but in bits, not bites. How would this work? Remember your Digital Echo file, that record of everything you do and say? Imagine it has a million elements in it. (It would have many more, but for now let's just say it includes a million things about you.)

Then imagine if you shared your Digital Echo with a billion other people on the planet. And if each of those billion people in turn shared a million of their life experiences, and you recorded them, you'd have an aggregate number of life experiences so large I had to look it up online. It's called a quadrillion.

Imagine what you could do with the combined learning of a quadrillion life experiences. With such an ability to learn from the actions of so many others, you could advance humanity at a rate that is almost incomprehensible.

Further, suppose a way existed for you to learn everything that *all people* did: what kind of camera the photographer shoots with, where people go to school and where they work and which restaurants they choose. And from every experience they have had in their lives, we would be able to infer what was successful and what was not successful. All these people and a billion more just like them would be logging every single thing that they do and it could be used for your benefit, so that you could learn. You could learn from their success and you could learn from their failure.

Think about this. It would be the seminal accomplishment of humanity. A recording of every cause and effect. A collective memory. No longer would we learn and forget, learn and forget, learn and forget, again and again, as a species. We could learn and remember. Everyone's life experiences would become the data to make everyone else's life better. How might this work?

To use a simple example: You are in San Francisco. You are not from there, and you want to go out for Italian food for dinner. You need an answer to a basic question: "Where should I go for Italian food?"

Back in the old days (the 1980s), you only had data—say, the Yellow Pages with its list of restaurants. You had no real knowledge and therefore no way to make a wise decision.

Then along came the web, and you had data plus knowledge. You could see which restaurants were rated the highest on Yelp, which ones certain reviewers liked, and so on. You were better off than before, in terms of making a knowledgeable decision. But you still were working with the biased, anecdotal opinions of a few people not very like you.

To attempt to make a wise choice today, you have to take that imperfect knowledge and apply your unique values: "I want a meal that tastes good to me, in a restaurant I think looks nice, for what I consider to be a reasonable price." But the web isn't able to automatically apply your unique values, so you do the best you can under the circumstances: You read a few reviews, get suggestions from friends, and talk to the concierge at your hotel. We all have had that turn out poorly! We all have experienced choosing the wrong restaurant—and odds are that we seldom have chosen what would have been the absolute best choice for us.

In the future, something very much like the Amazon suggestion engine, but for all of life, will change that. First, it will consider all your friends, people with whom you have actual intimate relationships, and it will look at where they go for Italian food. Not just where they have been, but where they have been more than once, from which the system reasonably infers they like the place. The system will also look for anything they've written publicly about this place (Yelp, Facebook, personal blog) and which superlatives they used to describe it.

Then my system will go out further and look at their friends and their friends and their friends and it will start asking, "Where did they go for Italian food in San Francisco more than once?" Then it will look at everybody in San Francisco. Where do they go for Italian food? And not just where do they go, but where is it that people drive the farthest to get to? The system has data from all their GPS records and infers that to drive across town several times for a place is a stronger vote than eating at the corner restaurant. And so we are interested in the Italian restaurants people drive across town repeatedly to frequent.

This system will look at all the restaurants across the country (even around the world) where you have dined frequently. It will look at all other people who like the same restaurants and see where they repeatedly go for Italian food in San Francisco. The system will weigh heavily the choices of people with Italian last names, and people who own restaurants—all these different factors, millions and millions of factors, all from the passively recorded life experiences of a billion people.

This system will look at all the Italian restaurants around the country that you already like and look at all the ingredients they order online and look for restaurants in San Francisco using the same set of ingredients. It will look at the size of your favorite restaurants, the prices of all the dishes. It will build a table of all the words used by people like you who have reviewed those restaurants and will look for San Francisco restaurants described with the same words. It will look at all this and a million other factors that would seem to be unrelated. And my system will come back with a single answer, something like, "You should go to Tommaso's on Kearny Street. The traffic to get there is not bad. The reservation system says they have availability. Here's the menu. Would you like a reservation?"

What's more, the algorithms used to make that recommendation are self-learning and will improve their suggestions over time. A day later, the system will ask, "Hey, what did you think of Tommaso's?" And you may say, "Meh." If it gets enough "meh" responses, the system knows it has to re-juggle all the stats and do it differently. Or perhaps the system won't ask you. It might just wait to see if you go to Tommaso's again the next time you visit San Francisco or scan your e-mail and conversations to see if you mention Tommaso's in passing and evaluate what words you used to describe it.

Over time, the algorithms used to sift through these quadrillion life experiences will become extremely sophisticated and extremely accurate. The system will be able, in an uncanny way, to inform you and your decisions. Of course, the system only shapes decisions insofar as you take its guidance, which begs the question: Will people follow suggestions they may not fully understand?

Sure they will. The doctor tells you to take this antibiotic and not that one, and you do. You don't necessarily understand how the doctor chooses one over the other, but you have confidence in the doctor, based on experience. Over time, we will feel that kind of confidence in this kind of system.

Today, I might be able to make a fairly wise choice for an Italian meal in San Francisco if I were willing to take a week off work and do nothing but research all the options and conduct interviews and apply my value set to the accumulated knowledge. None of us has the time to do that—but in the future, with my system, wisdom will operate at processor speeds.

You may be thinking that choosing the right place to eat Italian food doesn't constitute wisdom in a King Solomon kind of way. But I contend that only matters of degree separate it from the weightier matters we conventionally associate with wisdom.

"Where should I go to college?" is a much bigger choice that people face. Yet, just like the Italian restaurant search, it will be approachable through the aggregate life experiences of everybody on the planet. Where did they go to college? Where are people who are studying what you want to study going? What are their average salaries? How many of them have filed for unemployment since they graduated? What books are the professors reading? What have the professors at that college ordered online that you have ordered as well? How many people similar to you went to that college and are now on antidepressants? How many met their spouses at college and stayed married?

The system will look at people like you, who express the same preferences and make the same choices as you. It will look at where they went to college and what the outcome was. I could list a thousand variables that might affect your decision on where to go. We cannot deal with equations that big—but a computer will solve for that in a minute if it has enough data.

That brings us back to the need to share data—and to our online example with Amazon, and our offline example with our salesperson. When the salesperson rings up your purchase, no one tells him he had better forget what shoes he sold you with that suit and not to use that information to advise any future clients. Every time you buy a book from Amazon, its employees use your data—information about what you did on their site in the privacy of your own home—to try to sell other people more products. And no one is concerned or even notices much, because your association with that data is so removed from you. This gives me confidence that, in the wisdom-seeking systems of the future, people will be willing to share data to make the algorithms better.

Don't get me wrong: Privacy issues in the future will be thorny to work through. A world that records this much data about our lives is something akin to living in a TiVo world, where you can rewind to any moment in your life and play it again and again. These will be waters to navigate carefully, in order to make sure that the right to privacy, a cornerstone of a free society, is not destroyed.

But that has nothing to do with the *anonymous* sharing of data. Clearly, this already happens today, in a primitive form. The future system I foresee will not be different in substance, but only in degree. What will change is the amount of data that will be recorded, the speed of the processors, and the cost of storage and computation. And as people come to understand the enormous benefit of such a system, I am convinced we will permit data about our every movement, action, and word to be passively stored, and we will anonymously share that data for the betterment of society.

In some twentieth-century science fiction visions of the future, humans created friendly robot sidekicks with data storage capacity and computational speed the human brain lacked. The idea was that it would be great to make machines that behaved like us and, through that, we could harness their abilities.

But human beings are not machines. We cannot fashion them from machinery. What we can do—and should begin to do—is to track every choice and every outcome for every human being on the planet, and use machines to analyze that data. When human problems no longer are bound by the capacity and speed of our brains and the slow passage of time but instead are addressed at the speed of the fastest processors, change will be swift and profound.

As we move toward that future, it is a great tragedy that the experiences of all the people of the past are lost to us. We never will have the opportunity to learn from the details of their lives and the trillions upon trillions of trial-and-error learning experiences that humankind has repeated again and again. All the things they tried and failed, or achieved, we have to redo.

But as we do them yet again and capture them, we finally can begin to develop a planet-wide memory system. And then everyone can benefit, equally and perpetually, from everyone else's knowledge.

How the Internet and Technology Will End Ignorance

Ignorance, the root and stem of all evil.
—Plato

In the world of the future, the collective experience of everyone on the planet is recorded. All the decisions and outcomes. Millions of pieces of minutia per life, for billions of lives. The amount of data stored is so vast that even if we put a number on it, it would be beyond our comprehension.

In this world, all that data is processed using ever more sophisticated algorithms that apply the subjective values of each of us to the data and advise us on the wise decisions to make. These algorithms are self-teaching by way of feedback loops. They learn from trial and error.

Consequently, in this world we possess the perfect, personalized knowledge to make decisions about everything—what to eat, where to vacation, where to go to college, and what profession to enter. Obviously, knowing the wise course is one thing, and following it is another. But in this future world, in a way we scarcely can imagine now, we will almost always know how to avoid making mistakes because we will have all the world's knowledge available.

There are limits to this. For questions like whom you should marry or how to achieve peace in the Middle East, there simply isn't enough observational data to which we can apply this methodology.

But these are the exceptions.

In almost all aspects of life, the application of this process will bring improvements. In a profound way, our lives will be better. Our progeny will look back at us and wonder how we ever made any progress, having only tiny bits of anecdotal data and imperfect knowledge. They will feel like we stumbled sloppily into the future. When we consider the costs of all the wrong decisions ever made—a calculation I don't even know how to approach—we will think of it as a diminishing problem receding into the past.

In the future, every single person will have at his or her disposal the sum total of the life experience of everyone alive. In the years to come, the available knowledge will grow to include the sum total of the life experiences of all the people who have lived since the system came online.

In the past, knowing the wise thing to do was a power confined to a few. In the future, we will all have it. What we do with it has yet to be written. But in a world where great wisdom is available to everyone, the end of ignorance will be within our grasp.

THE END OF DISEASE

- Disease (and Cure) Defined

- "Could You Patent the Sun?"

- Dairymaids, Folklore, and Smallpox

- A Reason to Hope

- Disease: A Timeline

- We May Already Have the Answer

- The Promise of the Genome

- Information and Disease

- How the Internet and Technology Will End Disease

Disease (and Cure) Defined

*Our most basic common link is that we all inhabit this small
planet. We all breathe the same air. We all cherish our children's
future. And we are all mortal.*
—John F. Kennedy

The quest to end ignorance and the quest to end disease have two important similarities. Against both these scourges, history records that—even in challenging times, with primitive resources—humans have scored some amazing victories. And as with ignorance, we may already have much of the data we need to find solutions.

Armed with the data to develop medical knowledge and wisdom, and the technological tools to enable medical progress at an ever-quickening pace, we can confidently foresee a day when humanity will overcome disease.

Dictionary.com defines disease as "a disordered or incorrectly functioning organ, part, structure, or system of the body resulting from the effect of genetic or developmental errors, infection, poisons, nutritional deficiency or imbalance, toxicity, or unfavorable environmental factors; illness; sickness; ailment."

To that definition, I would respectfully offer this qualification: I would say that disease has a well-defined center and very fuzzy edges. Bubonic plague, to be sure, is a disease. But at times in history, left-handedness was thought to be a malady in need of curing (and in some parts of the world still is).

As an example near that well-defined center, consider infectious diseases. We do not call it disease when pathogens of a non-harmful or even beneficial type live in the human body. We do call it disease when pathogens such as viruses, bacteria, and fungi impair the function of the body.

The situation gets fuzzier, though, around that word "impair." To understand when something is impaired, we must know its normal function, since impairment is a departure from that. Two problems then arise. First, the range of "normal" for the human body's functions is both vast and subjective, and our bodies and their capabilities are so different from each other that trying to define a norm borders on the arbitrary. Second, we struggle to understand disease and impairment because we still do not know much about how the human body works, is supposed to work, or can possibly work. Some people's bodies break in ways that we don't understand. Some people have exceptional abilities we do not understand—for example, savants.

Consider Jedediah Buxton of Derbyshire, England, who in the 1700s was asked to compute the number one would get by doubling a farthing 139 times. He computed the answer in his head and recited the thirty-nine-digit answer in pounds. Consider Stephen Wiltshire, who could remember landscapes in such detail that he once drew an extremely intricate, thirty-foot panorama of Tokyo after only a short helicopter ride around the city. Consider Ellen Boudreaux, who can perform every piece of music she has ever heard even a single time—thousands upon thousands of songs.

We know for certain that these feats, and hundreds more like them, are true. We simply don't understand how it can be so. Perhaps we all have such remarkable abilities but are impaired in a way—maybe the rest of us have a disease to which these savants are immune. I'm not just playing with words here; rather, I am trying to make a point about the fuzzy edges of what is deemed a disease.

Now, back to the well-defined center. After the infectious diseases come the non-infectious ones such as cancer, Alzheimer's, and heart disease. These, too, impair the body, but without an underlying foreign pathogen. Clearly, we must also regard the various genetic ailments as being diseases as well, even though we know they, too, have no pathogenic component.

As we move out from that defined center, we come to disorders and disabilities—impairments of bodily systems that are brought about by injury, disease, or genetics. Next would come all the various syndromes, which are sets of clinically recognizable symptoms that occur together without a known cause. After these syndromes, we come to the entire spectrum of mental illnesses, from depression to paranoia.

And what do we say of aging itself? Is it a disease? An incurable, terminal disease? Now we are certainly on the fuzzy edges, a place where words, often fuzzy in their meanings, begin to fail us. A disease? A condition? A syndrome? A normal biological process? A result of our actions? A natural part of life? And what about mortality? Can that be prevented? Now we are asking questions beyond my pay grade.

So where does that leave us in our quest to end disease? I think we should aspire to this: to have such mastery over our bodies and our environment as to extract the best quality of life for the longest period of time that is both theoretically and biologically possible for every single member of the planet.

What would that look like? Under what conditions can we claim victory in this war on disease?

Since it is theoretically and biologically possible for infectious diseases to end, then the goal clearly includes the end of those. It would include ending all non-infectious diseases as well. All genetic conditions that one would reasonably wish to alter would also be altered.

Regarding disorders and disabilities: We should be able to repair, heal, or replace any part of the body not functioning at the level the person with the disability reasonably wishes it to. But I stress the word "reasonably." I might wish to run a three-minute mile like a futuristic Olympian and consider my inability to do so a disability, but it simply may not be an attainable goal for me.

Regarding the various syndromes: Over time we would expect to better understand their root causes, and consider them disorders to be cured to the extent the affected person wishes them to be. Likewise for mental illnesses: We should be able to cure them to the extent the person in question would wish them to be. (Again, within reason: I may view my less-than-200 IQ as a mental defect to be fixed but, again, that simply may not be possible).

And then there is aging. With the exception of *Turritopsis nutricula*—called the "Immortal Jellyfish" because it is believed to have no pre-determined lifespan—everything on the planet grows old and dies. Does this have to be the case? Is it possible to tweak our genome to remove aging? Is it possible to replace all our organs with freshly grown new ones created from our own cells? I do not know and certainly don't want to try to prove to you that the future will be like that. So how about this instead: What if I can show you a future where everyone on the planet will live in good health as long as it is possible for their body to live?

Let us put the bar there. By the end of disease, we accomplish all that the preceding paragraphs describe—the full spectrum of human ailments, vanquished from the globe. We will eradicate what we can, eliminate (slightly different than eradicate) all that is left, vaccinate against whatever we cannot eliminate, prevent that against which we cannot vaccinate, cure what we cannot prevent, replace what we cannot cure, and finally, as a last resort, treat what we cannot replace.

What a future that will be! A future without disease as we understand the term's meaning today. From its well-defined center to its fuzzy edges, all gone, sooner than you might guess—and beginning with some of the deadliest diseases, as we already have proven we can do. Read on.

"Could You Patent the Sun?"

When I was about nine, I had polio, and people were very
frightened for their children, so you tended to be isolated.
I was paralyzed for a while, so I watched television.
—Francis Ford Coppola, describing possibly the
only good thing to come from polio

Of all the celebrated accomplishments of science, I think none is more significant than the end of certain diseases, especially the scourge of polio. Let's look at how this happened.

Polio is a viral infection that can, in some individuals, enter the central nervous system and infect motor neurons, leading to muscle weakness and paralysis. It was recognized as a distinct condition in 1789, although records from the ancient world describe conditions highly likely to have been polio. In addition, images engraved in walls of what appear to be people infected with polio are found in Egypt dating back to at least 1400 BC. In 1840, a German physician published a seventy-eight-page paper clinically describing polio. In 1908, the polio virus was identified as the cause.

By 1910, polio spread dramatically around the world, paralyzing thousands each year. In 1916, the number of cases just in New York City was reported to be nine thousand. Epidemics in the United States in 1914 and 1919 prompted quarantine efforts in which "physicians and nurses made house-to-house searches to identify all infected persons," according to the book *Community Public Health Nursing Practice*. "Infected children were removed to hospitals and the rest of the family was quarantined until they became noninfectious. Parents were unable to leave their home to bury their child if the child died in the hospital."

In 1921, a dozen years before he would be sworn in as president, Franklin Roosevelt was diagnosed with polio. During his campaign and his time in office, the extent of the effect of his polio was kept from the public, but the fact he had the disease was commonly known. Interestingly, political cartoons of the era, both for and against FDR, showed him unaffected by the disease. Starting in 1934, Americans marked the president's birthday on January 30 by holding Birthday Balls around the country to raise money to fight polio. And near the end of 1937, Roosevelt created the National Foundation for Infant Paralysis to join in the fight.

In anticipation of the 1938 Birthday Balls, a popular radio comedian encouraged his listeners to send their spare change to the White House. His call for a "march of dimes" was a play on "The March of Time," a well-known newsreel series. The name and idea caught on, and by mid-January the biggest names of the day were promoting it on their shows: Jack Benny, Bing Crosby, and Rudy Vallee, to name but a few. On January 29, with donations pouring in, President Roosevelt took to the airwaves to extend his thanks:

> During the past few days, bags of mail have been coming, literally by the truckload, to the White House. Yesterday between forty and fifty thousand letters came to the mailroom of the White House. Today an even greater number—how many I cannot tell you, for we can only estimate the actual count by counting the mail bags. In all the envelopes are dimes and quarters and even dollar bills—gifts from grownups and children—mostly from children who want to help other children to get well. Literally, by the countless

thousands, they are pouring in, and I have figured that if the White House Staff and I were to work on nothing else for two or three months to come, we could not possibly thank the donors. Therefore . . . I must take this opportunity . . . to thank all who have aided and cooperated in the splendid work we are doing.

By the end of the four-month campaign, the White House would receive two million dimes. Soon the March of Dimes campaign became better known than the organization it benefitted. The fact it was accessible to everyone—after all, who didn't have a dime?—made it appeal to people of all ages and stations.

A few years later, with the United States again at war, most of its top medical minds were engaged in the war effort. On the research team of the eminent virologist Dr. Thomas Francis, who was working on a flu vaccine, was a young physician named Jonas Salk.

In his 1945 Birthday Ball address—which would be his last—President Roosevelt likened the fight against polio to the fight against the Nazis, who viewed the physically and mentally handicapped as inferior. Both, he said, were fundamentally wars waged for human dignity:

> Our national concern for the handicapped and the infirm is one of our national characteristics. Indeed, it caused our enemies to laugh at us as soft. "Decadent" was the word they used. . . . We will never tolerate a force that destroys the life, the happiness, the free future of our children, any more than we will tolerate the continuance on Earth of the brutalities and barbarities of the Nazis or of the Japanese warlords. We combat this evil enemy of disease at home just as unremittingly as we fight our evil enemies abroad.

After the war, in 1947, Jonas Salk was offered his own laboratory at the University of Pittsburgh School of Medicine. With a grant from the National Foundation for Infant Paralysis, he went to work on a polio vaccine.

Today, it is hard for us to imagine what that time was like. The disease struck people in childhood or in the prime of life. It often left them partially paralyzed, in wheelchairs or iron lungs (a term that's now all but forgotten and will likely send younger readers to Wikipedia). Parents kept their children at home, especially in the summer, and certainly away from public swimming areas. Nonetheless, in 1952, the United States had 58,000 new cases of polio, the most there ever would be.

But by 1952, there was also hope. Early versions of a "Salk vaccine" were successful on a few patients, so more extensive tests were planned—a vast field trial that involved twenty thousand doctors, two hundred thousand volunteers, and almost two million school children. One Gallup poll at the time said more people knew about the trial than knew the full name of the president.

On April 12, 1955, the aforementioned Dr. Francis, the monitor of the test, declared the vaccine to be a success. William O'Neill, in his book *American High: The Years of Confidence*, describes what happened next:

> Jonas Salk became world famous overnight and was showered with awards. The governor of Pennsylvania had a medal struck and the state legislature gave him a chaired professorship. New York City could not get him to accept a ticker tape parade, but eight Jonas Salk Scholarships were created by it for medical students. He received a Presidential Citation, the nation's first Congressional Medal for Distinguished Civilian Service, and honorary degrees and other honors in profusion.

By this time, one hundred million people had mailed dimes to the White House.

When legendary journalist Edward R. Murrow interviewed Dr. Salk and asked him who owned the patent on the vaccine, Salk replied, "Well, the people, I would say. There is no patent. Could you patent the sun?"

The dimes had worked. In the United States, polio cases fell to 5,600 in 1957, to 121 cases in 1964—and by 1979, there were none.

Hundreds of thousands of cases still existed, of course, in the rest of the world, even three decades after Salk's breakthrough. In 1988, the World Health Organization, partnering with UNICEF and Rotary International, announced the goal of eradicating polio by the year 2000—and although it is not yet gone, it is quickly disappearing. At present, there are about one hundred new cases reported per month around the world, infecting about the same number of people as die from lightning strikes.

The virus cannot live in immunized individuals, nor in nature. So if its person-to-person transmission can be interrupted, it truly can be eradicated from the planet. This goal is within our grasp—and with the vaccine presently priced at about thirty cents a child, shame on us for not ending polio once and for all.

As I was writing these words, my ten-year-old son came in and asked, "What are you doing?" I replied, "Writing about polio," and he asked, "What is polio?"

What an accomplishment that is!

Dairymaids, Folklore, and Smallpox

No man dared to count his children as his own
until they had had the disease.
—Comte de la Condamine, eighteenth-century
mathematician and scientist, writing about smallpox

In the century leading up to its extermination, smallpox killed about 500,000,000 people. Wars in that same period—the most destructive wars in all of history—took a fraction of that number. While difficult to know with any exactness, smallpox likely killed roughly as many people in that hundred years as have been killed in every war ever fought.

If 500,000,000 is still an inconceivably large number: Imagine a football stadium packed with spectators. A record turnout! One hundred thousand fans fill the stadium. Then imagine them all instantly dead. Next, imagine that happening every week for one hundred years. That is the dreadful history of the final, and deadliest, century of smallpox.

Now the disease is eradicated. Aside from two laboratory samples, one in the United States and one in Russia, it does not exist on the planet. Gone! In the last thirty years there has not been a single smallpox death or even a single infection.

How did this happen? In the eradication of smallpox, as in the near-elimination of polio, I find both fascinating lessons of history and enormous reason for hope.

Smallpox has been with us for thousands of years. It was mentioned by the Hindus more than three thousand years ago (and some suggest they even inoculated against it). It was described in China about the same time. The mummified body of Egyptian Pharaoh Ramses V, also from this same general period of time, shows what are believed to be signs that he died of, or at least was infected by, smallpox.

Around 430 BC, Athens, embroiled in the Second Peloponnesian War, endured three years of epidemics that wiped out a third of its inhabitants. The description of the illness given by Thucydides, alive at the time, reads like a description of smallpox:

> [T]he body was . . . reddish, livid, and breaking out into small pustules and ulcers. [I]nternally it burned so that the patient could not bear to have on him clothing or linen. . . . The body meanwhile did not waste away so long as the distemper was at its height, but held out to a marvel against its ravages; so that when they succumbed, as in most cases, on the seventh or eighth day to the internal inflammation, they had still some strength in them. . . . For the disorder first settled in the head, ran its course from thence through the whole of the body, and even where it did not prove mortal, it still left its mark on the extremities; for it settled in the privy parts, the fingers and the toes, and many escaped with the loss of these, some too with that of their eyes.

In the Roman Empire in the second century, it is believed smallpox was the Antonine Plague that spread at a rate of ten thousand new infections a day and eventually killed seven million people, including the Roman emperor. In the 800s, smallpox wiped out a third of Japan. We read about it in vivid detail, from around the year 900, in the writings of the Persian physician Muhammad ibn Zakariya al-Razi. In the 1200s it killed a third of everyone in Iceland. In the 1400s it killed millions upon millions of Aztecs, including the emperor Cuitláhuac. In the 1500s it spread all through Europe, in the 1600s expanded its foothold in North America, and by the mid-1700s regularly occurred almost everywhere in the world.

Two things were known at the time about smallpox, also called variola. The first was that people who got it and survived never got it again; that had been noted centuries before by the Persian physician and by numerous observers since. The second was that the disease clearly passed from person to person, though by what mechanism was not clear.

Based on these two bits of knowledge, a procedure emerged, independently in several parts of the world, called variolation. A practitioner took a scab from someone with a mild case, made an incision in the skin of a healthy person, and infected that person with the scab.

After variolation, sometimes people died from the smallpox they caught. Sometimes they became infected with other illnesses, and variolation seemed to start entirely new epidemics. But in other cases, variolation worked: The person who survived it did not subsequently get smallpox. That was progress.

An Englishwoman who saw the process in Turkey in the early 1700s brought it back to England, where it was proven to be effective. During the Revolutionary War, it made its way to the Colonies, where General George Washington—seeing his troops ravaged by smallpox while the British were immune—responded by variolating the entire Continental Army.

By the 1780s, though the procedure was certainly better than nothing, it still had a fair number of problems. Enter Edward Jenner, a physician in Berkeley, Gloucestershire.

Jenner had frequently performed variolations on patients. He also knew that, according to local folklore, a person could not get smallpox if they'd already had cowpox. An illness with no serious effects on humans, cowpox caused lesions on cows' udders, which then could spread to dairymaids' hands. When Jenner did variolations on milkmaids who had had cowpox, they never came down with smallpox.

Jenner reasoned that the pox contracted by dairymaids could be used to impart immunity to others. In 1796, he extracted fluid from the pox on the hand of a dairymaid named Sarah Nelmes—who had caught the condition from her cow Blossom—and injected the fluid into a cut in eight-year-old James Phipps's arm. James caught the cowpox, recovered, and then Jenner variolated him. Phipps never came down with smallpox.

The Latin word for "cow" is *vacca*. Thanks to Jenner, Nelmes, Blossom, and Phipps (which sounds like a rather odd law firm), today we have the word "vaccine." And Jenner had created this vaccine for smallpox without even understanding the basics of germ theory!

In 1798, Jenner published a seventy-five-page book detailing his discovery. By 1801, his vaccine had been widely adopted across Europe and he was able to write of it:

> A hundred thousand persons, upon the smallest computation, have been inoculated in these realms. The number who have partaken of its benefits throughout Europe and other parts of the globe are incalculable; and it now becomes too manifest to admit of controversy, that the annihilation of the Small Pox, the most dreadful scourge of the human species, must be the final result of this chapter.

Jenner was right. The goal was annihilation. In areas where Jenner's techniques were available, infections fell, and when inoculation became mandatory, they plummeted. However, there were many challenges. Cowpox was a localized condition, so fresh supplies were hard to get. Although the technique of growing cowpox on cow hides would come, transporting it was difficult due to lack of refrigeration. Because of this, inoculation was done arm-to-arm, that is, use Sue's cowpox to inoculate Bob, then when Bob gets it, use that to inoculate Jill, and so on. If the conditions weren't sterile—a word that was not even comprehended at the time—the inoculation didn't work, or worse, introduced a new disease.

But with time, technology worked through all these problems. A stable vaccine was developed, our understanding of the disease expanded, and technology moved forward. In 1958, with smallpox still killing two million people a year, the World Health Organization pledged to eradicate it. In 1967 the effort was intensified. Ten years later, in Somalia, the last natural case of smallpox occurred.

The scourge was eradicated.

A Reason to Hope

We will either find a way or make one.
–Hannibal, 197 BC

We can draw lessons and encouragement from the histories of polio and smallpox, on several counts.

First: It is possible to eliminate diseases. And if it is possible to eliminate two, then it must be possible to eliminate more, for it is not that we eliminated two of the easiest diseases, but two pretty tricky ones.

How do we know these weren't the easiest diseases to eliminate? Well, the diseases that human beings focus on are the ones considered most unbearable.

Smallpox affected the rich and the poor and it changed the course of history: It killed Queen Mary II of England in 1694, King Louis I of Spain in 1724, Emperor Peter II of Russia in 1730, and King Louis XV of France in 1774, and changed the succession to the thrones of nations a dozen more times. Polio, likewise, was an equal-opportunity scourge, and infected such notables as actor Donald Sutherland, author Arthur C. Clarke, Supreme Court Justice William Douglas, Congressman Jim Scheuer, and nuclear physicist Robert Oppenheimer.

Widespread diseases that affect children, celebrities, and people we know will simply attract more public attention and funding. We are most horrified by that which strikes closest to us and reminds us of our own mortality. I think that is the case with polio and smallpox, which means they weren't eliminated because they were easy, but because they were awful.

Second: When they successfully fought these diseases, Salk and Jenner didn't have anything like the technology and knowledge that are available today, even to an undergraduate. Jenner didn't even know about germ theory, that diseases are caused by pathogens, yet he made a vaccine that worked! Every day, we seem to be getting better at distributing medical resources and information. Every day, the world has fewer unreachable corners and a more interconnected population. If the smallpox and polio successes were achieved in a low-tech world, think how much more we can accomplish with vastly improved tools, infrastructure, and communication.

Third: It is always the case that diseases are eliminated first in the healthy, well-developed, rich countries, then gradually around the world. If my reasoning elsewhere in this book is correct, we are moving toward a future where there will be nothing but healthy, well-developed, rich countries with modern infrastructure. And as population rises, education rises, health rises, and wealth rises, more and more people will be working on these problems. Expect solutions in the future to come from countries you couldn't find on a map today.

The factors that enable us to solve for and eliminate disease are getting better all the time, like wind at our back, pushing us forward. Read on to see how that momentum has built over time, and continues to build.

Disease: A Timeline

Life is not merely to be alive, but to be well.
– Marcus Valerius Martial, first century AD

Our battles with diseases go as far back into history as we can see.

Medical matters were covered extensively in early Egyptian papyri. The Ebers Papyrus—which dates to about 1500 BC but is believed to be a copy of a document dating perhaps to 3000 BC—contains a list of remedies for

ailments and sections on diagnosis and anatomy. Egyptians' medical expertise extended to nutritional theory, surgery, dentistry, the construction of
prosthetics, and other specialties, according to the historian Herodotus,
writing around 450 BC:

> Medicine is practiced among them on a plan of separa
> tion; each physician treats a single disorder, and no more:
> Thus the country swarms with medical practitioners, some
> undertaking to cure diseases of the eye, others of the head,
> others again of the teeth, others of the intestines, and some
> of those which are not local.

Herodotus neglects to note whether Egyptian malpractice attorneys were
equally specialized.

In the Indus Valley region, a center of early civilization located near present-day India, we have found extensive evidence of surgery, specialization,
medical equipment, and even elective procedures.

Early Chinese civilization had an understanding of medicine at least as
far back as 200 BC, as can be seen in the text *Recipes for Fifty-Two Ailments*,
which gives remedies for conditions from snake bites to warts.

And then we come to Greece, the home of Hippocrates, the "Father of
Modern Medicine," who left us not just the oath that bears his name but also
a corpus of roughly sixty medical texts based on his teaching. Hippocrates
was remarkable not only as a surgeon but also because he systematized medicine in his spare time. He created many of the medical terms we use today,
such as acute, chronic, endemic, epidemic, paroxysm, and relapse. He formalized the structure of medical inquiry as an independent science. He laid
out how doctors should conduct themselves professionally, how to record
patient records, and even suggested matters of personal hygiene for physicians, right down to their fingernails.

Certainly some of the medical practices of the ancient world, such as
bloodletting and the use of leeches, seem to us at least misguided and at
worst, barbaric. Because of his unmatched contribution to science, we must
grudgingly forgive Aristotle for his error in maintaining that men have more

teeth than women. We must also excuse Hippocrates for his belief that the human body is composed of four basic substances called "humors" that must be kept in balance. And while it seems counterintuitive to us, many cultures reasoned that the best way to cure chronic headaches was to drill holes in a person's head.

(The use of such practices continued into the scientific age: While Jenner was inoculating people with his new smallpox vaccine, doctors were draining half a gallon of blood from George Washington for his sore throat, a procedure that hastened his death. And today's primary method for treating cancer is, in a way, very tenth century: Essentially, chemotherapy is a medical way of saying, "Let's fill you so full of poison either you or the cancer dies. Hopefully the cancer. But frankly, we have no idea.")

I use this brief overview to point out that for thousands of years, humans have treated medicine as a scientific discipline. Even in superstitious ancient cultures, an underlying understanding was that the human body would develop problems and that those problems would have predictable solutions.

When the ancients could not find these solutions, it was not for a lack of intelligence but for a lack of technology. Many of the treatments of the ancient world had high degrees of efficacy, all obtained without access to any modern knowledge or equipment. So these doctors were perhaps just as brilliant as those who have come since. Had they had the technology of our day, I wonder what they could have accomplished.

After the ancient era, advances in medicine came more quickly. The Byzantine Empire, in the 1200s, had a network of free hospitals with separate wards for different illnesses and fresh linens changed daily.

In 1543, Andreas Vesalius published *On the Fabric of the Human Body*, which corrected errors from antiquity and advanced the medical sciences. Three years later, Girolamo Fracastoro theorized that disease is caused by objects that can be transmitted from person to person by both direct and indirect contact.

In 1628, the first complete explanation that blood flows through the body in arteries was published. In 1676, Antonie van Leeuwenhoek, the "Father of Microbiology," pointed his handcrafted microscopes at all manner of items and became the first person to see, or at least record seeing, bacteria. From that point, medicine would never be the same.

In 1736, Claudius Aymand performed the first successful appendectomy on an eleven-year-old boy. In 1747, it was discovered that lemons prevent scurvy. Half a century later, nitrous oxide came into use as an anesthetic.

In 1816, we got the stethoscope. In 1818, a human blood transfusion. In the late 1800s, Gregor Mendel gave us our first glimpse into how traits are inherited. Louis Pasteur came along around this same time and proffered the germ theory of disease and a vaccine for rabies. At the same time in Germany, Robert Koch identified the bacteria that caused tuberculosis and the one that caused cholera. In 1879 a vaccine for cholera was invented. Two years later, an anthrax vaccine; the year after that, a rabies vaccine. In 1895, X-rays were used in medical imaging, and four years later, aspirin came along.

In the early 1900s, we learned about blood types, vitamins, and Alzheimer's disease, and invented the electrocardiograph. In the First World War, we learned to treat wounds by washing them with a germicide. In 1921, a tuberculosis vaccine was developed in France. The same year, a technique for treating diabetes, insulin therapy, was developed. In the 1920s, we got a vaccine for diphtheria, pertussis, tuberculosis, and tetanus. Then came Alexander Fleming and his penicillin, saving millions of lives.

In 1935, a vaccine for yellow fever was created. Dialysis came a few years later, then chemotherapy, then the defibrillator, then the polio vaccine; then came cloning, then a kidney transplant. The 1960s brought us hip replacement, the artificial heart, a liver transplant, and a lung transplant. It brought us a measles vaccine, a rubella vaccine, a mumps vaccine, and a heart transplant.

Pause here to take a breath. There will be a test at the end of this, consisting of only two questions: First, has the pace of advance increased or decreased? Second, will the pace of advance increase or decrease in the future?

In the 1970s, we got MRIs, laser eye surgery, CT scans, and antiviral drugs. The 1980s brought us a hepatitis B vaccine, artificial skin, DNA sequencing, and laser cataract surgery. The 1990s brought us a hepatitis A vaccine and artificial muscles.

The most recent decade, the first of the Third Millennium, saw an artificial liver, a face transplant, an HPV vaccine, a bionic eye, and, most impressive, the map of the human genome.

If the magnitude and increasing complexity of these creations fails to impress you, the sheer quantity should suffice. The number of medical patents issued in 2010 was more than fifty thousand, an all-time record—and it almost certainly will be broken next year, then the next, and again the next. The number of pharmaceutical patents issued in 2010 was also more than fifty thousand—also an all-time record, and also likely to be broken again and again in the years to come.

The pace of innovation and accomplishment is already fast but will grow even faster. We will do much more in the next twenty years than in the preceding one hundred. After that, more in five years than those twenty. Then more in one year than those five.

Given all this, do you really believe disease has a chance?

We May Already Have the Answer

Let both sides seek to invoke the wonders of science instead of its terrors. Together let us explore the stars, conquer the deserts, eradicate disease, tap the ocean depths, and encourage the arts and commerce.
–John F. Kennedy

A drug called bupropion hydrochloride—trade name, Wellbutrin—has been widely prescribed for depression and has a long, successful clinical history in treating it.

Some years ago, a few people taking Wellbutrin reported that their cravings for cigarettes diminished. GlaxoSmithKline, the makers, tested it and found out that bupropion hydrochloride was a highly effective aid in smoking cessation. So they repackaged the drug under the name Zyban, and it is now prescribed to smokers wanting to shake the habit.

Its makers had not conceived bupropion hydrochloride as a drug to help people quit smoking. It was only when users of the medicine happened to notice the positive side effect that this piece of knowledge was gained.

How many connections like that are there in the universe—causes and effects we cannot see because the sheer amount of data we encounter in the everyday task of living is overwhelming to our minds?

I think it is likely that the answers to almost all our medical problems could be found in the data we may already be collecting.

For instance: Imagine all people with skin cancer voluntarily shared their Digital Echo files on an anonymous basis. Imagine they also included their genetic mapping as well as every single thing they did in their daily lives. Every food they ate. Every exercise they did. Every song they heard. Everything.

With skin cancer, like all diseases, over time some people get better and some people get worse, and often we really don't know why. Imagine a computer culling through this massive amount of data, inconceivably large, and pulling out patterns. A finding might look like this: "People who eat radishes get better slightly more frequently than people who don't."

Now, you don't know if the radishes make the people get better or if something that makes people crave radishes also beats back skin cancer. So what do you do? Dig deeper into the data.

Then we see that only people in certain parts of the country are getting better. Why would that be the case? The data shows pockets where radish efficacy is substantially higher and others where it is nonexistent. The computers would then see that most people who got better bought their radishes in stores stocked from certain farms. And not just certain farms, but farms that used a certain pesticide. Not just a certain pesticide, but pesticides that contained a certain chemical.

The machines surface this information. We act on it. Brilliant doctors try to understand what is happening, and drug companies commission studies to see if this particular chemical, frequently found in radish pesticides, known to be harmless to humans, might just cure skin cancer.

So they run trials and find that in a majority of cases it does cure skin cancer; and yet, in some it has no effect. The machines again churn on the data and reveal that it is effective when a person has a certain common, though not universal, genetic marker.

Wow. Now you have this magnificent piece of knowledge: For people who have a certain genetic marker, this radish pesticide ingredient will cure skin cancer.

Findings of this kind are impossible today because no mechanism can decipher the complex interactions of everything on the planet with everything else on the planet. Today, we discover things like "Wellbutrin helps people stop smoking" through chance and dumb luck.

The same happenchance brought us the learning that children in schools with fluorescent lights get fewer cavities than those in schools with incandescent lighting. Why is this? Fluorescent lighting increases the body's production of saliva, which helps prevent cavities. Now, we stumble upon these kinds of causal associations almost as an accident. Not long from now, computers will systematically look through trillions upon trillions of pieces of data for these associations.

I mean no disrespect to the accomplishments of science when I note how they've been slowed by our limitations in processing data. Our brains weren't designed for that, which is completely fine—that's why we build computers. We also can't hammer nails with our hands, so we invented hammers. It is not to our discredit that machines can perform calculations so wondrously fast; rather it is to our credit that we conceived of and built such machines.

The complex interactions between things we hitherto didn't know were connected (like our fictional radish/skin cancer connection) will not be limited simply to medicine; and the benefit will not be limited to scientists. Anyone will be able to formulate a hypothesis and look backward in time across the entire population, dividing the world based on any factor. This method will allow us to treat the entire world as a controlled experiment in retrospect.

Say, for instance, you believe redheads cause more traffic accidents than those with other colors of hair. You can then divide the world into redheads and non-redheads and compare their accident records. But wait: Perhaps there are more redheads now than there used to be, thus making the average age of the redheads lower. Perhaps since younger people have more wrecks, you need to control for this. So you make sure that if your population of redheads had a million people with a certain distribution of age, the distribution in your non-redhead sample is exactly the same.

You continue and control for every variable you can think of—region, brand of car, income, vision, height, eye color, and a hundred other factors. Then you ask the computer for any other statistical anomalies between these two populations. The computer reveals that redheads go to the ER more often and break bones more often.

That sends you down another line of thought. Are redheads clumsier and thus get in more accidents? Or are their bones more brittle? And of the redheads themselves, are there factors among the clumsy ones that are different than the coordinated ones? Is it actually that blue-eyed redheads have the same number of accidents as non-redheads, but brown-eyed redheads are even more clumsy, accident prone, and traffic hazards?

You can see where this is headed. Instead of creating hypotheses and constructing experiments, then modifying hypotheses and retesting, we can make all of history a controlled test and then sift through the trillions of pieces of data for meaningful information.

Why do all of this? In the fictitious case above, perhaps it turns out that these brown-eyed redheads who are stumbling through life and getting all banged up all have a certain protein deficiency caused by the same genes that make them redheaded and brown-eyed. This protein deficiency is a key component of reflexes. The brown-eyed redheads have slower reflexes and should consider getting more Vitamin X (or whatever it is).

All kinds of anomalies are in the world. Why do people who win Academy Awards outlive people who are nominated but do not win? Is it because winning the award gives them more confidence? Or is it something about them that predates their Oscar triumph and helped them win? Why do first basemen live longer than anyone else on the team? It is said that tall people live shorter lives than short people. Why is this? Are taller people heavier and thus they die sooner? One study suggested the entire difference could be accounted for simply by the fact that when tall people trip, they fall further and are thus hurt more.

Though cases like these are not really how the science will be used, they illustrate the principle. In actuality, scientists will study far more subtle associations of diet, activity, genetics, and behaviors that might give us an insight into how to live longer, happier, and better.

My guess is we won't have to absorb all this information. For example, if the system (conspiracy theorists will call it "The System") determines that people like me are happier and healthier with more thiamine in their system, that will come up in my custom vitamin formulation, which also includes whatever nutrients I didn't get enough of that day. I can, of course, see everything in it, or if I prefer, set the system to "minimum supplements" or "maximum supplements" and let the system decide. But just as I would trust my doctor or nutritionist to create a custom vitamin formula for me based on all my medical records and health conditions, I would be a million times more comfortable letting the system do it based on every bite I swallow, every bit of my genetic code, and every byte of data about the billion people to which it has access. My body would be kept in perfect condition, constantly monitored and optimized—all safely because the system is built on collective memory and experience of the entire planet.

It will be the end of the age of anecdotal evidence, where because "Aunt Martha takes a teaspoon of honey every morning and hasn't been sick in years," I should as well. Now, what everyone on the planet eats and does, and the outcome of that, will be used to help us all.

Then we will come to understand the outliers better. Why do some people live to 120? They inexplicably seem to be the ones who eat a stick of butter every night before bed or chain-smoked Lucky Strikes until they were seventy. Why is this? What is it about them and their lives that made them live so long or so well? Is it all genetic? If so, which genes? Is it behavioral? Psychological? I am eager to know.

Why do some people keep their mental faculties so late in life? Some have suggested that doing crossword puzzles helps keep the mind active. In the future, we'll not only know if that is so, but why: Perhaps mental agility is a result of their extensive exposure to a chemical in pencil lead and newsprint that they got by doing all those puzzles. Or maybe smart old people just direct that energy to crosswords and it is not the crosswords doing the job at all . . .

In the future, we will know. We will know how to live our lives to best maximize any and all factors. We may not choose to—we may choose eating cheesecake and bacon over living an estimated extra 2.4 months longer. But the choice will be ours and will be made based on facts.

This future will begin gradually. More and more data will be passively collected. More people will participate. The passage of time will grow the repository. Successes will come, encouraging more data collection and more people to participate. Once this ball gets rolling, it will speed up and, because of it, we will all wake up each morning with a little extra spring in our step and sparkle in our eye.

Once the promise of this world comes to be, new ways will be created to measure even more data. Once we know how to use it, we will start logging it. I fully expect that in the future my silverware will scan my fingerprint while I am eating and will be able to recognize me and analyze every bite I take. It should know what the food on my fork weighs, run a chemical analysis of every bite I take, and log it in my Digital Echo file for my future reference. If I am trying to portion my meals better, I could ask it, through a verbal interface, to vibrate gently when I reach seven hundred calories in that meal. It would know all my food sensitivities and alert me if a single bite had these substances in it.

In such a world, everyone who wants to be a medical scientist can be. Anyone could sit down at his or her desk, formulate a hypothesis, ask the machine a question, receive an answer, and then modify the question until causalities are found. Then that person might choose to publish those results and others could verify them. This will all be made possible because the tools needed will no longer be specialized; the interface to this massive store of information will allow people to learn at a high level even without a deep understanding of medical science. Essentially, we will be able to run as many controlled experiments as we can imagine instantly and for no cost—and that will revolutionize medicine.

You could begin studying something you have noticed anecdotally in your own life. You could say, "When I eat corn dogs, I get a headache" and start studying that. What ingredients or combination of ingredients are in corn dogs? Are these ingredients in other foods as well? Does eating those foods cause you to get a headache? You won't have to go eat the other foods; the system will remember every meal you have had and will log your headaches. Then, you will search to see if other people have this same problem. You won't be able to identify the other people; you will simply see that 1,600 other people seem to have this same corn dog issue. You will then look to see what other factors they all have in common.

Groups of people will do science this same way. When the cost of recording all the data is zero, the cost of processing it is zero, and the cost of accessing it zero, then the many sciences, especially human health, will be democratized.

The world will still need ever-smarter specialists doing ever-more complex work. I am not saying the research scientist loses out to the florist in Akron, Ohio. I am, however, saying that the florist will be one of the millions of minds accessing the data looking for associations and testing hypotheses. She will be the one who figures out that people who use antidepressants (and are thus assumed to be depressed) disproportionately live in apartments with a certain kind of coating on the floor, which contains a chemical that likely causes depression. How would we ever know that today? How much potential is there in millions of discoveries like that?

Finally, this system will not just solve for human illness, but all kinds of other problems as well. Patterns in crimes will be discovered. That issue alone could fill an entire chapter. Why do some houses get broken into and others don't? Can the system learn to predict crime targets? We will be able to examine all kinds of social issues: Why are some areas poorer than others? Why do people in certain areas stay in school longer than those in other areas? And on and on and on. A record of all human activity, with anonymity safeguards in place, will allow us all to become part of the solution by putting our minds to work on the problems of the world.

I take great comfort in this. I believe in crowdsourcing—well, crowdsourcing cubed. I think the answers to life's mysteries are buried there in the data, waiting for the florist in Akron to coax them out.

The Promise of the Genome

*You try it. You try finding out why you're you
and not somebody else.*
—Ezra Pound

Here is a fact both sobering and embarrassing: Once human beings had a vague understanding of how genetics worked, our initial response was to invent the "science" of eugenics. It's even more embarrassing that the book about racial purity that Adolf Hitler called his Bible was written by an American, Madison Grant. And the worst of all: The United States of America, the "Land of the Free," forcibly sterilized over sixty thousand "feeble-minded" citizens during the seventy-five years it was practiced in this country in order to keep them from reproducing and cluttering up the gene pool.

This proves without a doubt that the science of genetics can be horribly perverted. But because it can be misused doesn't mean it cannot be used well. Metallurgy gives us steel with which we can fashion either swords or plowshares. Our challenge is to learn how to choose the plowshares, not to abandon metallurgy.

The sequencing of the human genome, completed in 2003, stands above all other scientific advancements because it is both profound in character and unmatched in terms of potential practical application. Let's look at this from its beginning.

In 1665, physicist Robert Hooke pointed a microscope at a piece of cork and noticed many small compartments he called "cells." A decade later, Antonie van Leeuwenhoek, the aforementioned "Father of Microbiology," aimed his microscope at pond water and found it to be full of life. This was an electrifying discovery to the whole world. Life existed at a scale smaller than the eye could see.

Over time, microscopes got better. Technology allowed us to peer deeper into the mysteries of the miniscule. In 1831, Robert Brown, a Scottish botanist, could see plant cells with such clarity that he noticed spots in the middle of them. He discovered the nucleus of the cell.

Better microscopes gave us more information, more ways to unlock the secrets of life. Less than half a century after Brown's discovery, German biologist Walther Flemming looked into the tiny nucleus of a cell and was shocked to see that it was made of even smaller components. He had discovered, and seen, chromosomes.

In 1902, an American named Walter Sutton noticed that chromosomes duplicated themselves before cells divided so that each new cell had a full copy of the chromosomes. He reasoned that perhaps the chromosomes were carrying the genetic traits of the creature. But no one had any idea of the mechanism by which this could be achieved. Then in the 1940s, another American, Oswald Avery, was able to show, through an ingenious method, that the genetic information had to be carried by the DNA. Again, no one knew how this could be, but the DNA had been identified as the agent.

Then the scientific race of the century was on, with this goal: to figure out how DNA conveyed genetic information. Everyone in biology weighed in. Code breakers and linguists were consulted, chemists and biologists patched up their differences and worked together, and scientific groups were formed to share information and theories.

In 1953, James Watson and Francis Crick announced to the scientific world that they had solved the puzzle. They accurately described the construction of DNA as a double helix and showed how its structure made replication both possible and reliable.

Fifty years later, the human genome was decoded. What exactly does this mean? Let's look at that.

In every cell of your body except your red blood cells exists a copy of your DNA, which is a recipe for how to make and operate your body. Uniquely yours. A strand of your DNA is a couple of molecules wide and, amazingly, six feet long. On it is the recipe to make you, a recipe written in a language which has only four letters, commonly called G, A, T, and C—and is three billion letters long.

Stop and consider that for a moment. In every cell of your body, and there are trillions of them, this six-foot-long recipe exists. It boggles the mind to hold this image and simultaneously think of how small a cell is. In fact, if you laid out all the DNA in your body, it would stretch from the sun to Pluto.

That three-billion-letter recipe for making you is what was sequenced—deciphered and written down—in the human genome project. That is what we mean by "decoding." We don't yet know what it all does. But we have a copy of it. Today, for just a few hundred dollars, you can get a copy of your genome. Of course, if you wanted to print it out and read it, the stack of paper would be many miles high. And yet, all of that is crammed into pretty much every cell in your body.

If you and I both had our DNA sequenced and compared the output, the information would be virtually identical. After all, we both have ten fingers, two lungs, and a tongue located in our mouth. But every now and then there would be a little difference. That difference gives me brown eyes and you blue eyes. Those differences are part of what makes us unique. Even identical twins, thought until recently to have identical DNA, actually have slightly different DNA.

Some chunks of your DNA do nothing useful (that we know of yet), but we call other chunks genes. They are essentially instructions on how to make proteins, which are what build and regulate your body. Every second, millions of cells die in your body and millions are born. Each of those new cells has a new copy of your DNA. Whenever a cell divides, all kinds of checks and double checks are performed to make sure the DNA copy is accurate. On chromosome 17 is a gene called TP53. (With more than thirty thousand genes in your body, you can't expect them all to have cool names.) TP53 makes a protein called p53 that is one of these quality-control mechanisms. It can stop a cell from developing so its DNA can be repaired, it can "order up" repair on a piece of broken DNA, and it can kill a cell whose DNA cannot be repaired. This is all very critical. This protein is key in preventing cancer, for instance.

While we have deciphered the genome in that we have written it all down, we aren't at all sure which parts do what, as noted before. Some of it is known, but the function of each of the thirty thousand genes has to be figured out one at a time.

How will all of this help us end disease? A number of ways, I think.

First: It will help us understand why certain people get certain genetic diseases. By looking at how the genome varies between people with a genetic condition and people without it, we can identify the troublemaking gene. Once we have identified it, we can understand how it is going about doing its damage. Understanding how the damage occurs, we are that much closer to finding a cure. We have already seen this method work. For example, a treatment for chronic myelogenous leukemia is based on an understanding that this cancer occurs when two particular genes fuse, go haywire (not the actual medical term), and order up a massive amount of white blood cells to be made. Knowing this allowed for the creation of a drug called Imatinib, which inhibits this process.

Second: Everyone who wishes to do so will be able to contribute his genome to a common database. Then, people could start reporting all their medical issues—headaches, halitosis, heart disease—and we will begin to see commonalities between genes and conditions we do not generally regard as genetic. By doing this, we will come to understand those conditions better and perhaps prevent them. If people with those conditions get better, information about their treatment can be widely shared with those who have the common genetic factors.

Third: We will learn what treatments not to use. Due to genetic factors we will certainly learn about in the future, some drugs and treatments do not work on certain people. We hear of treatments that work some percent of the time or we hear phrases like, "They are not responding to treatment." In addition to knowing more about what will work, in the future we will also know more about what won't work.

Fourth: We will be able to define illnesses better. Diseases are frequently diagnosed with broad terms based on a set of symptoms. In the future, our understanding of our individual genomes will allow us to gain vastly more specificity concerning which ailments we have and thus learn how to cure them. What we call "heart disease" will become hundreds of individual conditions each with its own cause and, hopefully, cure.

Fifth: We will understand correlations between lifestyle factors, quality of life, and genome. Most often, this is phrased in terms of what we should not do, as in, "Because I have a genetic predilection for diabetes, I need to watch my weight." However, I fully expect we will learn things about the opposite—what we may do, thanks to our genes. For instance, have you ever seen one of those people on TV who is turning one hundred and says he ate bacon every day of his life? My guess is that such people have some genetic factor protecting them against the adverse effects of bacon. If we isolate that—what I will term the "bacon gene"—then people with that gene will be able to eat bacon without concern. That's what I call progress!

Sixth, the furthest out but most promising: We will be able to fix the genes themselves. Whether this will be by growing working copies of the genes and administering them to a patient, by introducing a nanobot that fixes them, or by any of the dozen other methods currently being developed, I do not know. But my guess is that we will be able to do this and even make existing "good" genes perform better.

When we think of decoding the genome, we typically think in terms of the human genome. And as we have seen, understanding how we are made is certainly a huge advantage in our battle with disease. But scientists have been busy sequencing all manner of things. They have sequenced the cacao tree, the mosquito, coral, the Tasmanian devil, the bald eagle, the leafcutter ant, a germ that attacks wheat plants, and the extinct woolly mammoth. Additionally, we have deciphered the genome of diseases, from SARS to influenza. Even smallpox has been sequenced and is available for download.

Understanding the recipes that make our pathogenic enemies is a huge advantage. Pathogens are not intelligent, so we can certainly outsmart them. And if we know how they are made, we can destroy them. Imagine being Jenner and not even knowing you were dealing with microbes. Or imagine being Pasteur fighting rabies and knowing there must have been a microbe down there but that it was too small to see even with the best microscopes of the day. They had so much success with so little. We cannot only see our enemy but have deconstructed it to its very core. With all due respect to Nietzsche, we have looked long into the Abyss, but the Abyss has not looked back into us.

Knowing how these pathogens work down to the molecular level, we will soon be able to use computers to model their complex interactions with our bodies, our immune systems, and whatever other factors we wish to introduce into the equation.

As an example of what I think will soon be a flood of medical advances, consider a recent report on MSNBC.com headlined, "New leukemia treatment exceeds 'wildest expectations'":

> Doctors at the University of Pennsylvania say the treatment made the most common type of leukemia completely disappear in two of the patients and reduced it by 70 percent in the third. In each of the patients, as much as five pounds of cancerous tissue completely melted away in a few weeks, and a year later it is still gone.
>
> . . . Using a modified, harmless version of HIV, the virus that causes AIDS, they inserted a series of genes into the white blood cells. These were designed to make cells target and kill the cancer cells. After growing a large batch of the genetically engineered white blood cells, the doctors injected them back into the patients . . . Doctors had told Bill Ludwig, one of the research volunteers, that he would die from his leukemia within weeks. Then he got the experimental treatment a year ago.[4]

Imagine that: being told you would die in a few weeks and then being suddenly and dramatically healed!

---

4. From "New leukemia treatment exceeds 'wildest expectations'" by Robert Bazell from *NBCNEWS.com*, August 10, 2011. Copyright © 2011 by NBCNews.com. Reproduced by permission of **MSNBC Interactive News LLC.**

Additionally, we will at some point in the not-too-distant future have enough biological understanding of the genome and enough computer horsepower to model complex interactions in the body. You would know before you received a treatment how likely it was to work for you—not merely how likely it was to work for the larger population, but for *you*.

Beyond that, we will be able to genetically modify both plants and animals with great benefits that we can only now begin to see. Rob DeSalle and Michael Yudell note in *Welcome to the Genome*:

> Pharmaceutical companies hope that in the near future, farms will replace factories for production of some drugs. Already in the works are potatoes that are genetically engineered to contain a drug to treat cirrhosis of the liver, rice to treat cystic fibrosis, and tomatoes that produce an anti-hypertension drug. Research has also been conducted using bananas genetically modified to produce certain vaccines. . . . Potato-based vaccines for hepatitis B and the Norwalk stomach virus are currently in an advanced stage of development, as are vaccines against cholera (tobacco), rabies (spinach), malaria (tobacco), and HIV (tobacco and black-eyed bean).

How about modifying a flower to produce insulin? To address what it labels "the emerging global insulin crisis," SemBioSys Genetics has successfully attached human insulin genes to the oilbody in a safflower seed so that insulin can be harvested from fields of safflower, making the drug widely available and less expensive for diabetic people all around the globe. They claim they can produce one kilogram of human insulin per acre of safflower, which would be enough to treat 2,500 diabetic patients, and estimate they could meet the exploding global demand for insulin with only three commercial farms of genetically modified safflower.

Or how about cows producing human milk? Well, not literally, but close. Two enzymes called lysozyme and lactoferrin contribute to the antimicrobial and anti-inflammatory characteristics of human milk, which contains more of those beneficial enzymes than animal milk does. However, new and improved cows are now able to make milk with more of these enzymes. The hope for such technology is that this transgenic milk might heal people with Crohn's disease or irritable bowel syndrome and perhaps even save lives around the globe where children are dying from gastrointestinal problems that lead to diarrhea and dehydration.

How can we not be excited about the possibilities this offers? It boggles the mind, especially when you consider that this science is in its infancy.

Information and Disease

Health nuts are going to feel stupid someday,
lying in hospitals dying of nothing.
—Redd Foxx

We have explored how the Digital Echo files will allow everyone to study human illness. We have looked at the astonishing possibilities afforded by genomics. Cool medical advances are happening every day (see page 89). And in a coming section on robotics, we will discuss the molecular machines called nanites—tiny, molecular-sized robots that will swim around in your body fighting disease, repairing damage, and alerting you to problems (and will likely dramatically increase the human lifespan).

Now let's look at how the Internet will help end disease in a more traditional, suit-and-tie kind of way.

If you were a scientist in Jenner's time, your only form of communication was letter writing. You knew little of what any other scientist was working on. If you had access to a library, its stock of medical books and journals was very small. You basically worked alone. And yet, in that world, scientific breakthroughs happened.

If you were a scientist in Pasteur's time, you had more resources. You had a lab and science symposiums. You began to have an understanding of how things worked in biology, if very little idea why. Difficulty of communication was still a barrier, and technology was still highly limited.

If you were a scientist in Salk's time, you did calculations by hand and wrote observations in notebooks. You still worked almost exclusively with people in your lab or at least in your city.

Today, the Internet enables science to operate at an entirely different level.

First, through things like e-mail, instant messengers, and online video conferencing, scientists can communicate with each other instantly and freely. This is powerful; it allows the best and brightest to collaborate easily.

Second, we have the mobile revolution. Twenty-five years ago, I had never seen a mobile phone. Today, an astonishing 77 percent of the people in the world have mobile devices and thus access to all kinds of better care via telemedicine. Listen to Dr. Hamadoun Touré, Secretary-General of the United Nations' agency for information and communication:

> Even the simplest, low-end mobile phone can do so much to improve healthcare in the developing world. Good examples include sending reminder messages to patients' phones when they have a medical appointment, or need a pre-natal check-up. Or using SMS messages to deliver instructions on when and how to take complex medication such as anti-retrovirals or vaccines. It's such a simple thing to do, and yet it saves millions of dollars—and can help improve and even save the lives of millions of people.

As access becomes cheaper and better, and the whole world has mobile phones, more information can be delivered to people in remote parts of the world.

Third, pretty much everything we know is published on the Internet and can be found in moments, if not seconds. All scientific material from the past is making its way online. All books are being scanned. Medical research findings can be distributed electronically for peer review, and feedback can be instant. Scientists can get inspiration and insights from the discoveries of others and can avoid fruitless efforts by reading of others' failures.

Already, the most complex mathematics are computed in an instant, and the storage and examination of vast amounts of data is effortless. Distributed computing makes enormous computational problems affordable to solve. Cloud computing and software frameworks such as Hadoop give unimagined computing power to the scientist on the most modest budget. Computer software is constantly being created to allow scientists to model, visualize, prototype, and diagram. Computers can connect to and control highly specialized scientific instruments, and equipment can be accessed remotely.

Teams of scientists in different parts of the world can collaborate virtually. Complex projects can be carried out on multiple continents through project-management tools. Highly specialized experts are a few keystrokes away and can be hired for just a few minutes or hours at a time. With Skype and similar products, you can even see the person you are working with. For free. You can share your desktop and have whiteboard sessions on your computer. When you travel, you can take your work with you. Underutilized scientists in remote parts of the world can telecommute to other parts of the world where their skills are needed. The division of labor applied to science will yield substantial results.

More data will come online, from satellite images to sensor readings. When X-rays and CT scans and MRIs are publicly shared, anonymously, they will become a huge resource for scientists to study. When every lab report, every blood draw, every ECG, every everything is added to the body of scientific knowledge, the rolled-up data alone will have a big impact. And when more and more people have their medical history tracked over time, we will learn even more about how our bodies get sick and how they heal. When medical records leave the paper folders of the doctor's office and become highly standardized, more analysis can be done.

Imagine the day when we know enough about biology to create a computer model of the human body! When "human testing" is done almost immediately, but within the safe confines of a CPU. This will likely not ever be perfect, but any insight it can offer us is a gain.

Imagine if Hippocrates had a fraction of this. If Jenner had had e-mail, Pasteur an electron microscope, Salk a genetic sequencer. If the scientists of today had all I describe. I ask you again, does disease even have a chance?

FUTURE HEALTH: NINE COOL MEDICAL ADVANCES

As I write this list, the technologies on it aren't yet mature or complete. But they're at the leading edge of advances that will end disease, and they demonstrate what we are reaching for.

1. Bionic eyes are no longer solely confined to the pages of science fiction. Sufferers of *retinitis pigmentosa* can now enjoy partially restored sight, thanks to a device made up of a camera mounted on glasses, a processing unit, and electronic receivers implanted into the eye that stimulate nerves in the retina. As the receivers transmit electrical pulses to the brain via the optic nerve, the person wearing the device sees patterns of light and dark representing objects such as furniture or cars. Some wearers are able to read again, with text spelled out in dots of light. The device, the Argus II, has already been approved for use in Europe.

2. A gastrointestinal liner to treat obesity, already available in Europe, works by placing a barrier between food and the two-foot portion of the small intestine where the most calories are absorbed. The EndoBarrier tubing is easily inserted and removed endoscopically. This non-surgical therapeutic device has potential to help countless obese people and dramatically change treatment and outcomes for people living with type 2 diabetes.

3. We all have bacteria in our mouths, including *Streptococcus mutans*, that convert sugar to lactic acid and cause teeth to decay. But Dr. Jeffrey Hillman has isolated a strain of *S. mutans* that produces an antibiotic to kill other strains, thereby eliminating the bacteria that make lactic acid. A dentist would only need to introduce this bacterial strain to a patient's mouth once and it should out-compete the tooth-decay-causing bacteria for a lifetime.

4. Scientists in Japan have developed artificial lymph nodes that could replace compromised lymph nodes in immunodeficient patients. Even more, the scientists theorize that in time, the lymph nodes could be customized to create particular antibodies to fight diseases or allergies according to individual patients' needs.

5. A biomedical corporation in California has developed ingestible digital devices the size of a grain of sand that will measure medication adherence, heart rate, sleep patterns, physical activity, and stress levels. The microchips will wirelessly transmit this information to receptor patches worn on the skin, which will in turn wirelessly transmit the data to a computer and even the mobile devices of caregivers.

continued on next page

6. What if there were a device for those who have lost their ability to speak, that could read their mind and transmit those words to a cell phone or computer? You are probably thinking, "riiiight." Ambient Corporation's Audeo device is doing just that. As the user imagines sounding out the words she wants to say, her neurological signals communicate silently with a device worn on the neck, which transmits the electrical impulses to a computer or cell phone to produce audible speech.

7. You may think geckos are only for selling insurance, but they are advancing the medical sciences as well. MIT researchers were inspired by the carpet of "nanoscale pillars" on the paws of geckos and created a bandage with nanostructures on its surface to make it more adhesive. The gecko-inspired bandage will be flexible, waterproof, and biodegradable, unlike existing surgical tapes. Researchers also hope the material could serve as an internal drug-delivery patch.

8. Someday I hope we have contact lenses that give us augmented reality, over-laying images and information on the world around us. This should freak no one out—after all, you could just take the lenses out or turn them off. But we are a ways away. However, researchers are already developing smart contact lenses that will do everything from monitoring the wearer's blood sugar levels to dispensing medication to reporting warning signs of glaucoma. In Sensimed's Triggerfish lens, highly sensitive wires measure changes in the cornea's curve, indicating increases in pressure on the optic nerve, a sign of fluid build-up and glaucoma. Catching the disease early could prevent the irreparable damage that makes it a leading cause of blindness.

9. Smart Skin. Researchers have embedded electronic sensors into a flexible film, thinner than a human hair. Once again, the geckos have been at work. Instead of using an adhesive, the film attaches to your skin using the van der Waals force, the same technique that holds geckos to walls. The result is medical sensors that look like temporary tattoos, and cool ones at that.

How the Internet and Technology Will End Disease

All endeavor calls for the ability to tramp the last mile,
shape the last plan, endure the last hours toil. The fight to
the finish spirit is the one . . . characteristic we must possess
if we are to face the future as finishers.
—Henry David Thoreau

It is said that in ancient China, doctors were paid when their patients were well. After all, it was the doctor's job to keep you healthy, not to make money when you were sick. In fact, if you stayed sick long enough in that culture, the doctor had to pay you! I did not ask the American Medical Association their opinion of this arrangement.

A disease-free future for everyone is within our grasp. This might not seem to be borne out by history—until you consider the amazing trajectory of recent medical advance. The power of the Internet and associated technologies we have so far described, combined with our new understanding of the genome, dooms disease to eventual extinction. The additional possibility of access to all humans' Digital Echoes, to be studied for a million unnoticed causal correlations, will hasten the demise of disease as well and will increase quality of life and longevity.

To what length can the human lifespan be extended? Opinions vary widely; no one really knows. Some suspect we can be made to be healthy and energetic to the age of one hundred thirty and that's it. Others contend, and feel they have science to support, that humans can live beyond five hundred. Biomedical gerontologist Aubrey de Grey maintains that aging is caused by seven underlying factors, each of which can, in theory, be countered. He predicts that within twenty years, the first person to live to one thousand will be born.

In any event, this much is certain: We will see medical advances in the future that seem impossible today. From growing our own replacement organs to having nanobots swimming around our blood supply keeping an eye on things, we will have come very far from the world of Jenner, Blossom the Cow, and smallpox—and can envision the end of disease.

THE END OF POVERTY

- How Is Wealth Created?

- Scarcity

- Free Trade, Technological Displacement, and Outsourcing

- Chad Gets a Better Job

- Robots and Nanites and Jobs, Oh My!

- Wealth and Poverty in History

- Earning a "Living"

- Left Behind

- How the Internet and Technology Will End Poverty

How Is Wealth Created?

Wealth is the product of man's capacity to think.
—Ayn Rand

Dictionary.com defines poverty as "the state or condition of having little or no money, goods, or means of support." It lists synonyms including privation, neediness, and destitution, and antonyms including riches, plenty—and wealth.

To see how the Internet might end poverty, we must first look at wealth and three different mechanisms by which it is generated: the creation of things, the division of labor and trade, and technological advance.

The first mechanism is the creation of things, an old and familiar approach. If you take low-worth items or raw materials and apply labor to them to make something that has value, you have created wealth. By taking a block of marble and carving a statue, or taking a handful of seed and growing a cornfield, you have combined your labor and know-how with something of little value and have created something of more value.

The second way to create wealth is through the division of labor and trade. This, to date, has been the big one for humanity. And it really is composed of two separate components that need to be understood in their own right.

First, trade. How can it be said that trade actually generates wealth?

When you trade with someone in a free market, you are giving up something you have for something the other person has, which you value more. One can imagine two children each with a bag of jelly beans. Jill hates the licorice ones and eats all her jelly beans except the licorice ones. Jack loves the licorice ones but hates the pink ones, so eats all his jelly beans except those. One can thus imagine Jack and Jill meeting, perhaps while fetching water, and realizing they can trade their jelly beans and both have more of their favorites—Jack gets Jill's licorice ones, and Jill gets Jack's pink ones. Both are better off than they were, even though nothing new has been created.

You might remember the story of Kyle MacDonald, who famously traded up from one red paperclip to a house, one small exchange at a time between July 2005 and July 2006. With each trade he got something he valued more than what he traded away; and presumably all the people he traded with along the way also increased their value with each trade. Trading is not a "zero-sum game." Both parties must win for the trade to occur.

Trading is able to create value for two reasons. The first is that we all value things differently, such as in our jelly bean example. This is a good thing because it means that high degrees of utility (the economists' word for "happiness") can be achieved with a wide variety of goods. The second way trade is able to create value is because most goods have what economists call "decreasing marginal utility." That means that as you get more of them, you value each new one less. If you are in a desert dying of thirst, you value the first glass of water very highly, the second glass a bit less, and the 802nd not at all.

Puppies are like this, too. Going from zero to one puppy might increase your utility a great amount. From one to two, a bit less. The seventeenth puppy has negative utility—it doesn't even add a little happiness; it actually takes it away. So when people have excess goods, they are able to trade those goods away for things they want and suffer less of a decrease in utility than the amount they are increasing in their trading partners. It is safe to say that the man with seventeen puppies is creating more happiness by giving one each to sixteen friends than he is forgoing by his loss of puppies.

Direct trading is inefficient in most cases. Most cases aren't like our jelly bean example where each person had the items the other person wanted. That is why money was invented. It means I can trade you a good or service for an intermediate store of value known as money, and then trade that money to the person who actually has the goods I want. To be readily accepted as money, items must be nearly universally regarded as valuable (think of gold), be scarce, be difficult to counterfeit, and finally, be easy to transport, measure, and exchange.

Even with this technology called money, trade has been difficult. In most cases, you must be in physical proximity to (1) the items you are trading, (2) the money that will be exchanged, and (3) the person with whom you are trading. This is so that the goods can be physically inspected, the money can change hands, and price negotiation can occur.

If more trading can occur, more wealth is created. So even if no new goods were created tomorrow, we could still vastly increase the wealth of the world by allocating existing goods differently.

Governments (and thieves, for that matter) reallocate wealth—but they do it by increasing the wealth of one party at the expense of another party. One wins and one loses. Trade is not like this at all. Everyone wins in trade, because goods are reallocated in a way that increases utility to all parties involved.

To the extent that the Internet is able to increase trade, it increases utility. It already has increased both substantially and will do so dramatically more in the coming years. Consider just a few of the mechanisms by which the Internet promotes trade that otherwise would not have occurred.

1. **Online employment.** One form of trade is to exchange your labor for money. The Internet has only touched the tip of the iceberg here. Actually, the tip of the tip of the iceberg. From Amazon's Mechanical Turk to hiring programmers and designers living in other parts of the world, and in a thousand more ways, the Internet has enabled this form of trade to occur where it never could have occurred before.

2. **PayPal, Square, and the online use of credit cards.** The ability to instantly and, for a very low cost, reliably transfer money to anyone on the planet is a key ingredient in increasing the amount of trade that occurs online. We have seen this happen already, and it will get substantially better in the near future. I am fascinated by credit cards and the fact that the entire free enterprise system relies on the honesty of almost all people. Credit cards are able to work and charge low fees because almost all transactions are honest. If I get my credit card bill and call up and dispute a charge, the benefit of the doubt is given to me, that I am telling the truth. The vendor is usually made to "eat" the charge. Imagine if everyone frequently disputed charges: "I never got my order!" or "It wasn't what they promised it would

be!" or "Yeah, I got a box in the mail, but it was full of rocks." It would not take much of this for businesses to no longer take credit cards. And yet they do, because fraud is a small part of the overall picture. The free enterprise system requires the basic honesty and goodwill of most people. And it seems to work pretty well, as author Dean Koontz noted when he observed, "Civilization rests on the fact that most people do the right thing most of the time."

3. **Amazon and large online stores.** These stores are able to increase trade a number of ways. They offer millions of products at good prices, delivered tomorrow if that is what I want. They allow for easy return of merchandise that doesn't meet my expectations, decreasing my fear of making a bad purchasing decision. They provide information such as reviews and user ratings. They suggest other products a customer might be interested in. Could you have imagined a store like this if you lived a century ago? Such a thing is not possible without the Internet.

4. **Etsy and small online stores.** Etsy allows people to trade their crafts, items they have made with their own hands and materials. Most of these people have other jobs and obligations, so without something like Etsy, they might not be able to enter into these trades. Additionally, online stores powered by Yahoo and Google and Amazon exist where small vendors can set up storefronts and sell to the world, as a hobby or a livelihood. This has no offline corollary and is economically empowering to so many people.

5. **eBay and reallocating existing goods.** eBay is actually a little like direct trade. I take things from my attic and my garage and sell them to people who value them more than I do. Without the Internet, they would just gather dust. Even if this were not the case—perhaps I would donate them to charity—eBay does an amazing job of putting them in the hands of the person who values them the most. This works toward maximizing the utility that item can bring to someone. eBay is not alone in this regard. Freecycle, Craigslist, and a thousand

message boards achieve the same outcome. This is not possible without the Internet.

6. **Product information.** One failure of the marketplace is the misattribution of the amount of utility an item will bring a person. Good information on a product can mitigate this problem. I can find objective information and detailed specifications about almost any product online, up to and usually including the operation manuals. Often, a buying decision hinges on a piece of arcane information about a product that is difficult to locate. The Internet solves for this in a way no library ever could.

7. **Yelp, online product reviews, and trust.** I buy something because I have certain assumptions about how much happiness it will bring me. These assumptions are often wrong. To the extent that I get accurate information from other consumers of the product, I will tend to make better choices. Just as the Internet facilitates trade by providing objective information, it also does so by disseminating subjective information about products. This occurs through services such as Yelp, where customers rate businesses they use, and in product reviews posted on countless sites. Additionally, trust indicators such as eBay's and Amazon's feedback systems direct more business to reliable suppliers, thus increasing trade. This could not be done without the Internet.

8. **Smoother methods of communication.** The cost of interactive information exchange, such as asking questions about products you are contemplating purchasing, has fallen to nearly zero. All it takes is the cost of your time to type into the feedback form or e-mail. This is unprecedented in the history of commerce and could not be done without the Internet.

9. **Low-cost business websites hosted around the world.** No matter where you live, if you have access to an Internet connection, you can host an online store and sell to the entire world. The removal of all

the traditional barriers to opening a new business will most benefit those who had no means to overcome those barriers and will be an especially powerful force for nations with struggling economies. This could not be done without the Internet.

10. **The meritocracy of online business.** With the rapid flow of information about businesses and their products, along with the ease of "checking up" on a vendor, good businesses will get more business and push out the bad ones. This makes business a meritocracy and encourages business owners to focus on quality, service, and reputation since these are so easy for customers to check. This could not be done without the Internet.

11. **Google Adwords and the PPC business.** The pay per click (PPC) business is a way to advertise online to people who did a specific search in a search engine like Google or who are viewing content on a certain topic. This has allowed for the creation of millions of niche products that could never have found their market before. In the past, when most media was mass media, it was essential to create products with mass appeal. But today, trade is encouraged by specialization. For instance, I could hand carve bird calls and then advertise them only to people who are looking at online content about hand-carved bird calls or who search the Internet for information about hand-carved bird calls. This could not be done without the Internet.

(As I write this section, I am reminded of the Roman statesman Cato, who was known to end his speeches, regardless of the topic, with the phrase "Carthage must be destroyed." But I assure you I am operating on conviction, not reflex, when I end these passages with the assertion that "this could not be done without the Internet.")

As noted earlier, trade has been one of two great drivers of increased prosperity through history. The other is division of labor, worth discussing in some detail as it is an almost miraculous process.

Imagine that you personally had to create everything you wanted to use.

If that were the case, we would almost all be naked, walking around with sharp sticks, picking berries until we got so hungry that we started eating grub worms.

And yet, our lives are nothing like that. I have never so much as tasted a grub worm. Instead, we are surrounded by things we could not create ourselves. Not in one hundred lifetimes could I make a car. By "make a car," I mean really make a car: dig iron ore out of the ground, smelt it to steel, wildcat for oil, find oil and refine it into gasoline, and so on.

Forget a car. I could not in one hundred lifetimes make a working electric lamp, even knowing what I know now. If I were given ten thousand years to live and were left on a planet with nothing but natural resources, I could not make a light bulb or microwave or helicopter.

So how do these things get made?

In 1958, an American economist named Leonard Read wrote an essay called "I, Pencil," written from the pencil's point of view, about how no one on the planet knows how to make a pencil. No one. From mining the clay to make the lead, to the lacquer applied to the pencil, to the rubber eraser, to the metal band holding the eraser to the yellow paint, no one person knows how to make a complete pencil.

And yet pencils get made, more than a billion of them a year, and they are essentially given away. It requires the labor of thousands to make a pencil, and yet they are so inexpensive as to be almost free.

How can this be? It is because of the division of labor. When a person learns to do one job and specializes in that one job, she gets really good at it.

Adam Smith's book *The Wealth of Nations*, published in 1776, is the defining work of the free enterprise system. In it, Smith uses the pin industry to describe the division of labor:

> "To take an example . . . the trade of the pin-maker; [in which] a workman . . . could scarce, perhaps, with his utmost industry, make one pin in a day, and certainly could not make twenty. But in the way in which this business is now carried on . . . [o]ne man draws out the wire,

another straights it, a third cuts it, a fourth points it, a fifth grinds it at the top for receiving the head; to make the head requires two or three distinct operations; . . . I have seen a small manufactory of this kind where ten men only were employed. . . . Those ten persons . . . could make among them upwards of forty-eight thousand pins in a day."

Smith says that if one man tried to make pins by himself, he might make one per day. But if each of ten people specialized on just one-tenth of the task, they could together make 48,000, an increase in per-person productivity from one pin a day to 4,800 pins per day. And in this efficiency that is generated by specialization, wealth is created.

It doesn't matter that the person selling pencils doesn't know how the pencil is made; he only needs to know how to sell them. And it doesn't matter that the person who paints the pencils doesn't know how the paint is made, for his job is to paint them. The gains in efficiency obtained through this approach are one reason that cities are such powerful economic units: Cities bring people into proximity to each other and facilitate specialization and trade.

Returning to the three ways wealth is created: The first is by making things. The second is through the division of labor and free trade. And the third way wealth is created is through technological advance. Technology is simply the combining of other economic products in new ways. These new methods are considered advances if what they produce is worth more than the cost of their parts.

For instance, you may manufacture widgets from lightweight plastic. Someone comes along and invents a cheaper, lighter-weight plastic. You figure out how to make your widget from this new plastic. Your widget is now more technologically advanced. And because it is both better and cheaper, people using it will get more marginal utility (more increased happiness) than before. This increase in utility is the same as generating wealth.

For the foreseeable future, technological advance will drive the world of wealth creation—and it is capable of producing more wealth than everything that has come before it.

I noted previously that, even if the world stopped producing new things tomorrow, great new wealth could be created by trading, by reorganizing who has what. Yet as powerful as this concept is, it has a logical limit. There is an optimal distribution that can be achieved. Given perfect information, frictionless markets, and other theoretical impossibilities, a finite amount of utility can be achieved.

Technological advance, however, is not limited in that way. It may have some limit in theory, because there is an optimal arrangement of atoms in the universe; but for practical purposes, it has no limit.

This is because technology is cumulative. Once someone knows how to make a factory that can produce 48,000 pins a day with ten people, someone else can figure out how to make one that makes 100,000 a day with five people. Or five million a day with no people. Technology marches forward—perhaps not forever, but as close to forever as we can understand. This will bring vast amounts of new wealth onto the planet.

We won't talk at this point about the distribution of that wealth; that will come later. But for now, I want to leave you with a preposterous thought: In the future, a new Mercedes-Benz will cost just $50. And the mechanisms that will bring that about are also the ones that will end poverty forever.

To build a case for the end of poverty, we begin by discussing scarcity.

Scarcity

I wonder how much it would take to buy a soap bubble
if there was only one in the world.
–Mark Twain

Economically, we understand the world around us in terms of scarcity. Most things come in a limited supply, so some people have a thing and others do not. As my professors told me the first day I started studying economics in college (and never tired of repeating), scarcity is the central underlying assumption of all economic theory.

We all understand this. There is a finite number of baseballs, beanbags, and balloons. We can manufacture more of any of these things, but to do so requires labor and materials, and those are scarce as well.

We allocate scarce resources by pricing them. The theory of pricing means people who want items the most choose to buy those items instead of others they could buy.

We essentially view scarcity like the children's game "musical chairs." You have ten kids but only nine chairs. That's how life works. Only it's not set to music. You'd better scramble and get a chair even if it means elbowing little Timmy out of the way. Better him than you. Next round: nine kids, eight chairs. We inculcate the concept of scarcity at a young age, at birthday parties no less.

The notion of scarcity is so ingrained in us and so permeates the world today, it is difficult to imagine a world without it. And yet we do have some experience with situations where scarcity is nonexistent.

Think about breathable air. Humans require relatively little oxygen, and plants are constantly transforming the carbon dioxide we exhale back into useful oxygen. For all practical purposes, we have an unlimited supply of air to breathe. Because of this, it is free (and we are spared from television public service announcements urging us to take fewer and shorter breaths).

But in many areas, scarcity is so profound it has huge societal impact. Consider energy. Energy is expensive. Because it is expensive, people have to limit their consumption of it. A problem arises because of the strong correlation between standard of living and energy consumption. Why is this? There are a few reasons.

First, think of energy as the capacity to do work. If you are able to consume more energy, you can do more work and therefore create more. If you are a farmer and work alone, you can only plant as much land as you can personally plow. You can do just a couple of thousand calories of work a day, consuming only the energy produced by the food you ate. This is roughly the same amount of energy it would take to power a one hundred-watt light bulb. That's it. Now, if you acquire an ox, a new source of energy, you can plow more. The ox consumes about six thousand calories of energy, so now your combined output is four light bulbs' worth of energy. But if you get a diesel tractor (and presumably diesel fuel), the amount of energy you can consume goes up exponentially, and with that, the amount of work you can do. You could power generators that could light up a stadium.

In the United States, we consume vast amounts of energy—something like one hundred times the amount of energy we could generate per day by furiously pedaling on a stationary bike attached to a generator. Because of this excess energy we consume, we can essentially do one hundred times what we could do without it. It is as if each person has one hundred assistants working for him. This dramatically increases his output and thus his standard of living.

Additionally, and less abstractly, energy is needed to power refrigerators, purify water, transport food, manufacture medicines, print books, power computers, operate dialysis machines, and do a million other activities that are themselves embodiments of prosperity. Without energy to power these, prosperity plummets.

An ongoing debate is whether a high amount of energy raises a nation or region's gross national product (GNP) or whether rising GNP increases the consumption of energy. I suspect it is both; GNP rises, so we buy more energy, allowing GNP to rise so we can buy more energy. But the causality of this relationship is irrelevant to the point I want to make, which is this: An unlimited amount of free and clean energy would profoundly change the world. Poverty would be no more.

I won't base my reasoning for how the Internet and technology will end poverty on this idea alone. But think about how it could play out:

If energy truly were free and unlimited, you could, for instance, power tractors everywhere in the world. "Aha," you may say, "you still need the tractor, which is an expensive piece of machinery." But the price of the tractor would have plummeted, for a constellation of reasons. The labor to build it is now robotic and powered by free energy. What we need to make its parts—iron ore to make steel, rubber to make tires, sand to make glass, petroleum to make plastics—is generally a few cents' worth of raw materials. The cost derives from the application of huge amounts of energy, intelligence, and technology to obtain and process the raw materials: digging and smelting to create high-grade steel, harvesting and refining and molding to make rubber parts, and so on.

The point is that the cost of making almost everything is mostly energy and intellect, not raw materials. The energy—sometimes human exertion, sometimes mechanical exertion—has always come at a cost.

But what if that energy cost fell to zero? As my economics professors insisted, cost is determined by scarcity and demand. But is energy really scarce—or is it like air? Is it finite, or is it for all practical purposes infinite?

Fossil fuels are, without a doubt, scarce. But energy? It is essentially infinite. Even more so than air!

Vastly more energy than we need pours down on this planet in the form of sunlight. We just don't know how to capture it efficiently. Think about this: Nearly four million exajoules of energy is absorbed by the earth's atmosphere, oceans, and land each year. (An exajoule is roughly equivalent to a quadrillion BTUs or 174 million barrels of oil.) How many exajoules of energy does all of humanity consume each year? Less than five hundred. So four million come to the earth and we only need to capture five hundred.

Thunderstorms release tremendous amounts of energy. We can't yet capture it. Hurricanes release unimaginable amounts of power, as do earthquakes. We can't yet capture it. The wind in the upper atmosphere has extraordinary amounts of energy. Can't capture it. The earth has an enormous molten core that contains vast amounts of energy. Can't get it yet.

The oceans shift every day because of the pull of the moon, and these tides contain a huge amount of energy we don't yet know how to gather. Everyone knows water evaporates, rises, then falls to the earth as rain—but no one can even guess how much energy could be captured from this if we only knew how. Every day the earth heats and cools as night turns into day and back into night. We know how to power a clock with this energy but haven't yet cracked the code on doing it at scale.

We haven't even begun to figure out all the ways we might get unlimited free and clean power from nuclear fission or fusion or other ways to unlock the vast power stored in the atom. All around the world, scientists are racing to create hot fusion reactors. The United States is spending billions on fusion, the Chinese announced they are training two thousand fusion scientists, and a fusion research facility is being built in France that will cost US$20 billion. That is serious money! These scientists all know what a fusion breakthrough will mean to humanity . . . and to their bottom line.

And then technology opens up completely new ideas and methods for us. Consider what the eminent physicist Freeman Dyson suggests in *The Sun, the Genome, and the Internet*:

> An energy crop could be a permanent forest of trees that convert sunlight to liquid fuel and deliver the fuel directly through their roots to a network of underground pipelines. If these two advances could be combined, we would have a supply of solar energy that was cheap, abundant, and environmentally benign.

Think about that! A genetically engineered tree that converts sunlight into fuel and then pumps the fuel through its roots to where it is needed. A few such trees in the backyard behind your condo, cabin, or yurt would be enough to satisfy your power requirements.

So is energy scarce? Not by a long shot. It is abundant beyond imagination. What we don't know is how to capture it. But these are questions of technology, not of scarcity, and technology is about to rocket forward. One breakthrough is all it will take to change the world.

Skeptics may argue that we've heard this before, in the 1950s when the proponents of atomic power promised electricity so abundant it would be "too cheap to meter." That was indeed the hope for atomic energy in that era, and it did not pan out. But the point is, that is the kind of breakthrough we are working toward. That is what we expect to be able to do, because it is theoretically possible in a hundred different ways. That particular energy breakthrough didn't materialize as people hoped it would—but is that really an argument that no breakthrough will happen?

No. Each success has some failure along the way. I don't mean that in a motivational poster kind of way but in a literal sense: Failures (and what we learn from them) will help build the energy solutions for our future.

And in that future, I believe the world can have—in fact, will have—plentiful, free, clean energy that will result in dramatically lower costs for everything, everywhere.

Why do I think this?

A brilliant physicist named Richard Feynman (1918–1988) worked on, among other projects, developing atomic weapons. On the matter of trying to decide whether to join the team working on the bomb, he once wrote: "It kinda scared me when I realized what the weapon would be, and that since it might be possible, it must be possible."

Those final nine words stuck in my mind: *Since it might be possible, it must be possible.* What did he mean by this? Was it some kind of rhetorical flourish, just words that sounded good? I doubted that, as Feynman was precise in his usage of words. He had died by the time I read that passage in one of his books, so I couldn't write him, as is my normal practice when an author's words puzzle me. I find they almost always answer.

Here is what I think he meant: If you could see a theoretical possibility for something in physics—"something that might be true"—then given enough time, you eventually could achieve it in reality. If you could see a way it might be possible, then it *must* be possible.

I believe this is the case with energy.

We have a hard time seeing this world without scarcity because we are firmly planted in the worldview of scarcity. But technology and human innovation know no scarcity. They have no known preset limits. And like our example with energy, technology and human innovation could make other things that are now scarce—or that we think of now as scarce—not so at all.

Most raw materials in the world are essentially unlimited. We scratch at the surface of the planet with our feeble machinery and, because of the physical difficulty of getting at the raw materials, we term them scarce. At this writing, nickel sells for over $10,000 a ton—yet the core of the earth contains vast amounts, safely locked away from us. At this writing, gold sells for more than $1,000 an ounce and, despite the frantic efforts of human-kind, in all of history only about three billion ounces of gold have been recovered. That amount, if melted, would form a cube fifty-five feet on each side. However, locked up in ocean water—just suspended in ocean water—may be the equivalent of eight more such cubes. And beyond that, billions more ounces of gold may be buried beneath the ocean floor. So gold isn't scarce—only the gold we know how to recover is scarce.

True scarcity is uncommon. Most things simply appear to be scarce, and their seeming scarcity is just a shortfall of current technology. Remember when Janis Joplin sang "Freedom's just another word for 'nothing left to lose'"? Well, scarcity is just another word for "we don't know how to get it."

Food isn't really scarce. We compute the maximum amount of food the world can produce by beginning with total acres of land considered arable, but that is based on assumptions about the future of technology and agriculture. Water isn't scarce either; we have had the same amount forever. When we talk about it in terms of scarcity, we usually mean clean water in a certain location is scarce. But that, too, is a function of present technology.

So hold these thoughts, as we will be returning to them. First, many things in the physical world that we think of as scarce are not really scarce, just presently beyond our ability to capture. Second, as technology advances, it will make things in the physical world fall in price. And third, because most of those things' costs are bound up with the costs of energy, then if clean energy is no longer scarce or expensive—if it is, instead, free and abundant—the impact on the planet will be profound.

Free Trade, Technological Displacement, and Outsourcing

No nation was ever ruined by trade.
—Benjamin Franklin

Laborsaving technology has long been distrusted by those who make a living selling their (competing) labor. During the early Industrial Revolution, factory workers in France (or in some accounts, the Netherlands), were concerned that the mechanization of the textile industry would cost them their jobs. So they threw their *sabots*, a kind of clog shoe, into the machinery to break it—an act that gave us the word sabotage. Their behavior was by no means unique to history: In the 1830 Swing Riots of the United Kingdom, farmers vandalized the diabolical laborsaving contraption known as the thresher.

I remember visiting Egypt not many years ago and seeing a dozen men using scythes to cut the grass of a government building by hand. I asked my guide why they didn't use a lawnmower. He explained to me that with a lawnmower, one person would be able to do the job and eleven men would be unemployed. (I answered, "They should get jobs at the factory that would make the lawnmowers; it would pay better.")

Personal computers and the Internet have come under criticism in this regard. I knew typesetters who said computers would never duplicate their quality; travel agents who said the Internet would never replace them, and whose stockbrokers reassured them this was true. This displacement is in no way finished; in fact, it has hardly begun.

As we envision a world where machines do more and more work that people used to do, our minds naturally turn to those who would be displaced by technological advance. We'll look at their lives, and the social aspects of this change, in a coming chapter called "Left Behind." At this point, I will just say that people have long been distrustful of technology that clearly replaces the labor of humans (unlike, say, air conditioning, which replaced no one. No one threw his shoe into the air conditioner, I assure you.).

First, let's consider the macroeconomic impact of this change—the effect it will have on the net economic status of the planet.

Technological advances that displace human workers are similar in effect to two other concepts with which we are very familiar in the modern age: outsourcing and free trade. Both of these have political implications, and so it is with some hesitation I bring them up. My purpose in this chapter will not be to persuade the reader of any political doctrine of trade; please apply your own political and social values as you see fit. My purpose is to explain the net effect of free trade, technological advance, and outsourcing on the overall economic system of the planet.

The idea of free trade has divided people for as long as trade has existed. Wars have been fought over it—many wars, in fact. It is hard to see your widget factory close and your friends who work there become unemployed while your neighbors import widgets from another country by the load.

Outsourcing has a similar feel. We instantly empathize with those who have had their jobs outsourced to a distant land where people are willing to work for a fraction of the wages.

We have understandable emotional responses to all these situations. But in spite of the relative economic displacement they all cause, free trade, outsourcing, and technological displacement all have a positive net effect on the economics of the planet. If prices for an item fall, this is a net good. Since prices are a proxy for labor (you can, after all, buy labor with money), then lowering the amount of labor it takes to acquire something is a gain in efficiency and thus a gain in wealth.

Let's consider examples of how the effect is positive for some, negative for some, but the net is a gain in the overall wealth of the system.

If you figure out how to make widgets more efficiently by using a new technique that only requires half the workers, you are able to lower the price of widgets for all and are able to sell more of them. But it is quite likely you will need fewer workers. The net effect is positive, but the laid-off workers will probably have a hard time appreciating it.

A textbook example of this is Eli Whitney and the cotton gin. The cotton gin cut the cost of removing seeds from cotton. One person with a horse and a cotton gin could process as much as fifty people without the gin. Even though this allowed cotton prices to plummet and demand for cotton to increase, some of those fifty people got laid off, no doubt shaking their fists at the infernal gin as they stormed off the property.

We are sympathetic to the laid-off workers, but no one would suggest the cotton gin not be installed. If this were really the best choice, it would also be logical to blindfold the fifty workers so they would work that much slower and thus create twenty new jobs for blindfolded cottonseed removers. Then, make them all soak their fingers in ice water so they are numb and work even slower, creating another thirty jobs for cold-fingered, blindfolded cottonseed removers.

Let's look at another hypothetical. Consider a factory that makes widgets for a dollar each. A competing company decides to make an up-front investment and build a new factory in a distant land, high in the mountains where residents who choose to live there have less economic opportunity. They are able to produce widgets for ten cents, putting the Dollar Widget Company (with its unfortunate name) out of business. This situation echoes the cotton gin example: The Dime Widget Company is essentially a new piece of technology, just like the cotton gin, that dramatically lowers the cost of an item. Lowering the cost of something is an increase in efficiency and an increase in the wealth of the overall system.

Finally, consider the outsourced worker. Worker Chad lives in Chattanooga. He makes $10 an hour. He works from home and has a night job remotely monitoring real-time security cameras after hours at an office building. His job is to push a button if he sees anything suspicious. Worker Chang, located in China, is willing to do the same job, remotely, for a dollar an hour. Chad is regrettably but understandably replaced by Chang. The cost of monitoring falls and thus wealth is created. The cotton gin example is the same as if Chad were replaced by a gin.

It is tempting to argue this point—to say, "No, what really happened is the employer gained $9 an hour in savings, Chang gained a dollar an hour in wages, and Chad lost $10 an hour in wages, thus there is no gain in efficiency. Chad's wages were merely redistributed to the employer and Chang." It is tempting to say that but entirely wrong. Let's walk through it.

Unquestionably, the employer pocketed the $9 an hour in efficiency savings. That is completely real. He used to pay $10; now he pays one dollar. But Chad merely stopped selling his labor to the employer for that price. He still has his labor to sell and can go get a new job. If he replaces the job with another $10-an-hour job, then you must admit there was a true efficiency gain. The employer gained $9 an hour, Chang got a job, and no one is worse off.

AN EXCEPTION TO THE RULE: WHY FREE TRADE SOMETIMES HURTS THE NET WORLD ECONOMY

Fair warning: If this chapter has been tedious to you thus far, you may wish to skip this box, which clarifies an exception to the rule that the chapter outlines. But if you can tolerate it, what follows will explain why free trade sometimes hurts the (net) world economy. This is seldom discussed but very real.

The concept is known as "internalizing externalities." Externalities are the external effects an action has on society. Sometimes they are negative and sometimes they are positive. Economic theory states that to the degree people or businesses factor these effects into their decisions, more efficient outcomes happen. Consider two examples of this.

First, an individual example. You and your spouse both like Oreos. You, personally, are pretty happy with the generic knockoff, which saves you a dollar and tastes the same to you. You would tend to buy the store brand and pocket the dollar. However, your spouse hates the knockoff. She once bit into one and there was a paperclip in it and she is so scarred by this experience that she will only nibble at them carefully. If you buy the generics, she will launch into a depression that could last a week. So here is the situation: You are at the store deciding which ones to buy. If you did not internalize the externalities, you would buy the generic brand and save a dollar. After all, why do you need to internalize them? You are leaving town for a week and a day and will completely avoid your spouse's meltdown. However, being socially conscious, you look at the effect on the entire system, the externalities of your decision, and count those equally with your own personal factors when making the decision. Clearly, from a "big picture" standpoint, you should stick with the Oreos.

Now, a business example. Say a business makes widgets, and one of the by-products of making a widget is a gallon of mildly polluted water. And say the net cost to society of having a gallon of polluted water dumped into the river—the cleanup cost, or the economic impact of the gallon of dirty water—is $10. Further, say there is a technology that would allow the widget to be made without creating this gallon of polluted water—but making the widget this way costs an extra dollar. What should the company do? Well, from a societal standpoint, the company should pay the extra dollar because the cost of making the widget the "clean" way is cheaper than the cost the polluted water has on society. However, the company likely won't choose this outcome because the $10 cost of cleanup is not paid by the company but by society.

When businesses and people are made to consider the overall effects of their choices as opposed to only their individual effects, efficient outcomes occur. This is known as "internalizing externalities." This is one of the few areas in which government taxation actually leads to a more efficient outcome. In fact, I think you could replace the entire tax code with taxes that make the costs of products more in line with their actual costs to society as opposed to only their costs to individuals.

Imagine that world! Calculating the actual, societal costs of fatty foods, alcohol, cars, pet ownership, mercury thermometers, air conditioning, solar panels, razor blades, jogging shoes, and ten thousand other things, and incorporating those costs in the prices as taxes would lead to a vastly more efficient allocation of resources. You could finance the entire government and its (hopefully) noble agenda by this method alone. And you could feel good about it; after all, you would be increasing efficiency, not merely acting as a leech to the system.

It would work in the reverse in the form of subsidies. If jump ropes or board games or ice cream turn out to have positive externalities—that is, if they help society—a subsidy could lower the prices of these items.

To some extent, we have this in the form of high taxes on cigarettes, which are seen to have negative externalities, and a home interest deduction on income taxes, as home ownership is viewed as having positive social good. But there is no serious attempt to systematically calculate the externalities of everything with an eye toward replacing the tax code.

How does this play into our analysis? Well, businesses are very efficient and, over the long term, will choose a location less able to compel them to internalize negative externalities (or, more rarely, overly compensate them for positive externalities, as in cities offering tax breaks to businesses.) Therefore, rational-acting businesses will likely locate in areas that allow them to inflict negative externalities without requiring compensation.

What does all this mean? Say you have two countries in the world. One taxes businesses on their pollution, requires they provide medical insurance to employees, requires a safe work environment, mandates a minimum wage, and so forth. The country does so to force the business to internalize externalities. If the company pollutes, it should bear the cost of that pollution. The company should insure its workers because if uninsured workers end up in the ER, the burden falls on society, not the company. If workers are in unsafe work environments, they are bearing a risk that has a measurable negative cost. The country requires a minimum wage because workers paid below the poverty line have an added cost on society.

Say the second country requires the business to do none of those things. The business looks at this new country and decides to move there because, from their standpoint, they can save costs and be more efficient. So they move. But realize, no new net efficiencies are gained from this move. The cost to the system has not changed; costs have just been transferred from the business to society at large.

So the net-net is this: There are a hundred good reasons why outsourcing raises the overall standard of living of the world. But outsourcing to pollute, oppress workers, or have unsafe working conditions hurts the world's standard of living. This would suggest a policy of classifying nations according to their regulation and working conditions, and enacting legislation that discourages companies from relocating certain operations to places where they can inflict societal harm. This would have a tertiary benefit of encouraging governments to raise their level of consumer and worker protection so business can be outsourced to them more easily.

You might argue that since there is now a surplus of labor in Chad's neighborhood, the price of labor is lowered and Chad will only find work paying $9.75 an hour. But even in this case, the result is still a massive overall gain in efficiency.

But that is not what will happen. Chad's next job will actually pay more than $10 an hour. You are probably thinking, "How can we ever know that? This is all hypothetical." But I intend to show you how in the next chapter: "Chad Gets a Better Job."

Chad Gets a Better Job

Nobody got anywhere in the world by simply being content.
—Louis L'Amour

We have established that outsourcing, free trade, and technological advance all have the same effect on the system: They lower prices and increase net wealth. Outsourcing a job to get it done more cheaply and building a machine to do it more cheaply are really the same.

We also discussed the plight of Chad, the worker who lost his security-camera-monitoring job to Chang in China—who will soon lose it to a computer program who can look for suspicious behavior better and more cheaply. Someday the computer program will lose its job, although I don't know to what. But change is inevitable.

Now, to explain why I think Chad will be getting a better job anyway.

What determines how much money you or Chad or anyone gets paid? The minimum is either set by a minimum wage law or determined by the demand and supply of that labor. The maximum wage you can earn, though, is defined by supply and demand for labor, and by your negotiating ability, but it also has a cap. It is capped at the value your labor adds to the goods or services you create.

If you take something worth a dollar, spend an hour working on it, and your employer sells it for three dollars, no way in the world can you ever make more than two dollars an hour. Why would your employer pay you more than the value you are able to add?

Say the world has ten thousand burger flippers. They form a union and get laws passed that no burgers can be flipped except by a union member. Then they all agree to set the price per flip at $1,000. This action makes the price of a burger go up by $1,000 and drops demand to zero. All burger flippers just lost their jobs. The burger flippers don't add $1,000 of value. It doesn't matter what the law or the union or their mothers think about it: They can't get a thousand dollars per flip.

Now, think about machines. What do they do exactly? Machines multiply our labor and increase our ability to do work.

Machines therefore expand our ability to add value.

Machines thus increase our maximum potential wage.

If you are a wage earner, then you should love machines. Machines—which still need you as an operator, as far as we can see—magnify your productivity. And thus, when it comes to negotiating, machines magnify your ability to extract a higher wage.

Think of all the machines you use to do your job. Your car, a ball-point pen, your computer, a dolly, and so on. What would happen to your productivity if they all disappeared? And if your productivity fell, then your salary would fall as well.

Who do you think makes more money: the person who hauls bricks on his back or the person who operates the forklift that moves the bricks? Clearly the latter. His labor, amplified by the machine, allows him to add more value and thus extract a higher wage. Who do you think makes more money: the one person who operates the cotton gin we discussed in the last chapter or one of the fifty people he replaced? The former.

Machines could, in theory, do all kinds of jobs in the world. We only have people doing this work because we have not yet developed the technology to get machines to do it. Thus, someone has to tighten the bolt on the automobile assembly line, and her wage is limited by the value her action adds to the car. No matter how good she is, how dedicated she is, the assembly line worker's wage is capped.

And that leads me to a statement I consider so important that I've italicized it for emphasis:

Any task that could be done a machine is, by definition, dehumanizing to a human doing it. If a machine can do it, then the task does not take advantage of anything that makes people different from machines. This does not ennoble the machine; it dehumanizes the person.

I am not saying if you enjoy manual labor and being exhausted at the end of the day, you shouldn't do it. I am not saying if you love digging ditches, you should do something else. If you like having sore muscles at the end of a day or working a job that requires little of your mental capacity so you can contemplate Nietzsche, hey, more power to you. I am saying that, on balance, these jobs exist not because people love them, but because we do not yet know how to make machines to do them.

The minute we do, the people doing those jobs should become operators of the new machines—and get big raises because their productivity just shot way up.

If every job that could be done by a machine was done by a machine tomorrow, the standard of living of virtually everyone on the planet would rise. All people would have tools to make them more productive.

I think most people want this. This leads me to my second italicized statement:

The number of people who feel challenged by their work is depressingly low. The number of people who want to be challenged by their work is encouragingly high. How many people do you know who say their job stretches them to their maximum potential? How many people do you suppose would like that?

I think a lot would. And that brings me to my final italicized point:

The most underutilized resource in the universe is human potential.

Many tasks in life have to be done. Frankly, no one wants to do them, so the only way to get people to do them is to pay them. But what if a machine did everything people really don't want to do? What if machines did all the things they could in theory do? What if everyone had a job only a person could do?

Only a person can do a job if it requires creativity or empathy, compassion or understanding or humor. Only a person can do a job if it requires a sense of justice or a sense of wonder or any of the thousands of things a machine will never be able to do. Maybe the job requires athletic ability or beauty or poise or diplomacy or trustworthiness or loyalty or kindness or cheerfulness. Perhaps it requires musical ability or style or sassiness.

No machine will ever be an interior decorator. No machine will be a politician. No machine will ever star in a Broadway musical. No machine will ever be a kindergarten teacher. Machines cannot and never will do these things.

Chad is lucky. He is freed from being a stand-in for a machine. Now he can go forward using machines to increase his productivity and to magnify his humanity. And he will find he is capable of adding far more value than as a set of eyes watching a screen. Don't get me wrong: I love technology. I love machines. They make wonderful servants, but I think they have really terrible jobs. And the sooner we get machines to do the things they can do, freeing up people to do what they can do, the happier and wealthier we all will be.

Have I convinced you that replacing people with machines frees people from the bondage of doing machine work? It is a profound thought and, I believe, an irrefutable one.

Humanity augmented with technology will lead to ever-increasing productivity. The next chapter will explore how far this can go, how many of our daily tasks machines could assume.

Robots and Nanites and Jobs, Oh My!

The factory of the future will have only two employees, a man and a dog. The man will be there to feed the dog. The dog will be there to keep the man from touching the equipment.
—Warren Bennis

The history of the world is a history of rising prosperity.

Prosperity can happen anywhere. We sometimes assume it must be fueled by abundant natural resources and mineral deposits and land—but if this were the case, Brazil would be the richest country on the planet and Japan the poorest. Those things were never necessary for prosperity and even less so in the Internet age. But I consider three ingredients key to a prosperous society. They are:

1. **Rule of law.** Everyone has to believe there are rules and that they apply to everyone. No one will play the game if the rules only apply to one team.

2. **Respect for property.** Once someone has something, no one should be able to take it from him or her. If this is not the case, people will not trade their labor for things that can easily or capriciously be taken away.

3. **Individual liberty.** Everyone must be free in his associations, able to start businesses, enter into contracts, travel freely, speak openly, and exercise other such freedoms.

In parts of the world where these three ingredients exist, we have seen prosperity rise. Conversely, in places where prosperity has not risen, lack of these ingredients plays a significant role. Although nations create governments to establish such protections, history shows that all too often, governments fail to do so. The fact that an unprecedented number of Earth's inhabitants today live in poverty is an indictment of governments, not a reflection of some underlying natural limit. If there can be a USA, a Germany, and a Japan, then every country can be rich. The prosperity of some does not require that others be poor. In fact, the poverty of some limits the wealth of all.

Prosperity has risen dramatically in the last two hundred years because of increasing division of labor and massive increases in technology—for example, the nearly five-thousand-fold increase in pin-making productivity in Adam Smith's *The Wealth of Nations*. As technology and the division of labor were applied to virtually every industry, increases of efficiency resulted in dramatically better products, lower prices, and productivity increases that left five-thousand-fold on the low side of average.

However, there are limits to how much prosperity and efficiency the division of labor can create. In the end, the speed at which a human operator can move has a physical limit. The ten men who make the 48,000 pins a day could not, simply by dividing the labor further or training even harder, increase that to 480,000. People simply cannot move that fast.

Enter the robots.

As I have pointed out, technology may in fact have limits, but we do not know what they are. We are about to enter a world where robots do more and more of our work for us. All the jobs that can, in theory, be done by machines—the jobs that I think suck the life force out of people—will in fact be done by machines.

"Robot" is a term almost one hundred years old, created in fiction before becoming a reality. (Karel Capek, an acclaimed Czech playwright, coined the word to describe the mechanized workers in his play.) The word is broad in its meaning and I use it in its broadest sense, as a mechanical device built to independently perform a task. It is differentiated from, say, a screwdriver, which does not perform any task on its own but requires a human operator. To that extent, the contraption that automatically metes out the daily allotment of cat food for your pet is a robot. This is not a flawless definition, but it will serve our purposes here.

And when I say robots, I don't mean androids, which are people-shaped machines doing the work of people. People are not machines (see my thoughts on that, on page 120), so modeling robots after our bodies makes about as much sense as modeling machines after radishes or daisies. Depending on function, robots can come in all shapes and sizes, and I see no compelling reason to make them like humans. (Of course, some people will do so for novelty's sake in the same spirit as those who like to put sweaters on their dogs.)

We have reached the point where many items can only be made by robots. No human can solder a billion transistors on a computer processor, so your computer needed a robot in order to be built. Recently, my ten-year-old son and I visited the factory in Denmark where Lego building blocks are made. They still have the hand-operated machine from the 1940s that was used to make the first Legos, but it is of course now a museum piece. The

LET ROBOTS BE ROBOTS

As robotic technology advances, we are being forced to readjust our expectations of machines' capabilities. What we should not try to do, in my opinion, is give them human traits. Let me offer my reasoning on this.

We have fallen into the habit of anthropomorphizing computers and robots for a simple reason: The more we program them to do things that we presently do, the more we think of them as being like us. People play chess, so that object playing the Grand Master must be a person. Nope. It is a machine.

A second reason we think of robots as mechanical people with personalities is that historically they have been portrayed this way in entertainment media. From the time mechanized workers were first called "robots" in a 1921 play, there has been high drama—and even higher comedic value—in portraying robots as metal people. From Data on *Star Trek* and C-3PO in *Star Wars* to Twiggy in *Buck Rogers*, robots are wise-cracking sidekicks and sage philosophers reflecting on "the human condition." In this regard, they are little different than talking dogs in cartoons.

Seeing Scooby-Doo in cartoons doesn't change our expectations of canine behavior because we have so much experience with real dogs. But what if dogs didn't exist and your only experience with them was watching Scooby-Doo? Your natural expectation would be that they would talk, at least as well as Scooby does. When you imagined dogs being "invented" in the future, you would naturally imagine having conversations with them.

It is altogether possible that many people would want to have conversations with their dogs mainly because they regard their dogs as sentient. But I know of no one who would want to have a conversation with a computer program pretending to be his dog. Okay, maybe for novelty value. But in terms of wanting to converse with robots at an emotional level, I just don't see it.

Let's do a thought experiment about this. Pretend you have called an airline or a cell phone company and reached that automated voice system that tells you to speak your question and it will try to answer it. Now, pretend that automated agent is perfect: It has perfect inflection, it can make small talk, ask you about the weather, be polite, and giggle at your jokes. Would you care? Would you want that?

I wouldn't. I might enjoy that kind of banter with a real person I will never meet, talking to me from a distant state. But that's because I would be sharing the experience with another human being, and human beings form connections with other human beings. I'm not about to waste my best material on a machine! A stranger? Sure! But not a machine.

Machines are not persons and so cannot have personalities. Artificial surrogates for human companionship are always vastly inferior to the real thing; we crave connections with people, not machines. No matter how convincing the machine is, once I know it is a machine, I won't care about it anymore.

So, spare me your cute robots with human names. Just make the things work.

robots I watched making Legos had no human operators because no human can keep up with them.

In *The Lexus and the Olive Tree*, back in the 1990s, Thomas Friedman observed the following:

> I was in Tokyo on a reporting assignment and had arranged to visit the Lexus car factory outside Toyota City, south of Tokyo. . . . At that time the factory was producing 300 Lexus sedans each day, made by 66 human beings and 310 robots. From what I could tell, the human beings were there mostly for quality control. Only a few of them were actually screwing in bolts or soldering parts together. The robots were doing all the work.

And the move toward robotics is accelerating, as Douglas Mulhall notes in his book *Our Molecular Future*:

> As the new century arrived, there were about 750,000 robots in the world, and their numbers were growing at a rate of 25 percent annually. One in 10 automobile-manufacturing workers was a robot. Their prices had dropped to a fifth of what they were in 1990, both in real terms and compared to the cost of human workers.

But wait (as they say on late-night TV commercials), *there's more!* The field of nanotechnology brings even more advances. Generally defined, nanotechnology is the field concerned with creating machines along the scale of a nanometer, a billionth of a meter. Nanotechnology is not the stuff of science fiction: More than one thousand nanotechnology products are on the market today with hundreds more coming out each year.

I hesitate to start talking about nanotechnology for fear I will not be able to stop—the entire field is amazing to me! Because nanites are so small, they require little in the way of raw materials, just a few molecules here and there. Similarly, they require little power, so they either can be powered cheaply or can power themselves from their environment, with a little heat or sunlight. They will be able to self-assemble and can be made to do all kinds of things that boggle the mind.

To "go nano" is to directly manipulate reality at the atomic level. We need no far-out scenarios to see how this will change the world.

First, imagine all the jobs they could do inside us. They could investigate what ails us, rebuild what is broken, fight disease, and enhance our abilities. Choose whichever of those you are comfortable with, but let me illustrate with a single example.

Currently there is no known cure for type 1 diabetes, in which white blood cells mistakenly attack cells in the pancreas that produce insulin. But researchers at the University of Calgary have created a vaccine, made up of nanoparticles thousands of times smaller than a cell, that has been effective when tested in mice. The vaccine nanoparticles are painted with a protein that helps keep the white blood cells from attacking the pancreas without damaging the overall immune system. Researchers also discovered the vaccine was able to restore normal blood sugar levels without using insulin. Not a cure, but it sure beats insulin shots. And the principle at work in this technology could lead to a cure for other autoimmune diseases such as multiple sclerosis and rheumatoid arthritis.

Clearly, what nanites will do inside our bodies in the future is almost limitless and will change medicine forever. But let's move on to other jobs they can do outside our bodies.

In the future, we will paint surfaces with substances full of nanites that will absorb sunlight and turn it into electricity, transforming any object we paint into a clean energy creator. The nanite-painted objects will do this job better than anything we have now because when you work with things at the molecular level, you get a lot more surface area to collect energy. Plus, they will be able to convert heat to electricity as well, so anything that heats up will become an energy source.

As Mulhall views it in *Our Molecular Future*:

> Molecularly-constructed photovoltaic cells—thermal or otherwise—will also be applicable to irregular surfaces. They

may be painted on to everything from the inside of a furnace to the roof and walls of a house. Such cells could be combined with logic circuits to create photo-optical computers that carry their own power source with them. Most consumer electronics could go off the grid. Homes and offices would be free from an outside electricity source. Monthly energy bills could drop to near zero. Use of fossil fuel and its destructive impacts could be dramatically reduced.

But wait, there's more! Nanotechnology will give us metals that don't bend, or bend and yet remember their original shape. Paints that warn of overheating. Medical surfaces that detect pathogens. Windows that can't be broken and can switch from opaque to clear. Coatings that keep wood buildings from burning. Smart creams that let your skin absorb an optimal amount of sunlight. Frictionless coatings that never wear out in machines that last for centuries. Fertilizers that don't poison but discourage germs.

How about this: Nanobots that convert sea water into fresh water? We live on a planet that is two-thirds water, but we seem to have trouble figuring out how to get the salt out of it. Does anyone really believe this problem will persist? Or how about nanites that process each piece of trash in our garbage and turn it into something useful? Or nanites that clean up any toxic chemicals they find and turn them into harmless agents?

When we can build at the molecular level, we can build things I cannot imagine today. What I describe above is using a new technology to solve an existing problem. But more than that, nanotechnology will create new opportunities that we cannot now see.

As much as I would like to continue with speculations about molecular-sized machines, I have a larger thesis to prove. I branched off into this discussion of robots and nanites to give an idea of the kinds of massive gains in efficiency with declining costs. This is almost the definition of wealth creation.

Over the course of history, the division of labor has increased human productivity immensely. If I had to put a number on it, I would say ten-thousand-fold. The concept is difficult to quantify or even grasp because essentially, without it we could not make anything we use on a daily basis. Not toothpaste or roads or libraries or light bulbs or aspirin or mirrors—not even Legos. I could no more make a paperclip than I could make a Boeing 747. But we can get some sense of the scale of the increase of productivity if we think of the level of prosperity we have now—and compare it to what we would have if we had to make every single thing we needed by ourselves.

If we obtained this ten-thousand-fold increase simply by allowing specialization and dividing work up among *people*, then what astronomical gains will we achieve by outsourcing that work to robots capable of working with unimaginable precision at unimaginable speed?

Let that sink in: By dividing work up among people so they could specialize, we went from bows and arrows to Apollo moon missions. People specialized, technology advanced, and as a result, men walked on the moon. And that was almost half a century ago!

Now, things have shot forward. We can build machines to specialize even further. Robots are free from the physical limits our human bodies have. Robots can perform thousands of operations flawlessly every minute. Robots can manipulate matter smaller than we can even see, and robots can effortlessly manipulate objects that weigh many tons. Robots can work without ceasing in environments where the temperature is a thousand degrees.

These robots can be powered by computers capable of performing a billion calculations a second. They can be connected to sensors whose sensitivity dwarfs anything a human can do.

We can build these machines to do an incomprehensibly large range of tasks.

In the past, we simply had division of labor among people. Bob made paint, Beverly made nails. Now we can have something completely different: division of labor between machines and people. Bob will make paint, and a "Nailmaker 2000" will make nails. Beverly made one hundred nails a day. The Nailmaker 2000 makes one hundred thousand an hour. Oh, and they are smart nails. After they have been nailed into something, tiny nanite spikes grow out from the side of the nails, making them impossible to remove. Oh, and they change color if they detect structural weakness in the material to which they are affixed. And they are coated with a substance that gives off an inert gas if they are exposed to fire, so they are effectively a fire abatement system. And they are so cheap as to nearly be free.

So, how many thousands of times more will this increase our productivity?

Before you commit to a number, think of this. The pace of advancement in the field of robotics and nanotechnology roughly doubles every couple of years. Everything we have talked about relating to the Internet and technology is coming to bear on robotics and nanotechnology. These fields are about to explode with innovation and advancement.

In 2007, the National Academy of Sciences published a six-hundred-page report called "Rising Above the Gathering Storm: Energizing and Employing America for a Brighter Economic Future." It contained this observation: "Economic studies conducted even before the information-technology revolution have shown that as much as 85 percent of measured growth in U.S. income per capita was due to technological change."

The report also cited a mid-1950s report that found 85 percent of economic growth was attributed to technological change *in the period 1890 to 1950.*

Taken together, those findings suggest that almost all economic growth in the last 120-plus years was from technology. I find this very easy to accept. And after accepting it, I apply it to the future and project that technological advance—and the economic growth it promotes—is poised to proceed at an astonishingly faster pace. If the rate of technological advance is increasing dramatically—and I know of no one outside of a mental institution who disputes that—then it follows that economic growth will increase dramatically as well.

In fact, we are already seeing this. As Gregg Easterbrook notes in his book *Sonic Boom,* "In 2001, global average per-capita economic production was $5,000; by 2008, the average was $8,000, a 60 percent increase in less than a decade."

We still have a thousandfold increase in productivity before us. If so, what does this mean?

If you can build a Mercedes a thousand times more efficiently across the board, then instead of costing $50,000, its price will fall to $50. Put another way: If you make $40,000 a year today, the purchasing power of your salary will go to $40,000,000 a year.

I am sure at this point some of you are rolling your eyes, thinking that I am resorting to linguistic games or arithmetic trickery. A Mercedes for $50? Really? Come on!

Please bear with me and keep your mind open for a minute longer. I'll make this case for you.

When I was thirteen in 1981, I got a Commodore VIC-20 computer. It had 4K of memory and cost my parents about $200. (Thanks, Mom and Dad! It was worth it.)

Fifteen years later, I got a computer with 4,000K (or 4MB) of memory, one thousand times the memory of my trusty VIC-20. The memory for that computer cost me $40 per MB, just under $200.

Fifteen years after that, I got the computer on which I currently am typing. It has 4,000,000K of memory—once again, a thousandfold increase over its predecessor. This 4,000MB (or 4GB) of memory cost a bit more than $200.

So I saw, in real dollars, the cost of computer memory fall to one one-millionth of what it was thirty years ago. That would be like the price of a Mercedes falling from $50,000 to a nickel.

I remember that in 1993 I needed a big hard drive at work and got a 1GB drive. A lengthy discussion ensued around the office as to why I needed such a large drive because it was so expensive—something like $2,000. Now, less than twenty years later, a drive one thousand times larger is $70. That's probably like $50 in 1993 dollars. So a thousandfold increase in capacity at one-fortieth the cost is like the $50,000 Mercedes dropping to a buck and a quarter.

You might be saying, "Well, sure. Everyone knows that has been happening for computer stuff. But that won't happen with the Mercedes."

My response: Why not?

If the labor to build the Mercedes becomes completely robotic and computerized, then why won't we see that same increase in efficiency? Certainly the labor component of assembling the Mercedes could fall to nearly zero. So why not the other components?

I have only three possible answers.

One would be to argue that energy costs will remain high. That could be true, but I don't think so, for reasons laid out in the chapter on scarcity. I think no matter what, energy costs will fall dramatically in the future, probably to near zero, because the economic incentives to unlock that technical puzzle are so overwhelming. In the past two centuries with very little technology, we've come from whale oil and wood to solar and nuclear. Imagine what we can do in the future with a thousand times more technological advancement.

The second would be to argue that the cost of materials to build the Mercedes won't fall by a thousandfold. Again, the materials to build the car are abundant; their cost is high because of technology deficiencies around retrieving and refining them, not an underlying rarity. I think we will see commodity prices plummet in the coming years.

Finally, you might argue that fees paid as royalties to the owners of the intellectual property needed to build the Mercedes for $50 will not fall by a thousandfold. I doubt this, though. Technical breakthroughs in the future will come very rapidly, each one used to increase quality and lower costs in order to compete in an ever more competitive marketplace. Technical workarounds will prevent technical monopolies in the future. The ability of patent holders to extract monopolistic profits from innovation will fall in the future, because technology will simply move too fast and be too disposable. Innovating will become table stakes just to stay in business, and innovation will be used to lower prices, not to increase them. (There may be exceptions to this, such as in the field of biotech and genetics, yet as tempting as it is to go down those fascinating rabbit holes, I will stay on topic.)

So there it is: the $50 Mercedes. I know that sounds preposterous—but only based on our assumptions that the future will be like the past. Let's continue to explore how it may be radically different.

So, will we get a thousandfold increase in other areas? Let's look at a few. And remember, it can be obtained both by a plummeting cost and an increasing value of the thing to you.

BUT WAIT, THERE'S MORE: THE $1 SUPER PAN OF THE FUTURE

Most things we buy are worth more to us than the money we spend on them. If they weren't, we would keep the money. There is a chili I love called Wolf Brand chili. It costs about $2 a can. I would happily pay $10 for it; I love it that much. So every time I buy a can, I make $8. This is not Enron-esque accounting chicanery. This is basic economics.

(Of course, I can't go buy a thousand cans for $2,000 and have them worth $10,000 to me. As we discussed, due to decreasing marginal utility, each additional unit of a thing you get is worth a bit less to you than the ones you have already. At the margin, if I buy a can of Wolf Brand chili, I make $8. Makes me hungry just thinking about it.)

Consider the pan you most often cook in today. Let's say you paid $30 for it and you love it. It is worth $50 to you. Buying that pan increases your wealth by $20.

Now, consider the New Super Pan. It will be better than any pan you own today. It detects salmonella, E. coli, and all kinds of harmful chemicals in your food. It will analyze and record the nutritional content of your meal. In fact, it will remember everything that has ever been cooked in it so that when you are trying to recreate last week's risotto dish that you improvised, it will tell you that you added a bit more salt and less chicken broth.

This pan's nanite coating means to clean it, you just wipe it with a nanite rag that doesn't stain. The handle doesn't heat up. It alerts you when the food is about to start burning and needs stirring. It triggers your house's fire system if it detects it has caught on fire.

This pan will cost a dollar. Man, that's one cool pan.

How much would you pay for that pan today? Yes, I know this sounds like one of those bad infomercials. But surely a pan that warns you if your house is burning down or your food will kill you has to be worth $200 to you. Imagine the people who avoid food poisoning because of the pan—what will they say it is worth to them? $2,000? And the people whose houses or lives it saves? They can't even put a value on it; they wouldn't sell it for a million dollars.

So, let's say on average the pan is worth $2,000 to everyone who uses it—all the way from the people who just think it is "cool" to the people whom it saves from food poisoning to the people whose lives and houses it saves. Its social good, on average, is $2,000 a pan.

Buying this pan for a dollar basically gets you a $2,000 benefit. Your old pan only got you a $20 benefit, so this pan delivers one hundred times the wealth. So whether you are rich or poor in the future, you will own this pan and get this benefit. This is a form of wealth.

Food. Yes, I see the cost of food falling a thousandfold. I think in the future, food will be free. (If you can reserve judgment on that statement, I'll explain my reasoning in the book's next section.)

Computers. As I have already addressed this extensively, let me focus here on a specific economic aspect: how the falling price of computers will have an even more profound impact as more and more items have computers in them. When computers are in your clothes, medicine, eyeglasses, wallet, tires, walls, makeup, jewelry, cookware, tennis shoes, binoculars, and everything else you own, those things will do more than you can imagine—the stuff of science fiction.

Imagine when a five-cent computer in your shoe warns you that the way you are walking will lead to spine problems. Imagine when the twenty-cent computer in your eyeglasses begins filtering out high levels of radiation the moment it is detected, and the dime computer in your skillet warns you of salmonella in your eggs (see box at right). Each of these wonders is coming, and a million more. And each of these items will fall in price.

Housing. Yes, I see the cost of housing dramatically decreasing. Houses will be built by robots using materials not yet invented that are cheaper and more energy efficient. Labor will fall, material costs will fall, materials will be better, stronger, greener, prettier, lighter, more malleable, and just altogether better. Of course they will be. How do we know this? Housing is a huge industry that will reward innovative products that are truly better. Thus, it will be a prime target for technology and all its powers to double and redouble, again and again, forever.

The house of the future won't just be better than the house you have today. It will do things you don't expect a house to do. First of all, it will keep you safe. It will monitor for levels of CO_2, smoke, fire, odd variants in temperatures, chemical emissions, and so on. It will know everyone who is supposed to be in the house and alert you when someone else is in the house (replacing the family dog of old in whom we never fully placed our trust). It will have windows that cannot be broken and doors that cannot be forced. It will know sex offenders, who must register publicly, and warn you when they come to the door. It will verify the credentials of any service people who come by. Your home will be your castle, and in your castle you will be secure.

But your house will do more. It will passively recognize you by recognizing your face or your voice or your breathing pattern or the pattern of your footsteps or, most likely, your scent. The house will know where everything in it is; you will never again lose your keys or your child's favorite stuffed animal. It will alert you when you have mice or termites. The house will need scheduled maintenance but will remember when and will ask you for permission. It will be self-repairing. Its walls will be moveable by a professional, so it can be redesigned in a day. Its windows will darken at your command; its air will be automatically purified. If you ask it to run your bath, it knows you like the water at 104 degrees. You only need to say, "Going to bed," and the entire house will be put in night mode.

Let me clarify in terms of "talking to your house." Your house will not be "smart" insofar as it will not seem alive to you any more than your garage door opener or your web browser does. As I observed a few pages ago in "Let Robots Be Robots," an intelligent system like this won't be creepy because we do not want it to be creepy. We just want it all to work, to do what it is programmed to do.

This house will be cheaper to build than a house today and worth vastly more to you for all the cool things it does. How do you put a price on this house?

I would love to write more and more about this topic, about how things will get better and cheaper in the future. Not 20 percent better and 20 percent cheaper, but a thousand times better. About clothes, and how robots will weave garments that never wear out from materials not yet invented that will cost very little. How those clothes will monitor my health, my hydration levels, and even my body odor. I will be able to change their color. I will probably absorb vitamins through my skin as my shirt detects I need them.

I would love to go on about transportation in the future and how much better it will get—how we will look back in amazement at an era where, when people turned sixteen, we gave them a certificate that allowed them to propel six thousand pounds of metal down the highway at 70 mph, with disastrous results in one hundred thousand cases a year. I would love to write about how all the time that drivers waste driving will be returned to them to

car did back in 1911, for the simple reason that cars are so much better now. A poor person with free access to the Internet at the library is wealthier than a poor person with free access to just a library.

But this is merely a footnote, an asterisk in the record book of humanity. Given that inequalities in income are likely to grow, how I can I contend that we will see an end of poverty?

Let's address that by looking at two phenomena: the changing definitions of poverty over time, and the effect of a large gap between the incomes of the rich and poor.

The definition of poverty has both absolute definitions and relative ones. For an absolute definition, I'd offer the Dictionary.com wording that began this section, or this restatement of it: "the economic state where one cannot reliably fulfill the basic requirements of life." If you regularly don't have enough food for yourself and your family, or you do not have the clothing and shelter to protect yourself from the elements, then you are in poverty. No one disputes this.

Defining poverty in relative terms is trickier. In Beverly Hills, your poor neighbor might be one who had to buy the 14K-gold back scratcher instead of the diamond-encrusted platinum one everyone else is buying. (Obviously, my tongue is firmly in my cheek as I type this; people would not regard the poor neighbor as "in poverty," but they might sloppily use the word "poor" to describe her.)

My relative definition of poverty is "the state of being unable to reliably purchase a bundle of goods that allow one to participate in the economic norms of one's society." An elderly person reduced to eating dog food may be getting enough calories to fend off starvation and avoid being regarded as impoverished by our absolute definition. But the relative definition certainly kicks in here. As a culture, we have decided that eating dog food is outside of the economic norm and thus regard it as poverty.

In 2009, in the United States of America, the poverty threshold for a single person under sixty-five was about $11,000 a year; the threshold for a family group of four, including two children, was about $22,000 a year. This per-person threshold actually exceeds the average income of three-quarters of the countries on the planet, including Mexico, Russia, and Brazil, and is about 20 percent higher than the average income of the entire planet. Think about that: Poverty in the United States is defined as higher than the average income of the planet.

Compare the U.S. threshold to the poverty level in India as defined by its government, which is roughly $130 a year. By the government's calculation, about 40 percent of India's population, or half a billion people, are below that level. And according to widely used estimates, roughly a third of the planet's population lives on less than two dollars a day, an amount which must be regarded as close to absolute poverty.

Compared to that absolute standard of poverty, the poor in the United States are famously well off, many with cell phones, TVs, Internet access, and other modern comforts. This speaks to the fabulous wealth of this country and how our expectation of material possessions has risen so fast that we have redefined poverty to include what once were deemed luxury items. I wish the whole world were like that!

Because fate and nature unequally distribute ability, ambition, and opportunity, people's financial outcomes vary greatly. Thus the world has rich people and poor people, and history is full of conflict between the two groups. Though I think Karl Marx overestimated its importance when he identified this conflict as the fundamental struggle of history, it certainly has been a constant.

Tensions between the rich and poor grow higher under the following five circumstances:

1. **When the poor perceive their ability to become rich as restricted.**
   If there is mobility between the rich and poor, and the attainment of wealth is at least aspirational, the poor buy into the system more.

2. **When the rich believe the poor will not honor property rights.**
   When the rich believe the poor will revolt and seize their property, they react by trying to impose draconian restrictions on the poor. When there is widespread recognition of property rights, acceptance of who owns what, less tension is between the rich and poor, by both parties.

3. **When the poor believe the rich are beneficiaries of different legal status than the poor.** If the poor believe they have less justice than the rich, they buy into the system less.

4. **When the rich are demographically different than the poor.** If all the rich are left handed and all the poor are right handed (or some other shared trait), the system seems less meritocratic and thus less just, and the poor buy into the system less. When the poor see people like themselves (in terms of race, religion, age, gender, etc.) getting ahead, they buy into the legitimacy of the system more.

5. **Finally, when the poor see their income shrink while the income of the rich rises, they will buy into the system less.** However, if they are getting wealthier over time, even if the rich are getting wealthier faster, the poor will tend to accept the system more.

These conflicts are probably as old as civilization. Plutarch's *Life of Solon* describes Athens in 594 BC:

> At that time, too, the disparity between the rich and the poor had culminated, as it were, and the city was in an altogether perilous condition; it seemed as if the only way to settle its disorders and stop its turmoils was to establish a tyranny. All the common people were in debt to the rich. For they either tilled their lands for them, paying them a sixth of the increase . . . or else they pledged their persons for debts and could be seized by their creditors, some becoming slaves at home, and others being sold into foreign countries. Many, too, were forced to sell their own children (for there was no law against it), or go into exile, because of the cruelty of the money-lenders. But the most and sturdiest of them began to band together and exhort one another not to submit to their wrongs, but to choose a trusty man as their leader, set free the condemned debtors, divide the land anew, and make an entire change in the form of government.

BEYOND ROBIN HOOD: WHY RADICAL APPROACHES TO WEALTH REDISTRIBUTION DON'T WORK

History has witnessed numerous attempts, through radical methods, to raise up the poor by extracting wealth from the rich.

One is to hyperinflate currency, which is a massive transfer of wealth from creditors to debtors. Creditors loan out money worth a lot, only to be repaid in money worth less. As currency is inflated, prices rise. Governments respond to that inflation by freezing prices. It happened in the United States as recently as the 1970s.

When inflation gets really bad, shopkeepers respond by refusing to take the inflated currency at all. When that happens, refusal to accept the currency is swiftly outlawed and punished harshly. Shopkeepers close their shops to escape this catch-22—and that too has frequently been outlawed and punished. At that point, people flee the land looking for a better deal. This, too, has been outlawed in the past and was in fact part of the legal structure that created feudalism and serfdom, a lightly modified version of slavery that forever tied people to the land on which they were born.

This dance has happened more times than a weary historian can count. It is one of the many examples of how history repeats itself—not for any mystical reason, but because people make the same decisions over and over again when put in the same situation. I referred to it as a dance, but it is a dance to economic death. It wrecks economies and never, ever works.

A second method of radical redistribution is to increase marginal tax rates to a point that is confiscatory. The United Kingdom famously did this after World War II by raising marginal tax rates on earned income to more than 99 percent and, for some other kinds of income, to more than 100 percent. That meant for every pound someone made, he owed more than a pound in taxes.

It was a calculated, deliberate move to wipe out the wealthy. Families who owned great houses were able to keep them if they opened them to the public, acted as guides, and only lived in a small part of them. The rich, of course, got very clever about where they earned and reported income. Confiscatory tax rates also never work. They invariably lead to shrinking economies and remove incentive for the most productive people to work.

A third radical method of redistribution is called land reform, which is actually a polite term for taking land from one person and giving it to another. This approach has a long and mostly negative history. It comes up everywhere, even the United States.

Land reform recently made the news in Zimbabwe, where it was cruelly implemented with disastrous effects, including dramatically lowered food production, flight of capital from the country, increases in poverty, unimaginable inflation, and, of course, wholesale murder and theft.

In 1980, the Zimbabwean dollar was worth about the same as the U.S. dollar. Now the Zimbabwean dollar has undergone four re-denominations (the process of shaving zeros off the currency to make a more manageable new currency. Today one U.S. dollar would get approximately 10,000,000,000,000,000,000,000,000 of those 1980 dollars.

Other methods of redistribution are even more direct. Sometimes countries simply nationalize industries, so that an enterprise once owned by a private company, often a foreign-based one, is taken over by the government or "the people."

When industries are taken *without* payment to the property owner, it has a certain legal term. Where I come from the term is "thievery," but believe it or not, they don't call it that. When a nation-state does it, they call it "expropriation." They see themselves as defining law, not breaking it. I beg to differ, but I am seldom consulted when such decisions are made.

Expropriation is an act that simultaneously violates two of the three ingredients for prosperity that I have enumerated: private property and rule of law. Expropriation often is accompanied by infringements of the third ingredient, individual liberty, as well. Cuba expropriated all foreign-owned corporations after its revolution in 1958. Economically, that hasn't turned out as well as they had hoped.

Nationalization and expropriation are wealth-extraction methods that typically only work once. Once a nation shows its willingness to seize foreign-owned property at will, foreign investors are reluctant to do business there again. Long term, this hurts nations more than expropriation has helped them.

Sometimes the poor cut out the middleman of government entirely. They riot, steal, and then kill, torture, or humiliate the rich. The French Revolution was a particularly macabre affair, where the degree and cruelty of the retribution reached heights (or would it be lows?) seldom seen in Europe since the fall of Rome.

In no case did these methods and efforts secure a long-term solution to poverty.

In one understanding of economic history, the rich get ahead, and the gap between them and the poor widens. The factors I describe above kick in: The poor perceive themselves locked into poverty, deprived of justice, or feel they have the economic deck stacked against them. Because many more people are poor than rich, they revolt or elect a new leader or strike; they exercise the power of their numbers in such a way as to force a redistribution of wealth (see facing page).

Such radical redistribution attempts are dangerous games, for the rich are creators of economic opportunity, not just for themselves, but as employers, for society. If the poor remove rich people's incentives to produce economic gain, the rich, who behave somewhat rationally, will stop producing. This is a straight shot to economic poverty for any country desperate enough to try it.

Here I'll make a point that I believe to be a historic constant and to which we will be returning: If property rights of the rich are respected and tax rates, while high, still allow for indefinite gain, then the rich will keep producing. They will simply complain about the tax rates and keep on working.

One way that society keeps a lid on the powder keg of tension between the rich and poor is through the welfare state. In its most basic form (which I'll discuss here for simplification's sake), it is a guarantee of a minimum income above the poverty line for every citizen.

Cynics view this as the rich paying off the poor to keep them from revolting. These payments, the cynics would argue, bribe the poor to back the system. Although the poor may not believe that wealth is attainable for them, they do not want to rock the boat and risk disrupting the system that guarantees them at least some income.

Optimists view the same system as a form of social justice whereby the benefits of civilization, markets, technology, and modernity, which all disproportionately benefit the rich and talented, are more equitably distributed to the entire society, even those shortchanged by fate.

The cynic would read the optimist's view and say "Toe-may-toe, toe-mah-toe." The optimist would probably try to hug the cynic. Historian Will Durant summarizes the situation thusly: "[T]he concentration of wealth is natural and inevitable, and is periodically alleviated by violent or peaceable partial redistribution. In this view, all economic history is the slow heartbeat of the social organism, a vast systole and diastole of concentrating wealth and compulsive recirculation."

So far we have looked at poverty and how it is redefined as societies grow richer. We have surmised the future widening of the gap between the rich and poor, and looked at how that has played out in history. We have looked at factors that increase animosity between the rich and poor and situations in which they can live harmoniously. Now let's look at the role of government, both philosophically and historically, which also changes over time.

If governments are created to protect the life, liberty, and property of their citizenry, what all does that entail? When nations are young and when they are poor, they usually focus on two things: the military and civil order. The most pressing concern is securing their own survival. Nations can do this by acquiring enough military might that an attempted land grab would cost their neighbors more than they would get if successful.

Once borders are secured, nations turn to social order. This usually comes in the form of protecting their citizenry from crime. Preventing violent crimes and crimes against the weak usually take precedent over fraud and economic crimes.

Wise nations then work on making a stable and valuable money supply. They coin money in honest and accurate measures and allow this money to trade freely on open markets.

Next, nations work to expand justice in the society and provide infrastructure to promote commerce. This might be the adoption of commercial standards as well as the creation and operation of a civil court system and laws. They develop methods for the accurate measuring and recording of boundaries of land as well as the sale thereof. They institute legal protection for copyrights, patents, and trademarks. They codify laws regarding libel and slander. Further, they provide for the registry of births, marriages, and deaths of the citizenry so that, as the agents enforcing justice, they can ensure that wills are carried out and inheritances passed.

People broadly agree that government should do at least this much. Some believe this is the beginning and end of the role of government.

Others more broadly interpret the concept of securing life, liberty, and property. They would say, "If government is obligated to protect its citizens from a foreign invader, then it is obligated to protect them from a criminal. If you would expect government to arrest someone who tried to murder you and put him in jail, how much more so would you expect them to try to stop a bacteria that is trying equally as hard to kill you."

And by such an argument, they bring in the government as a healthcare provider. They might continue by saying, if they are Americans, "the Constitution of the United States authorizes it to 'promote the general welfare.' This is a deliberately subjective term each generation is expected to redefine. Didn't Thomas Jefferson, author of the Declaration of Independence, believe the Constitution should be rewritten every twenty years so that no one was governed by a document they had no say in creating?"

Those favoring limited government answer back, "What you describe leads to tyranny and poverty. No one should decide what someone else should value or spend his money on. Government is the servant of the people, not the master. The more it grows, the more heavy-handed it becomes and the more it tramples the very rights it purports to protect. You are right to quote Jefferson, but you chose the wrong quote. He distrusted government and said 'that government governs best which governs least.'"

In any case, this argument goes on ad infinitum, until one calls the other a "socialist" and the other responds by calling his opponent an "idiot." In a heated moment the phrase "jack-booted thug" slips out, and it is all downhill from there. Civility is the second casualty of political debate. The first is empathy.

I will spare you my thoughts on this debate because they are irrelevant to the topic at hand. Instead, forget which is "right" for the moment and simply consider the flow of history, for better or worse. As national income increases in a given country, the size of government as a portion of gross national product (GNP) rises and the range of services people expect the government to offer rises. Direct payments are made to an increasing number of citizens and the size of those payments rise.

This seems a bit counterintuitive. You would think that when nations are poor, they need high tax rates to guarantee basic services to their people.

Then, as a nation grows wealthier, tax rates could fall in terms of percentages because the nation is making so much more money.

But this is not the case historically. Whether you look at a single country over a span of time, or a group of countries at a specific point in history, the result is the same. The higher the average income of the people (as expressed through per capita GNP), the higher the tax rate. Roughly speaking, if you look at the poorest forty nations in the world, who have an average income per person of about $1,500 a year, their effective tax rates are about 20 percent. In other words, the government taxes and spends about $300 per person per year.

On the other hand, if you take the forty richest countries, each person earns on average around $33,000. So you might suspect the tax rate is only 1 percent. That is all the government needs to tax to bring in the $300 per person per year. But no. The tax rate is actually much higher. It averages 40 percent, or $13,000 per person per year.

The math works the same over time. As per capita income rises in the United States, the tax *rate* does as well, not only the gross tax receipts.

Simply put, as income rises, we buy more things, including more government. In fact, we don't simply buy more government, but we give it a disproportionate amount of our increased income. Wealthy nations by and large elect their rulers, so quite clearly a majority prefer to spend incremental income buying more government services, even services that do not benefit them directly. It is safe to say that more than a majority of people in rich nations feel this way. Almost everyone does, it would seem. The tax rates when the "conservatives" are in power are very little different than when the "liberals" are in power. The variable seems to be who is taxed, not the level of service the government offers.

It seems that as national income rises, people choose to create larger governments that offer more entitlements and have more expansive powers. It is a tale that history repeats with surprising consistency.

Historically, and one can certainly make the case in the present time, this ultimately bankrupts societies. The very well documented corn dole of ancient Rome is one of many cases. Established by a ruler of the Roman Republic named Gaius Gracchus (158–122 BC), the dole began as the state selling grain at half price to anyone willing to wait in line for it; there was no means test. Something like fifty-thousand people applied for it. After the death of Gracchus, a conservative government under Sulla withdrew the subsidy, but shortly afterward, in a period of great unrest, restored it, and two-hundred thousand persons stood in line.

In 58 BC, Clodius Pulcher ran on a "free grain for the poor" platform as he tried to become tribune. It worked. When Julius Caesar came to power a decade later, he found 320,000 on the rolls. He worked to apply a means test, pared the rolls back, then died; the rolls swelled again, and his successor again tried to bring them in line, but it was hard. Once a benefit is established, it creates a constituency fiercely dedicated to defending it. We've seen this: If you are running for president of the United States, merely using the words "freeze" and "Social Security" in the same sentence has the retirees of the nation heating up pots of tar and emptying their down pillows.

The Roman story went on. Three centuries later, it became a hereditary right and came with a daily ration of two pounds of bread ("Hey, you don't expect us to cook the free grain, do you?") and occasionally included meat, olive oil, and salt.

Why do I say this ultimately bankrupts nations? It seems that we can afford to spend more on government as income rises. What's wrong with that? All is well and good until things turn down for a nation. Like a TV star that doesn't scale back his expenses after his show is cancelled, these benefits expand, not contract, during periods of economic decline, for two main reasons. First, more people need them. Second, less political stability during these times means governments are less likely to anger the majority with unpopular legislation like the end of subsidies.

But the big question is whether these same economics would apply in a world one hundred times richer than we are right now. Would it bankrupt that world? I do not think so. I think those economics are driven by a fundamental scarcity which has been the historic norm and thereby the only one we know. All economic and political theory, from left to right to center to weird, is based on scarcity.

Our biggest takeaway from history, therefore, is not the disastrous results of increases in the welfare state, but the propensity of governments to tax and then redistribute wealth as wealth expands. No student of history would argue this point, regardless of his or her politics.

So think about this. Countries whose average income is $1,500 tax at 20 percent. Countries where it is $33,000 tax at 40 percent. Now, suppose I am right and incomes effectively rise dramatically. Let's say, to keep the math simple, they go up thirtyfold. So today, you make $33,000 and pay 40 percent tax. Tomorrow, you get a thirtyfold raise and are now making a million dollars a year. Or, at least you have that purchasing power. So, how much in taxes would you be willing to pay? Or, put another way, what if you had to pay 60 percent in taxes?

Well, on the one hand, you would be kind of cheesed-off. After all, that's the government taking more than half of what you make. What nerve! But think of it this way: Before, you made $33,000 and paid 40 percent in taxes, so you were left with $20,000 in take-home pay. After your raise, you made $1 million, paid $600,000 in taxes, and were left with $400,000—twenty times more after-tax income.

I think what would happen is this: You would grumble for a few days, mutter a few choice words about "blood-sucking politicians," and then get back to work—which, in this case, is spending $400,000 a year.

That is something like what I expect will happen, but on a worldwide scale.

I wrote this section, hypothesizing a future 60 percent marginal tax rate, before I read the following quote in *Esquire* magazine's "What I Have Learned" column, from conservative commentator Bill O'Reilly:

> Yes, I get angry when the federal government spends $100,000 on a study to find out why people don't like beets. I wouldn't mind [paying] 60 percent of every dollar I make in taxes if it was helping somebody in the street who wants to clean up his life, or giving some kid a school lunch and an after-school program. I'm more than happy to do that. It's a philosophical thing. If I work hard for my money, I don't want to see it wasted.

Now, let me pose a different question: In the vastly-more-prosperous future, what will "working hard for our money" even mean?

Earning a "Living"

In the 24th century there will be no hunger, there will be no greed, and all the children will know how to read.
—Gene Roddenberry, creator of Star Trek

Why do we have to work for a living? The answer rests in the phrase "for a living." We have to work at jobs to create wealth because as we live our lives, we consume wealth. If you want to eat a banana, then you have to create a banana-amount of wealth. You have to do a banana-amount of work.

But does it have to be that way? Let's think about that for a moment.

First, think of the concept of interest. We understand that you can, in theory, save and save and save and then live off the interest of your savings forever. In fact, your children, their children, and their children forever could live off that interest. Conceptually we get that. Now, consider the child that lives off the interest payments of all the money her parents saved. Are those interest payments to the child "welfare?" Most people would not term that welfare, which has become a loaded phrase associated with the state making a payment to individuals.

Here's a second example. Some stocks reliably pay dividends, portions of a corporation's profits paid out in cash to its shareholders. Some stocks pay dividends very regularly: Coca-Cola, for instance, has paid a dividend every year since 1920. So let's say your parents bought Coca-Cola stock their entire life, left it all to you, and you are able to live off the dividend payments of the stock. In fact, you have no other income. Is that welfare? No. Is there anything wrong with you collecting this dividend check for which you did no work at all? No. Your parents saved money. They used that money to buy part of Coca-Cola in the form of common stock. It was theirs to do with as they pleased and they chose to give it to you.

Now, consider the Alaska Permanent Fund, a fund established in 1976 where a portion of the revenue from the sale of oil from Alaska's public lands is deposited. Each year a payment is made to each resident of Alaska. The payments are substantial, about $1,000 per person. Now, is this welfare? I don't think so. This is simply returning to the people a portion of income from land that is publicly owned. The people in Alaska who get the checks don't work for them. They get the annual check regardless of what they do. They may have just moved to Alaska from another state. They aren't responsible for the oil being in Alaska and do nothing to extract the oil from the earth. And yet, this is not considered welfare. No stigma is attached to the checks. In fact, the fund, which is now worth almost $30 billion, is regarded as an example of responsible governance.

I describe these three situations because each, in its own way, illustrates how I think the future will play out regarding income and wealth.

I think that incomes will rise dramatically to many times what they presently are, in real dollars. As incomes rise dramatically, marginal tax rates will also rise. In other words, the average person will make more money, pay a higher percentage as taxes, but still bring home vastly more than before.

Because human ability is distributed unevenly and technology multiplies ability of the talented, the spread between the rich and poor will rise more and more. Why is this? In a world where only one tool is invented, a hoe, there will be no billionaires. The ability of the hoe to magnify ability might double someone's productivity but doesn't increase it a millionfold. Before recorded music, the best musicians made a good living but weren't extremely wealthy. Once technology allowed for the recording and sale of records, their income shot way up—they could use technology to magnify their ability. Bill Gates could make his billions because computers, with the right software, could vastly increase productivity. Therefore millions of people were willing to pay hundreds of dollars for the software to make them more productive.

So the poor will get richer, and the rich will get vastly richer.

In a world of economic superabundance, people will no longer tolerate poverty. Or, put another way, they will redefine poverty dramatically upward. In that world, everyone will be guaranteed a minimum income.

This income will not be regarded as welfare. It will be regarded as interest payments on the accumulated riches of one thousand years of technical and material progress. It will be regarded as a dividend of the work of the one hundred prior generations that got the world to this point. It will be seen as a distribution like the Alaska Permanent Fund is perceived: your fair share of the extreme abundance that civilization created. People will think of it as their birthright—their payment for having the foresight to have been born at the correct time in history.

This may grate on our nerves, striking us as a bit lazy, because we are so rooted in scarcity. But it really is no different than me thinking it is my birthright to be able to have freedom of speech. Somebody else—actually, a lot of somebody elses—worked really hard for a long time to build the United States and its freedoms. I enjoy those freedoms much like an interest payment or dividend, and I call it "my right" to free speech.

When all the factories run themselves, when energy is free, when scarcity is ended, when material needs are all met, it will be a different world.

As civilization and technology advance, people begin to create more than they consume. Some become wealthy. Some become so wealthy, in fact, they can live off the interest (the productivity) of their assets, not just their own labor. Is there a logical end to that—a physical or economic law of some kind that says only 10 percent or 20 percent or 30 percent of people can ever be this wealthy? No, not at all. All it takes is so much wealth that it is self-sustaining—that the productivity of that wealth can support everyone.

This is not socialism. Socialism is a flawed and unjust system. In a world without abundance, socialism removes the one reliable creator of abundance—the individual profit motive—and that results in a lower standard of living for everyone.

But in a world without scarcity, socialism can't even exist.

In a world without scarcity, or that has scarcity at such a trivial level it is hardly noticeable, all the conventional theories and dogmas lose their meaning.

This world will gradually come to us. We will know it is coming when we see more and more jobs once filled by humans being filled by machines. We will know it is coming when we see the prices of more products fall while their quality increases. We will know it is coming when formerly scarce items, such as commodities, fall in price.

As we start heading toward this world without want, there will be sizable disruptions in the normal fabric of life. Some people will have a hard time adjusting to the new reality. As we consider the lot of those left behind, it becomes clearer how the end of scarcity will have a profound impact on the world.

Left Behind

We cannot solve life's problems except by solving them.
—M. Scott Peck

When I talk about this future, a future in which machines will do more and more of the work people do now, I always get some variant of the same question: "What about the people who lose their jobs to machines and don't have any other skills? What will they do?"

The implication is always that some people are simply unable to do any job that a machine cannot do. What about them? It is a legitimate question that deserves a carefully reasoned answer.

First, I would contend that the size of this problem is substantially smaller than many people would guess. We see with our eyes many people doing mind-numbingly boring jobs and assume that is all they are capable of doing. This is wrong. Simply because only so many jobs can, in theory, be replaced by machines does not imply anything about the ability of the people now doing them.

As I've said earlier, the most underutilized resource in the universe is human potential. I also argue that most people in tedious jobs know they are capable of more than what they are doing and they want more challenging work, especially if it also pays better.

Pretend there is a spectrum of jobs from the best in the world down to the worst and everyone agrees on the order. Further, assume the best job pays the most and is the most fun, and the worst job pays the least and is the least fun. Let's say the best job is "movie star" and the worst job is "manure hauler." To the extent this world is a meritocracy, the most talented will be the movie star and the least talented will be hauling manure.

First, it would be tempting to assume the person hauling manure can only do that, and if that job disappeared he would have no useful skills. But in describing that job spectrum, I never said anything about his absolute ability—I said only that he was at the bottom of the list relative to others. He might be ambitious, well read, smart, and love to draw. But the manure is not going to haul itself, and so the job falls on him.

Now, what if the bottom half of jobs disappeared and were replaced by robots who did them for almost free? Well, wealth would expand dramatically, and the people who had those jobs before could get new and better jobs, such as managing the army of manure-toting robots. (Hey, it may not be your idea of a dream job, but it keeps you on the best side of the manure sack.)

As a historical precedent for what I am describing, consider the shift from the agricultural economy to the industrial economy. In the agricultural economy, virtually everyone was a farmer. If you were male and born on a farm, you were almost certainly going to be a farmer. By the time you were fifteen, you learned everything you needed to know to be a good farmer. And so at an early age, you took a wife, started having children, and supported yourself by farming. By the time your sons were fifteen, they, too, knew everything they needed to know to be a farmer, and it all continued.

Then along came the Industrial Revolution, and I am sure it all seemed very foreign. Wealthy factory owners probably wondered if farmers, moving into cities to work in factories, could learn all the new skills required in an industrial economy. The farmers had to learn what it meant to be paid by the hour and to take instructions from supervisors; how to do a task and then the next day, learn a completely new task and do it instead. Working in a factory required learning a whole different rhythm of life. And yet, we know of no cases of mass "left behind-ness," of people unable to learn how to function in this environment. People are highly versatile, great at learning new things, naturally curious, and naturally enjoy new things. So these former farmers got jobs in factories, learned to repair equipment, solved problems, became line managers, suggested improvements to processes, and got paid for their effort.

It may seem intuitive at first glance, this idea that somehow there are only so many jobs and if you replace people with machines, people have fewer jobs. But upon reflection, it is entirely inconsistent with our experience. Cars replaced horses; did the stable boys remain out of work? Automatic elevators replaced elevator operators; are the elevator operators roaming the streets unemployed? The Internet replaced travel agents; are they all unemployed?

In every sort of human endeavor that ever has existed, jobs have been eliminated by machines. Long ago, almost everyone farmed. Then machines came along and gradually put 80 percent of the population out of work. Telegraph operators used to have to send every message by hand. Then came the phone. Candlemakers made light before the light bulb. Young boys used to manually set up bowling pins after each frame. Not anymore. Lamplighters used to light street lamps every night, before the accursed electricity came along. The iceman delivered ice for your icebox until the electric freezer put him out of business. Thousands and thousands of women were switchboard operators before direct dial phones were in use. People used to sweep the streets at night until a machine replaced them. This list is unending.

This idea that there are a finite number of jobs misses the point entirely of what makes a job. Jobs are created when someone starts a business that takes a thing, adds labor and technology to it, and makes a new thing. However much value the labor can add to the thing is the amount of wage the person can earn. If a million people lose their jobs to a machine, then entrepreneurs start businesses that hire those people to do other things. Because there are more machines now—and as we noted before, machines magnify human effort—then anyone using a machine can get a higher wage than anyone not using a machine.

Today we are on the cusp of a substantially more profound shift in work life. We still have people in boring, dead-end jobs only because we haven't built a machine to do the work. But soon, we will.

As I've already said, I believe we will be experiencing so much prosperity in the not-too-distant future that no one will have to work. No one.

There will be so much wealth that a minimum income will be guaranteed to everyone. It will be regarded as a human right—a dividend for being born a human being, your share of the inheritance that all the prior generations accumulated. It will not be welfare (or, at least depending on how you define the term, it will not be perceived as welfare).

In that world, people will choose one of two paths.

I call the first one the *Star Trek* path. In one episode of television's *Star Trek: The Next Generation*, Captain Jean-Luc Picard thaws out a wealthy man named Ralph Offenhouse who had been cryogenically frozen in the twentieth century. At one point, they have this exchange:

> **Capt. Picard:** This is the twenty-fourth century. Material needs no longer exist.
> **Ralph Offenhouse:** Then what's the challenge?
> **Capt. Picard:** The challenge, Mr. Offenhouse, is to improve yourself. To enrich yourself. Enjoy it.

In the prosperous future, one group of people will rise to this challenge. They will take advantage of the freedom from financial want that the modern age gives them and will focus on improving themselves and the world they live in. When they no longer must consider the economic consequences of what they do with their time, they will follow their passions and do what they love.

The other group will follow the *WALL·E* path. *WALL·E* is a 2008 Pixar film set in the future of a world without want, with all of humanity occupying giant cruise ships in space. At one point, we hear an advertisement for one of the ships:

> The jewel of the BnL fleet; The Axiom! Spend your five-year cruise in style: Maided on twenty-four hours a day by our fully automated crew, while your captain and autopilot chart a course for non-stop entertainment, fine dining— and with our all-access hover chairs, even Grandma can join

the fun! There's no need to walk! The Axiom: Putting the "star" in executive StarLiner!

In this world, humans have grown fat, stopped walking, and fill their days with non-stop entertainment and food.

When those are the paths people choose between in the future—a *Star Trek* path or a *WALL·E* path—some will choose one and some will choose the other. Just like they do today.

But it is my belief that many more people will choose the first choice. Freed from worry about losing a job they do not enjoy, encouraged to follow their dreams and passions, I believe most will want to do just that. I think most people around the world will seek personal excellence.

We've all seen stereotypes of "the common man" coming home from work, popping open a beer, sitting mindlessly in front of the television until bedtime—then repeating that sequence the next day and the next and the next for thirty years. Like most stereotypes, it is an oversimplification. But many people's lives do follow humdrum, dispiriting patterns because we employ too many people doing work that machines should be doing. Their work is literally dehumanizing.

If someone's job demands she turn off her curiosity, her creativity, her judgment, and all the other things that make her human, why in the world would one expect those things to magically snap back on at 5:00 p.m.? If your job numbs your mind by day, why would anyone expect it to instantly come to life at night?

Imagine if all the people with boring, dead-end machine jobs were told they never had to work another day in their life at a job they did not like. Now they could find what really satisfies them and do that.

We all know the stories of people who win the lottery—and let's face it, far too often no good comes of it. In a few years, the money is gone and they are worse off than before. This pattern suggests freedom from financial want would be bad. But I am not talking about a state of affairs where overnight someone with a "machine job" gets unlimited wealth. I am talking about a world of abundance where children are not raised to do a job a machine could do but instead are raised to find out what they are passionate about and to do that.

What a difference it makes when people have hope—real hope, hope for a better tomorrow. Maybe you remember this story from the early 1980s (or, if you weren't yet born, maybe you've heard about it since). It goes like this:

In 1981, a businessman named Eugene Lang returned to the elementary school he had attended fifty years earlier in East Harlem. He was to give a talk to the graduating sixth-grade class. His prepared speech could be summed up as "Work hard and you will succeed."

But before he spoke, he chatted with the principal of the school who informed him that only a quarter of these students would finish high school. This struck Lane so much that he changed his speech. He told the kids about seeing Dr. Martin Luther King Jr.'s "I Have a Dream" speech in 1963 in Washington, DC. He told the kids they should dream their own dreams, and he would help them achieve them.

Then he dropped his bombshell: He promised free college tuition to any of his audience that stayed in high school and graduated. He hired a full-time program coordinator to work with the kids and he then partnered with a local organization that provided support to the kids through high school graduation.

So what do you think happened to these kids? Kids who now had a real reason to hope and believe in their future? Well, of the sixty-one original ones, the organization has stayed in contact with fifty-four. Of those fifty-four, 90 percent graduated high school or got their GED (not the 25 percent the principle had predicted to Lang years earlier), and 60 percent went on to college. Almost all of the students hold fulfilling jobs and many of the ones that are now parents vow they will be sending their children to college.

The success of this program has caused it to spread around the country. There are now about two hundred "I Have a Dream" programs in twenty-seven states helping 15,000 "Dreamers." This is the power of hope. Not hope as an empty wish, but hope as rational thing, a reasoned belief in a better tomorrow.

Perhaps if this world without meaningful scarcity burst upon us tomorrow, many would choose the *WALL·E* path. Who can blame them? They work at jobs they do not like, doing work a machine should be doing. They dream of time off. They long for retirement. People in these jobs know two states: working, which they do not enjoy, and relaxation, which is far better. So yeah, if you told them to choose between working and not working, many would choose to relax.

But over time, these dehumanizing jobs are what will be "left behind," not the people who perform them. The idea of having to "earn a living" will be completely foreign to us.

Imagine the transformation. As children, we had all these things we liked to do that interested and excited us. But as we grew up, reality set in that market forces did not allow those activities to pay enough to support us, so at some point we all figured out we had to "earn a living." And that meant, for too many of us, ditching what we loved to do and doing the work of a machine.

Remember Chad from earlier chapters? It turns out that he loves to paint. But sadly, other people don't think his work is any good. Truthfully, it is pretty awful. In fact, let's say his own mother considered donating the portrait he painted of her to Goodwill but decided not to because "the poor have enough problems already." Thus, because Chad is not good at painting, he cannot paint for a living. Instead, he gets a job monitoring security cameras, which pays $10 an hour—until, of course, he loses that job to Chang.

This is the state of much of humanity. They have something they love and want to do, but if market forces are not such that they can support themselves doing that, they have to do something else.

In the future, all people will be able to follow their passions without regard for market forces.

The rich have always had this luxury. They don't really worry about whether playing polo or building orphanages or any other chosen pursuit can pay the bills, because they don't need it to pay the bills.

What if everyone on the planet had that luxury?

Often when I discuss this idea with people, they bring up an objection

I have come to call The Spoiled Rich Kid Problem. It goes something like this: If everyone is "rich," then doesn't everyone just become the idle rich? Won't all people (or at least most people) waste their lives on narcissistic, hedonistic pleasure?

I don't think so, and I'll explain why with another thought experiment. Imagine you live in a large trailer park and you have four young children. Everyone you know lives in the trailer park and they all have about the same level of income. Nobody is particularly snooty in this world, right? One day, a tornado comes, lifts up your trailer with everyone in it, flies it around the world to the poorest nation on Earth, and drops it in the middle of the village. Now all of a sudden your children are raised in what seems to everyone to be the lap of luxury. You have windows! A door! Electricity (hmm, I guess the trailer was solar powered), a refrigerator, air conditioning. Now everyone wants to be your friend. Everyone wants to come in and enjoy your AC and play on your Wii. Your children actually might grow up feeling privileged, better, and even a bit snooty. And yet their wealth hasn't changed. Only their relative wealth is different.

In my experience—admittedly, generalized and anecdotal—what sometimes makes children of wealth take that hedonistic, narcissistic route is their sense that they are part of a privileged class. So when I think of a world where everyone is rich—not just some privileged few—I imagine everyone pretty much forgets about the wealth. I base that expectation in part on the fact that today, many of us already live in more comfort than the richest king in the world did two hundred years ago. We control the temperature of our surroundings, eat food from around the world, and own possessions no king could have imagined. Plus, we have powers formerly attributed to the ancient gods; we can fly, talk to people in other places, and see what is happening elsewhere. But we take it largely for granted—and I think that is just fine.

In a future where everyone has plenty, there may still be those who choose the *WALL·E* path. It is their right—but it is my belief that these people will be few. In my experience, people who challenge themselves and strive for goals are happier and healthier than those who don't. People who live their lives following their passions seem more full of life and energy than anyone else. It is contagious and would be even in a uniformly wealthy world. And in that world, no one is left behind.

Now, to address the challenge of getting there. As we transition from one set of economic realities to another, there will be severe disruptions along the way. Economic changes that have long-term positive benefits for society often have short-term negative ones. Of particular concern are those who have come to be called "the bottom billion," the poorest people concentrated largely in developing-world nations whose economies now rest mostly on work that machines will be made to do. Citizens in these countries are grateful for any job that pays anything at all, and their primary concern is simply survival. As machines displace people, they will be the most vulnerable, and sadly, will likely be the last ones to arrive in the world I describe above. But eventually, all of humanity will get there for the simple reason that compounding exponential economic growth fueled by technological advances will produce vast abundance for all.

How the Internet and Technology Will End Poverty

One ought, every day at least, to hear a little song,
read a good poem, see a fine picture, and, if it were possible,
to speak a few reasonable words.
–Johann Wolfgang von Goethe

Let us summarize.

Trade and the division of labor have given us vast amounts of wealth. We live in a place and time where we own thousands of things we could not have made. And we got them all, more or less, by trade and the wealth generated by our work doing some function for which we are trained.

Technology has made us ever more productive. Even using extremely primitive technology, we have made marvelous progress. For instance, up until recently in the long march of time, our primary method for storing information was on pieces of wood sliced extremely thin and bound together with thread—an approach not far removed from papyrus, a four-thousand-year-old technology. Until relatively recently, the main sensors we used for scientific study were called "our eyes," and we mainly communicated only with people in the same room. For computations, we developed processes that required us to perform many intermediate, error-prone steps to achieve an answer.

And yet, in that world, the Wright brothers flew a plane, a blood transfusion was performed, the speed of light was measured, and an uncountable number of human accomplishments were achieved.

In an 1843 report to the U.S. Congress, the Commissioner of the Patent Office, Henry Ellsworth, made this gloomy prediction: "The advancement of the arts, from year to year, taxes our credulity and seems to presage the arrival of that period when human improvement must end."

That period when human improvement must end? Ellsworth was wrong. There is no such period and never will be. Technology has no limit we know of. Thus it has unlimited ability to continue raising the world's standard of living, by making things better and more efficient and by doing so with less and less cost.

As machines do ever more things that we used to do, we will have more choices for how we spend our time. Social structures will change, and the purpose of education will be to learn to reason and find one's passion.

The free enterprise system—the greatest creator of wealth the world has known—will continue to produce the material gains we enjoy today and to reward most those who serve their fellow humans best. Jobs done by people will be only the ones that require uniquely human capabilities to do. These jobs can be market jobs that have the potential to make a person vastly richer, creating more and more wealth on the planet. Or these jobs can be divorced from economic realities, as the struggling painter or actor decides simply to do what he loves and live off the minimum income afforded by this planet-wide prosperity.

As technology enters its explosive period of growth, with the Internet and associated technologies flourishing in a Moore's-Law-like manner, it will create immense amounts of wealth. And if history is an accurate guide, that wealth will be partially redistributed to the poor—even the poorest of the poor, the bottom billion.

Even if I am too optimistic in describing a truly post-scarcity world, wealth will unquestionably continue to grow, thanks to technology and free enterprise. I know of no case in history that says otherwise. Taxes will rise, and social programs will grow. Poverty will be redefined upward until, for all intents and purposes, poverty as we know it today no longer will exist.

THE END OF HUNGER

- A History of the Hungry
- Nutrition
- Enough Food Already
- Why Is There Hunger?
- Agriculture 1.1
- The End of the Farmer
- Genomics
- Information and Agriculture
- Food as a Human Right
- Beyond Hungry to Healthy
- How the Internet and Technology Will End Hunger

A History of the Hungry

Love and business and family and religion and
art and patriotism are nothing but shadows of words
when a man's starving.
–O. Henry

I almost cut this entire section from the book. I reasoned that if I could show how poverty will end, then of course hunger would end as well—how many rich people do you hear about going hungry? But food, famine, and hunger occupy a special place in our discussion of scarcity: There seems to be a collective, vague sense that the planet can only support so many people and that we must be close to that theoretical maximum. After all, so many people are hungry for no apparent good reason, in a world that's so wealthy and where we're virtually all against hunger. So the problem must be that we have stretched the planet past its ability to feed its inhabitants, right?

Wrong. This simply is not the case. To prove my case, I need to first address hunger in history, what has caused it, and what have been its results.

Dictionary.com defines hunger as "a compelling need or desire for food . . . a shortage of food; famine."

Hunger can be classified as three different types. They are not distinct buckets but rather broad characterizations: actual famine, weaponized famine, and structural famine.

Actual famine is what we think of in history, where a certain region simply does not produce enough calories to support its population, and additional calories cannot be imported in time to alleviate the hunger. As a general rule within a population, the higher the percentage of those involved in agriculture, the more at risk the system is to hunger and famine. A society with only 2 percent of the people working in agriculture has become so efficient and productive that it takes very little effort to feed everyone (and the system could generate surpluses if needs be). By comparison, if a country has 99 percent of the people working in agriculture—if it is barely feeding itself, even with everyone working at that—then it is living at a subsistence level, the very definition of poverty. One bad plague or invading horde would leave pretty much everyone starving. In the modern age of communication and cheap transportation, food can be moved around the planet relatively easily. But before the twentieth century, this was not the case and actual famines were much more common.

Weaponized famine occurs when hunger itself is used to gain a political or military end. This would be the case in a besieged city or a nation using the food supply to keep its citizenry in check.

Structural famine exists when enough food is technically on hand or able to be imported, but some portion of the population is economically separated from it. In other words, food is present, but some cannot afford it. This kind of hunger is common and generally is what has triggered food riots, now and in the past. People riot when convinced that food is unjustly being kept from them. In the days immediately before the storming of the Bastille, riots occurred because the price of a day's bread was raised to a full day's wage. The poor, knowing there to be bread but being economically unable to get it, rioted. The result was the French Revolution, its Reign of Terror, and blood in the streets (as well as, ultimately, the creation of the metric system).

A hungry populous can be politically volatile, especially if it is used to being well fed. This fact was understood in ancient Rome, where people had a curious lack of interest in science and technology except when it pertained to the military and the building of roads. The empire infrastructure was optimized for moving the army, not freight. Thus, in the event of famine in other regions, Rome's leaders sent soldiers, not food, to control the potentially unruly population.

Because it will figure prominently in the rest of this section, let's take a deeper look at structural famine, whose responsibility it has been to care for the hungry and how that has shifted throughout history.

After touring the United States for more than nine months in the 1830s, Alexis de Tocqueville returned to his native France and penned the two-volume *Democracy in America*. It is fascinating reading to this day because the things he notes about the American character are still very much with us. He writes how in Europe when there is a problem, people turn to the government to solve it, but in America, they form what he calls "voluntary associations"—what we might term charities and nonprofits. He writes:

> Americans of all ages, all conditions, and all dispositions, constantly form associations. . . . The Americans make associations to give entertainments, to found establishments for education, to build inns, to construct churches, to diffuse books, to send missionaries to the antipodes; and in this manner they found hospitals, prisons, and schools. If it be proposed to advance some truth, or to foster some feeling by the encouragement of a great example, they form a society. Wherever, at the head of some new undertaking, you see the government in France, or a man of rank in England, in the United States you will be sure to find an association. I met with several kinds of associations in America . . . and I have often admired the extreme skill with which the inhabitants of the United States succeed in proposing a common object to the exertions of a great many men, and in getting them voluntarily to pursue it.

No government is involved in these organizations, which are instead driven by a combination of religious and civic motives. One is equally likely to see the Chicago Garden Society teaching illiterate men to read as to see the Methodist Women's League providing crutches to injured sailors.

This combination was powerful. Instead of piety being expressed simply in a multitude of unrelated individual acts, it expressed itself in group action. I personally think the establishment of charitable organizations was driven by the same spirit that drove the creation of new businesses: If you started a business to make a product, it would follow that you would start one to solve a problem. Even today, nonprofits in the United States are often incorporated and their governance looks very businesslike, with boards of directors, budgets, and annual reports.

This can-do, care-for-our-own spirit permeated the nation. In a speech to the House of Representatives at this same time, Congressman Davy Crockett told the story of getting chewed out by a constituent for voting for a $20,000 emergency relief bill for the homeless in a city just wiped out by a fire. Crockett said his constituent reasoned that "the power of collecting and disbursing money at pleasure is the most dangerous power that can be entrusted to man. . . . [W]hile you are contributing to relieve one, you are drawing it from thousands who are even worse off than he."

Half a century later, this concern about the role of government still existed. In 1887, President Grover Cleveland vetoed the Texas Seed Bill, which Congress had passed, appropriating $10,000 to purchase seed to give to Texan farmers who had just been wiped out by drought. In his veto message, he explained why:

> I do not believe that the power and duty of the general government ought to be extended to the relief of individual suffering. . . . The friendliness and charity of our countrymen can always be relied upon to relieve their fellow-citizens in misfortune. . . . Federal aid in such cases encourages the expectation of paternal care on the part of the government and weakens the sturdiness of our national character, while it prevents the indulgence among our people of that kindly sentiment and conduct which strengthens the bonds of a common brotherhood.

This all began to change in the twentieth century for a variety of reasons. Much change was due to the efforts of William Jennings Bryan, who received the Democratic Party nomination for president three times, in 1896, 1900, and 1908. Barely a decade earlier, Cleveland, also a Democrat, had said essentially, "Look, the government shouldn't be helping the poor Texans; that's the role of charity." But Bryan, a devout Presbyterian, believed government should be a major force in what we would today call social justice and the welfare state. And he used his decades of dominance on the national scene, as well as his fantastic oratorical ability, to advance that belief and essentially invent the Democratic Party we know today.

Another significant factor in changing government's role relative to the needy was the establishment of the income tax and the Federal Reserve System under the Democratic President Woodrow Wilson. This structurally facilitated a substantial expansion in the role of government. Then came

World War I, which utilized these institutions and greatly expanded the size of the federal government. After this came the Great Depression, which so overwhelmed the social support structures that Americans turned to the government for help and have never turned back.

Thus only recently has our expectation been that the primary actor in disasters is the government. In fact, if the government doesn't do a really good job with delivering aid, it comes under blistering criticism, as was the case in the aftermath of Hurricane Katrina in 2005. The private sector, church groups, and community organizations are seldom criticized for not doing enough because, in the minds of the public, the responsibility for leading these efforts has shifted.

That notwithstanding, de Tocqueville's "voluntary associations" are still alive and well in the United States. According to the National Center for Charitable Statistics, more than 1.5 million 501(c) charitable organizations exist in the United States. And that doesn't even count the many other charitable organizations that have not filed for this tax-exempt status with the federal government.

In the modern era, what we have seen around the world is a general increase in social services and the welfare state over time. A duty to feed and provide for the poor is taken on by the government more and more as national income rises.

An important point to make here is this: *Historically, the welfare state only emerges to solve problems that private charities either cannot or will not solve.* Rarely in history has a government wrested away a functioning, privately funded solution in favor of a government entitlement. In other words, civil government steps in to take over roles traditionally provided by private charity only when charities no longer provide the service. Governments create entitlements due to public demand for them, and public demand exists where the need is not filled.

Thus opponents of the welfare state must recognize that it has arisen out of a real need. They may offer any number of objections to it—arguing that this is not government's legitimate role, or that governments do a poor job at it, or that it creates false incentives and inefficiencies, or that it actually hurts the poor. But it is hard to deny the underlying need.

"ARE THERE NO WORKHOUSES?"

To see how governments have tried (with mixed success) to address poverty and hunger, consider the history of England.

Prior to 1600, government legislation relating to the poor was primarily concerned with keeping the able-bodied employed and punishing unemployment. Penalty for vagrancy rose over the years from time served in stocks, to whipping, to branding, and then to death.

Around 1600, the Elizabethan Poor Law came into effect and lasted more than two centuries. The system had an office, Overseer of the Poor, in each of 1,500 parishes. The thought was that the overseer, being local, would be able to separate the lazy from the truly needy. The system provided for some amount of charity and public works, and was financed by a "poor rate"—a property tax. Liberality and wealth varied by parish, so the enterprising poor would relocate to the more generous parishes. This abuse resulted in an overhaul of the system that sought to tie the poor to their original parish.

By around 1700, the workhouse movement was under way. Workhouses both lodged the poor and gave them work. Since many of the poor were not able-bodied, the workhouses were not profitable institutions. Ultimately, workhouses would provide shelter to more than one hundred thousand paupers.

The system was revised in the 1830s because it was viewed as discouraging work by interfering with the laws of supply and demand relating to labor. The new system prohibited any relief given to the poor outside of a workhouse while simultaneously lowering the quality of the workhouses to discourage the poor from using them except as a last resort. This involved making the poor wear prison uniforms and only providing enough food to avoid starvation. The theory was that life in the workhouse had to be worse than life outside the workhouse, otherwise it would be overrun with the poor. When the economy entered recession, the workhouse conditions had to be worsened more.

This system remained in place until the early twentieth century, when it was gradually replaced by government legislation that established the modern welfare state.

How is this need filled without government involvement? One example would be the Amish. The members of this community neither pay nor collect Social Security, and fought hard to be exempted from participating in that system based on their religious beliefs. Some may have objected to their opting out—but no one dared assert that if they did so, there would be old Amish women eating dog food with no one to care for them. The Amish have no need for Social Security. They have social security.

In any case, as the song says, *The times, they are a-changin'*—and they are changing in a manner that governments probably can't keep up with. As the world grows wealthier, I believe more individuals and non-governmental entities with more innovative solutions will roll up their sleeves to tackle our problems. It is a shame that de Tocqueville's voluntary associations aren't more prominent around the world today—but in the future, they may be. Remember that statistic from earlier in this chapter, counting some 1.5 million 501(c) charities in the United States? That number is 30 percent higher than it was only ten years ago. De Tocqueville would be impressed.

Nutrition

What some call health, if purchased by perpetual anxiety about diet, isn't much better than tedious disease.
–Alexander Pope

In 1989, late-night talk show host David Letterman—famous for his Top Ten lists—produced a list predicting what would be the "Top Ten TV Shows in the Year 2000." Number six on that list: "Oat Bran: The Silent Killer."

As the saying goes, we laugh because it is true. We have grown cynical getting on and off the "____ are bad for you" bandwagon. (You fill in the blank: Eggs? Potatoes? Pork chops?) We wonder if "bad" cholesterol is actually "good" and still don't know whether it's the carbs or the fat that makes us fat.

In discussing nutrition, not only is there little agreement on the nature of the solutions, there is often disagreement on the nature of the problems. And one person's solution may be another person's problem. This is the case on genetically modified crops and many other issues where passions run high.

Why is this the case? Why is civility so lacking in discussions about food, nutrition, and food policy? Why are people so quick to vilify those on the "other side" of the issue—and why do we even think in terms of sides? I realize I may get e-mail from every constituency in the food debate, accusing me of being a shill for every other constituency. If this chapter angers the Right and Left, the Greens and Browns, the capitalists and socialists, the nutritionists and farmers, I apologize to all in advance. I mean no offense. I take no side other than to be against hunger.

As we consider how the Internet and related technologies can end hunger, it is necessary to address the issues of food and nutrition—including why they are so divisive.

First, nutrition is a very primitive science. That is not to say it is a pseudo-science, some poseur who has thrown on a white lab coat and snuck in the back door of a convention of real scientists—far from it. There is undoubtedly a cause and effect between what we eat and our health, but I believe it is still poorly understood. That problem stems not so much from the nutritionists as from an inability to structure meaningful, controllable experiments. It is almost impossible to execute a pure, controlled study of anything relating to nutrition because there are simply too many variables to consider. I am not only what I eat but am also what I do, what I drink, what I think about, and more.

In addition, how food affects us unquestionably has a lot to do with genetic factors, and because everyone has a different genetic makeup, different foods affect each of us differently. If that were not enough to tax nutritional science, add the challenge of needing to study the effects of nutrition over long periods of time to get meaningful results. Add to that how food itself is changing, our food choices change, our lifestyles change, and all along the way we are aging. Then, factor in how income, region, and religion influence what people eat and their nutritional outcomes. And finally, consider how nutrition affects other relative and subjective factors in our lives such as energy level and mood. At every turn, this becomes more difficult to study.

Because of this, the nutrition aisle of your bookstore has more contradictory advice than perhaps any other part of the store. By one count, presently thirty thousand weight-loss diets have been published (when it would seem like a dozen or so might suffice). As we noted earlier, people no longer disagree simply about what values to apply to a set of facts—rather, they disagree as to the nature of the facts themselves. Given so many different nutritional theories and viewpoints, most people base their own nutritional philosophies on a combination of two factors: personal experience and social/political worldview.

If someone notices that she gets a headache when she eats MSG—or artichokes, or grasshoppers—that first-person, anecdotal experience will shape her nutritional philosophy. This makes a great deal of sense: If nutrition isn't governed by universal laws (as physics is) and instead affects different people differently, then the way you will know certain things is by learning through trial and error, through your own experience.

This approach, however, has a couple of downsides. First, it is only useful for factors that are immediately bad for you, not factors that will kill you in ten years. And second, people are really bad at connecting cause and effect in their lives when it comes to things like this. We tend to notice every time the expected effect is triggered by the cause, but may not notice all the times it isn't. In other words, you might not notice the time you ate the MSG and didn't get the headache. Or, we gravitate toward anecdotes like, "I take my vitamin C every day and haven't had a cold in years." Well, yeah, but you also drink a Coca-Cola every day, too. How do you know that isn't doing the trick?

Nonetheless, we all draw these anecdote-based conclusions to some degree, and no one could expect us to do otherwise. But it leads to different judgments: If I experience X as bad and you think it is good, in essence you are saying, "You are wrong and I am right." And that can be hard to hear.

The second way people choose a nutritional theory is to develop it from their overall social and political understanding of the world. Whether you are for the organic food movement or against it, for genetically modified crops or against them, for corporate farms or seed banks or raw food or anything else, is influenced significantly by your larger view of politics. I can generally tell you someone's beliefs on nutrition if you tell me what they think of green energy, yoga, SUVs, George W. Bush, alternative medicine, holistic healing, and vaccines, none of which have anything to do with food. This is how people are. In areas of uncertainty, we form our opinions on the basis of assumptions in other parts of our life.

For instance, if you think large corporations are greedy and evil, then when you read about how large corporations produce low-nutrition food or are putting family farms out of business, you will believe it. When you read somewhere else that food produced by large corporations saved millions of lives, you won't believe that. If you think "Western medicine" is a business whose goal is to keep you sick to sell you medicines, you will tend to move away from genetically modified foods and favor organic. If you love "Western medicine" and think all acupuncturists are "quacks," then you are not likely to heed (or even appreciate) your friend's well-meaning efforts to get you to drink your own urine for its health benefits. Again, this is because without compelling, widely accepted facts, we use things we've learned from other parts of our lives to make our decisions.

So when talking nutrition, people come to the table bearing their core life assumptions (which in their own cases they honor as "experience," while in others' cases they may deride as "baggage"). So if you challenge one of their beliefs about nutrition—and I use the word "belief" deliberately—then you are, in a way, attacking the very system they embrace. The subtle interplay of everything involved in nutrition is vastly more complex than our minds are able to handle. So our ability to find cause and effect in that—and to really discern fact from fallacy, what's good from what's bad for us—is highly suspect.

The Internet will solve for this problem.

Computers, especially computers of the future, will have no trouble handling all the variables that influence nutrition, though there will be millions of them. When everyone's Digital Echo (along with their genetic information) is anonymously available for computers to study for patterns, computers will be able to treat the entire planet as a single controlled experiment because they can normalize for all the variables. This will produce extremely specific nutritional information for just you, will add years to your life, and will increase its quality as well.

At that point, we will have much clarity into the true cause-and-effect relationship between diet and health. In the future, massive new amounts of information will begin to resolve the debate, instead of just adding noise to it as too often occurs today. And because agriculture is a technology, subject to technological advance, advances in agriculture will quicken and multiply, leading to improved nutrition and decreased hunger and famine.

Some methods and technologies that show promise to end famine are controversial. But in the future when we have more and better information, if it turns out that some of these methods are not net gains, we will know that and look elsewhere for solutions. The system will be self-correcting and will have a bias for means that are proven to work. So the current frustrating situation, where so many people have such wildly divergent understandings about nutrition, will fade away.

Then we can focus our energy on an area now so inefficient that technological advances inevitably will produce dramatic gains: agriculture.

Enough Food Already

The fault, dear Brutus, is not in our stars, but in ourselves.
–Cassius, in William Shakespeare's Julius Caesar

We already produce more than enough food to feed the planet.

Three of the world's best-known experts on food and agriculture—Frances Moore Lappé, Joseph Collins, and Peter Rosset—wrote a classic book called *World Hunger: Twelve Myths*. In it, they say this:

> The world today produces enough grain alone to provide every human being on the planet with thirty-five hundred calories a day. That's enough to make most people fat! And this estimate does not even count many other commonly eaten foods—vegetables, beans, nuts, root crops, fruits, grass-fed meats, and fish. In fact, if all foods are considered together, enough is available to provide at least 4.3 pounds

of food per person a day. That includes two and a half pounds of grain, beans, and nuts; about a pound of fruits and vegetables; and nearly another pound of meat, milk, and eggs.

It then continues with this extraordinary fact:

The American Association for the Advancement of Science (AAAS) found in a 1997 study that 78 percent of all malnourished children under five in the developing world live in countries with food *surpluses*.

Can this really be true? Let's look at some countries.

Start with India, which has more chronically hungry people than any other country. According to the FAO (the United Nations Food and Agriculture Organization), in 2005 India had 237.7 million undernourished people. That's a quarter of all the hungry people in the world. According to the ITC (the International Trade Centre, a joint agency of the World Trade Organization and the United Nations), India annually imports US$2 billion worth of food—and exports US$8 billion worth of food. That's right: India is a net food exporter to the tune of US$6 billion a year.

Next comes China, with the second highest number of hungry people at 130.4 million. Food imports: US$9 billion. Food exports: US$22 billion. They export US$13 billion more food than they import. In fact, China produces more food than any other country in the world, triple the amount the United States produces.

Pakistan has the third largest number of hungry people with a total of 43.4 million. Food imports: US$1.4 billion. Food exports: US$1.6 billion.

More than half the hungry people in the world live in just these three nations—nations that are all net food exporters.

In an article called "The Paradox of Hunger in the Midst of Plenty," Ghanaian writer Santuah Niagia notes "the irony . . . that many of the countries in which hunger is rampant export much more in agricultural goods than they import. The countries of sub-Saharan Africa, with about 213 million chronically malnourished people, continue to export food even during the most severe droughts. During one of the worst droughts on record, in the late 1960s and early 1970s, the value of the region's agricultural exports—US$1.25 billion—remained three times greater than the value of grain imported."[5]

Nations with high percentages of hungry citizens are not universally food exporters, and we will explore this more later. My point here is that currently the planet is producing enough food to feed everyone on it.

"Perhaps that is the case now," you may be thinking. "But what about as population grows?"

I am glad you asked.

The United Nations has estimated that Earth's population will pass nine billion by 2050, and ten billion by 2100. But even as the population grows—and even without any of the kinds of big, technological breakthroughs I will discuss later—the planet should have no trouble making more than enough food for everyone.

In his book *The Ultimate Resource 2*, economist Julian Lincoln Simon observes that "the capacity to feed people with an ever smaller small land surface has been developing rapidly for decades. In 1967, Colin Clark estimated that the minimum space necessary to feed a person was 27 square kilometers, a then-optimistic figure that had not been proven in commercial practice or even large-scale experiment. Now a quarter of a century later there is commercial demonstration of land needs only a fifth or a tenth that large. It is most unlikely that this process of improvement will not continue in the future."

British scientist Matt Ridley, author of *The Rational Optimist*, also offers a formula for feeding the nine billion even without any technical breakthroughs. And he even projects that if farmers followed his plan, "it is quite conceivable that in 2050 there will be nine billion people feeding more comfortably than today off a smaller acreage of cropland, releasing large tracts of land for nature reserves. Imagine that: an immense expansion of wilderness throughout the world by 2050."

---

5. From "The Paradox of Hunger in the Midst of Plenty" by Santuah Niagia from *News from Africa* website, October 2002. Copyright © 2002 by Santuah Niagia. Reprinted by permission of **NewsfromAfrica.org**.

"THE GREAT DIE-OFF" AND OTHER (FAULTY) PREDICTIONS

Projections of the earth's imminent collapse under the weight of population are centuries old. Consider Thomas Malthus, the poster child of bad predictions. In the nineteenth century, Malthus wrote that humanity was doomed to starve in the future because population would continue to grow unchecked and land is finite. Eventually, he reasoned, the hungry hoards would overwhelm the beleaguered food supply.

We can easily make allowances for Malthus; he had no basis on which to predict the astonishing explosion of human technological capacity that was the Industrial Revolution. But his more modern followers have been similarly mistaken, as writer Cormac Ó Gráda observed in *Forbes* magazine:

"As for predictions about the famine's future, it is worth noting that past prognostications have rarely been on the mark. In the late 1960s, biologist Paul Ehrlich famously predicted that in the following decade 'hundreds of millions of people' would starve to death 'in spite of any crash programs embarked upon now.' In the following decade, fear of global overpopulation prompted hard-line (and high-profile) Malthusian writers to predict the 'Great Die-Off' in which some 4 billion people would perish."

What actually happened? Well, in the developed world, the percent of people needed to farm fell from more than 90 percent to today's 4 percent. At the same time, the percent of income we individually have to spend on feeding ourselves plummeted as well.

How did Malthus and others get it so wrong? They underestimated the promise of technological advances in agriculture—both those we've already seen (e.g., the mechanization of the farm, invention of high-yield hybrids, new forms of fertilizers) and those yet to come.

We all understand intuitively there is plenty of food in the world. And that fact is driven home by its generally low price in most locations. Just half a century ago, Americans on average spent more than 20 percent of their income on food. Now the number is in the single digits.

I can go to Sam's Club and buy a twenty-pound bag of rice for $10 and a twenty-pound bag of pinto beans for $13. If I go down the spice aisle and drop another $5 on spices to help stave off food fatigue, then pick up a jar of multivitamins on the way to the checkout line, I am still out the door for $30. These foodstuffs alone contain sixty thousand calories, or two thousand calories a day for a month, for a total of $30. Now, I am no fan of beans and rice (even if well-seasoned) three times a day, but it staves off starvation for $1 a day. And that is paying full retail prices in an air-conditioned Western supermarket; by the ton, this food costs much less. Even at the retail price, we could feed all the world's hungry for a billion dollars a day or $365 billion a year. This is less than one-half of 1 percent of world GNP.

I am not suggesting this course—this is not a Marie Antoinette "Let them shop at Sam's" retort. The point I am trying to make is that on a global scale, neither the cost of feeding the hungry nor the fundamental lack of food can possibly be the major issue.

The United States produces more than US$100 billion worth of food and is able to export more than US$40 billion of it each year, yet only 2 percent of our workforce works in agriculture (down from 40 percent a century ago). And the American farmer produces key crops, such as wheat, very inexpensively. At one point, Tiger Woods got a dime for every box of Wheaties cereal with his photo on it, while the farmer was paid only a nickel for the wheat in that same box—and the farmer still made a profit.

Given these agricultural strengths, is there anyone who believes the United States alone couldn't produce an extra $365 billion worth of food, at full retail price, if there were a ready buyer for it? After all, China grows more than three times the amount of food we do in the United States, with less land under cultivation. Today, producer nations are making more food than ever, using fewer people and costing less money. And yet hunger persists— not because of agricultural failure, but because of social structures.

As the FAO declared in an oft-quoted report, "Widespread and persistent hunger is a fundamental contradiction in today's world." The problem is not that the world doesn't have enough food. The problem is that the poor don't have enough money to afford the food. Keep this in mind because we will return to it: *In the modern age, people starve to death not because they have no food but because they have no money.* To me, this makes the problem of hunger that much sadder in the present—to realize that the planet has enough food, just not enough generosity. But in a real sense, it also makes the problem that much easier to solve in the future.

Why Is There Hunger?

The world is very different now. For man holds in his
mortal hands the power to abolish all forms of human
poverty, and all forms of human life.
—John F. Kennedy

If you visit the United Nations Food and Agriculture Organization's website and go to the FAQ section, you will not find an entry for "Why is there hunger in the world today?" This certainly qualifies as a frequently asked question, and in the previous chapter we gave its simplest answer: "Because the poor cannot afford food." Bringing an end to poverty, then, will also help bring an end to hunger. But hunger has numerous and complicated causes and can only be eliminated by addressing the chief ones.

So, why is there hunger in the world today? In part, for the following reasons:

Crop yields are highly volatile and unpredictably so. This leads to the proverbial "lean years" and "fat years." In the lean years, harvests are small and farmers sometimes don't even produce enough to have surplus to sell. In lean years, the economics of using fertilizer, diesel-powered irrigation, and other technologies that involve out-of-pocket expense simply don't work. Then again, don't the fat years make up for all this? Well, no. In the fat years, agricultural prices are pushed downward by the abundance, often below the cost of harvesting and transporting the crops. To make matters worse, when Western nations have fat years, their governments often shore up prices to support domestic farmers by buying up the surplus and sending it abroad as aid. This food aid has devastating effects on local farmers, including one described in the book *Enough: Why the World's Poorest Starve in an Age of Plenty*:

> Bashada, a young man in his twenties, was tending his own lentils on ten acres of land stretching along the Djibouti road when he spied the food-aid caravan. He had once welcomed American grain and beans and peas. The previous year, his family received about 65 pounds of wheat and other food aid to make it through the drought. But this season, the rains returned, and his corn, beans, and lentils looked good. He believed he might reap a surplus, especially in lentils. Now, he saw American food aid as a threat. "If we have a good harvest, I think these American lentils will only hurt our price," Bashada said.

And in regions such as these, sophisticated financial systems such as crop insurance, to mitigate against these possibilities, simply do not exist.

Agriculture as an industry requires infrastructure. Farmers need to have supplies of seed, fertilizer, tractors, and fuel. They need to be able to irrigate without relying solely on rain. To harvest their crops, they need equipment and suitable storage facilities. They need trucks to transport their goods and roads to drive the trucks on. They need markets to sell goods in and stable currencies. All of these are sorely lacking in areas where hunger is most prevalent. Without this, it is impossible to farm at scale. You can be a subsistence farmer and perhaps produce some excess, but given the prior observation about the fundamental volatility of farming, you will always be at risk of not producing enough.

International aid strategies have often worked against each other. There is some debate as to whether the poor should even try to feed themselves. Those who argue they should not say there is no way for poor countries to compete with mechanized Western farming and the extremely high yields it produces. Instead, the poorest nations should simply resign themselves to importing their food from abroad and instead get jobs working in cities in factories. In essence, they would become like Japan, which exports essentially no food, imports US$44 billion in food annually, but still enjoys a high standard of living. Others say poor nations need to develop free markets in agriculture and strongly discourage government intervention. Still others argue for a system of government price supports, incentives, and subsidies, as is found in the United States and Europe. And of course there are those who believe poor nations can and should be self-sufficient when it comes to food production for a variety of cultural, economic, and ecological reasons. Regardless of who is "right," the harm comes if you try to do all these things at once. Going back and forth between these strategies is problematic, to say the least.

Farm subsidies in developed nations combined with high-tech farming keep global food prices low, which discourages indigenous agriculture. Cheap food is great for the poor but bad for the poor farmer. If poor nations decide to pursue what I will call the Japan strategy, importing all their food and developing other industry, then they become huge fans of farm subsidies in other countries. In that case, the subsidy goes straight from the taxpayer in the other country to the purchaser of the subsidized crop. If, on the other hand, they want self-sufficiency in agriculture, then farm subsidies in other countries are bad for them. In that case, they have to compete with rich, high-tech, government-subsidized industries. As the authors of *Enough* observe:

> Farm subsidies in the United States and Europe, for instance, started out as a vehicle for helping poor farmers recover from economic calamity or war. But over the years they have grown to be a matter of addiction. By 2007, the world's rich, developed countries were paying $260 billion to support their own farmers, making it impossible for competing unsubsidized farmers to grow strong in places such as sub-Saharan Africa. On top of that, the international financial institutions controlled by the United States and Europe have long forbade African governments from subsidizing their own farmers if they are to receive any loans.

As nice as it would be for the Japan strategy to work in the developing world, I don't think these countries can count on it. Heck, even Japan only recently allowed imports of rice and taxes the imports at 500 percent in order to protect their rice farmers. Food security is a real issue, and nations that do not at least produce some kinds of food are at risk. Say the poor decide they cannot compete with a modern farm, so they move to the city and get a job at a factory. Now, what do you suppose happens when agriculture prices shoot way up? The cost of their imported food doubles, and I guarantee you the foreign-owned factory won't double wages as a result. In societies where a large percentage of income is necessary just to buy food, having volatile food prices will mean hunger sooner or later, no matter how good the factory jobs are.

During the Great Depression in the United States, many unemployed Americans simply left the city and went back to farm life, sometimes living with relatives. While this was a highly inefficient use of their labor, the result was very little hunger—which would not have been the case if the United States had imported all its food at that time.

Land ownership and urban populations. When few people own land and most people live in cities, it is quite common to have high degrees of hunger in a nation that is exporting food. It makes perfect sense, actually. Imagine a hypothetical nation, Country X. Country X has a few very large farms and no small ones. The very large farms grow corn. Country X has ten million citizens, half living in cities and half in rural areas. The urban half clearly have no opportunity to farm. The rural half could, in theory, farm, but they own no land; they probably work for wages at one of the large farms. So let's say the large corn farms all have a great year and a bountiful crop comes forth. But because Country X is so poor, its citizens can't afford this expensive crop, so the farmers sell this commodity on the international market to the highest bidder. Thus all the corn is exported and all ten million citizens of Country X go hungry.

This is basically the situation in many of Earth's chronically hungry countries. In Africa in particular, aid, loans, expertise, seed, and agricultural credits have been linked to growing export crops as opposed to cheap indigenous crops like sorghum, millet, and root vegetables. Large urban populations to feed and a lack of widespread land ownership compound the problems. In a similar situation in Haiti, the authors of *Enough* described how "farmers stopped growing rice and instead drifted to factories making underwear. Food production plummeted, but as long as prices remained low, the country could import what it needed, paying for food with money earned from exporting the underwear made by former farmers."

But the problem, of course, was that food prices went up, the people went hungry, and riots ensued.

Those are only some of the most significant factors contributing to hunger in the world today. Africa, where half the world's hungry citizens reside, has additional challenges. It has a large number of landlocked nations without ports to access the international markets, both for imports and exports. Indigenous animals are not well-suited to be domesticated and assist in farming. Crops native to Africa are not the staples of the world. And finally, the area has been plagued by epidemics, never-ending malaria, severe drought, frequent civil wars, unstable currencies, and government corruption.

And yet, I remain very optimistic. Let's see why.

Agriculture 1.1

Civilization as it is known today could not have evolved,
nor can it survive, without an adequate food supply.
—Norman Borlaug

While agriculture itself is a technology, it is, in its most basic form, extremely low tech. Push a seed into the ground with your thumb, water, check back over a couple of months, and eat the food you find.

Of course, we have progressed far past this primitive state. (Well, I personally have not; I have regressed from this state. I push the seed in the ground, water it, and wonder why nothing grew. But the industry as a whole has shot forward.)

This notion of progress, however, brings up an interesting question: Just how advanced are we? If agriculture were a mode of transportation, would we be a wooden cart pulled by a donkey or an F-16 jet?

I think we are still at the donkey stage—and this is good news! It means we have plenty of room for improvement. We can still make plenty of progress.

Let me explain this characterization. Ever since we've had agriculture, people have been employing technology to make it better. When so many people farm and so much depends on it, innovation will happen. The rate of innovation is increasing rapidly, though. If you look back across the span of time, you see wood plows being used in 4000 BC, then irrigation five hundred years later. An iron plow comes three thousand years later in 500 BC, along with intensive row cultivation. A couple of centuries pass and improved harnesses come along. A couple of hundred years later, we see the Romans doing crop rotation. Six hundred years after that, we get the windmill for irrigation.

A thousand years later, the Industrial Revolution transformed the world, including the world of agriculture. The cotton gin, steel ploughs, tractors, combines, and a thousand other inventions would forever change the farm. The advances were not merely mechanical but chemical as well. In the early 1800s, fertilizer companies sprang up using bone meal as the principle agent. By the late 1800s, superphosphates were all the rage and eighty factories were manufacturing this high-yield fertilizer from coprolites (that is, phosphate-rich fossils of ancient animal dung—I kid you not). By the early twentieth century, most manufacturing of fertilizer had switched to the synthetic production of ammonium sulfate and ammonium phosphate. After World War II, the Green Revolution drove the uses of these fertilizers ever higher.

Since then, the changes have become more about intellectual property and technique. The 1970s saw the introduction of hybrid plants; the 1980s, research into genetic engineering; and the 1990s, the widespread production of genetically modified seeds. The 2000s saw the rise of commercially viable seeds created by transgenesis, that is, the insertion of DNA from one species into another species. Now we are in the 2010s where, at present, the annual number of patents being granted in agriculture exceeds twenty thousand.

By describing how we've gone from breakthroughs every few centuries, to every few decades, to twenty thousand patents a year, have I convinced you that Moore's Law, or something like it, is driving the rate of change in agriculture ever faster? It seems a clear-cut case. And yet in two aspects of agriculture, major inefficiencies still exist that, taken together, have huge impact. First are the inefficiencies in the natural processes of agriculture. Second are the inefficiencies in the human processes—that is, the techniques by which we practice agriculture.

To consider the great opportunity we can find in these inefficiencies, let's begin by talking about Norman Borlaug.

Norman was born in 1914 in Cresco, Iowa. To pay for his college education, Borlaug would periodically put his education on hold to find work. During the Depression, he worked for the Civilian Conservation Corps (CCC), which provided manual labor jobs related to the conservation and development of natural resources in government-owned rural lands. Workers made $30 a month, $25 of which went to their parents. Over the CCC's nine-year life, its workers planted nearly three billion trees, built eight hundred parks, and constructed roads in remote areas.

Many of the people Borlaug worked with at this time were poor, even starving. He later recalled, "I saw how food changed them. . . . All of this left scars on me."

While in college, Borlaug heard a lecture by Elvin Stakman about plant disease in wheat, barley, and oak crops. Stakman had determined that immunity to these diseases, or at least resistance, could be bred into crops. This speech was a pivotal event in Borlaug's life.

In 1940, at the request of Mexico's president, the Rockefeller Foundation joined Mexico's agriculture ministry in a joint venture to spur economic growth. This Cooperative Wheat Research Production Program, in which Borlaug took part, aimed to boost Mexican wheat production. In the first ten years of attempting to make better hybrids, Borlaug's group made more than six thousand crossings of wheat. Borlaug also promoted the process (which proved wildly successful) of having two wheat-growing seasons in Mexico: one in the highlands, then another in the valley regions.

Throughout this time, Borlaug constantly battled wheat's arch-nemesis: rust, a fungus that feeds on wheat, oats, and barley. In 1953, he developed a method to make strains of wheat highly resistant to a single form of rust. And although rust was highly adaptive, by making ten or so different wheat varieties resistant to different forms of rust, Borlaug helped farmers reduce the risk of crop loss to a minimum. To further enhance yield, at the same time Borlaug bred wheat strains with short, stubby stalks, which were able to better handle more weight of grain.

Here's how the results were described in Wikipedia (yeah, I'm not embarrassed to cite Wikipedia—I verified the numbers, as I always do, and found them to be accurate):

> Borlaug's new semi-dwarf, disease-resistant varieties, called Pitic 62 and Penjamo 62, changed the potential yield of spring wheat dramatically. By 1963, 95 percent of Mexico's wheat crops used the semi-dwarf varieties developed by Borlaug. That year, the harvest was six times larger than in 1944, the year Borlaug arrived in Mexico. Mexico had become fully self-sufficient in wheat production, and a net exporter of wheat.[6]

Based on this unprecedented success, samples of Borlaug's seeds were sent abroad. In 1962, some of them were grown in India, and based on the results, Borlaug was invited to India. Even though foreign aid, especially from the United States, was pouring into the country, scenes of famine and war greeted Borlaug when he arrived, bearing a thousand pounds of seed.

Although there was cultural opposition in India to Borlaug's methods and seeds, the famine was so bad by 1965 that the government stepped in and urged the project forward. Although Borlaug and company encountered many obstacles, they pressed on, planting seed at night illuminated by flashes of artillery fire. And the initial yields were the largest harvests in the history of South Asia.

The harvest was so overwhelming that there was not enough storage, transport, or harvesters to manage it. Government buildings were converted

6. Excerpts about Norman Borlaug courtesy of Wikipedia, http://en.wikipedia.org/wiki/Norman_Borlaug.

into silos to hold the abundance, as other countries in the region placed orders for massive amounts of these seeds.

Again, from Wikipedia:

> In Pakistan, wheat yields nearly doubled, from 4.6 million tons in 1965 to 7.3 million tons in 1970; Pakistan was self-sufficient in wheat production by 1968. Yields were over 21 million tons by 2000. In India, yields increased from 12.3 million tons in 1965 to 20.1 million tons in 1970. By 1974, India was self-sufficient in the production of all cereals. By 2000, India was harvesting a record 76.4 million tons (2.81 billion bushels) of wheat. Since the 1960s, food production in both nations has increased faster than the rate of population growth. Paul Waggoner, of the Connecticut Agricultural Experiment Station, calculates that India's use of high-yield farming has prevented 100 million acres (400,000 km²) of virgin land from being converted into farmland—an area about the size of California, or 13.6 percent of the total area of India.[7]

Because of this—because of Mexico, India, Pakistan, and a dozen other countries that Borlaug's work transformed—he is credited with saving a billion lives. Wow! This was a guy from a small town in Iowa who failed his 1933 entrance exam to the University of Minnesota. But if ever there was a textbook case of one guy making a difference, this is it. By the time Norman Borlaug passed away in 2009 at the age of ninety-five, he had become one of only six people to have won the Nobel Peace Prize, the Presidential Medal of Freedom, and the Congressional Gold Medal.

Consider for a moment how much Borlaug accomplished *with almost no technology*. He didn't have computers or even a calculator. He didn't have genome sequencing. He couldn't splice genes. He lacked a satellite phone, a smart phone, a cell phone, or even a phone. He had no way to collaborate

7. Excerpts about Norman Borlaug courtesy of Wikipedia, http://en.wikipedia.org/wiki/Norman_Borlaug.

with scientists in other places, no Internet, and no library. He couldn't develop new irrigation techniques, invent new machinery, or create new fertilizers. He basically followed old agriculture; he planted a lot of seed and hoped for rain. All he could do was cross strains of wheat, much in the same fashion as Gregor Mendel did in the 1800s.

And do you know how he crossed the grains? He would pollinate a wheat stalk, then cover it with a trash bag to prevent contamination by other plants. A trash bag was the highest-tech object Borlaug had.

If he was able to transform agriculture around the world and save a billion lives with so little technology, how much more should there be for us to accomplish?

In the opinion of author Jack Uldrich, "The future is all about getting the right seed, with the right characteristics, planted at the right time, and then nurtured with the right inputs for the right duration, so they can be harvested at the right time in order to maximize yield and profits." Obviously, we have many areas ripe for substantial improvement.

Plants themselves are pretty inefficient machines, at least from the standpoint of being good food sources for us. From our point of view, the job of the plant is to convert sunlight into energy and store that energy in a tasty way; then when we eat the plant, we get that energy. How good a job are the plants doing?

To deal in generalities, plants capture, on average, about 5 percent of the solar energy that falls on their leaves. Operating at basically 5 percent efficiency, they are less than half as efficient as solar panels now on the market. And solar cells presently being developed in laboratories are doing several times better than the plants. Additionally, of the energy the plant absorbs, it only stores one tenth of it in the potato or bean or whatever part we eat. From our standpoint, the plant wastes all the rest of its energy on riotous living: growing roots and leaves, soaking up water, separating carbon molecules from oxygen ones. Pretty much just goofing off.

Similarly, our agricultural processes aren't so hot. We stick a bunch of seeds in the ground and then treat a thousand acres of corn pretty much as a single unit. Farmers don't optimize per plant but per farm. What if the farmer could give every stalk of corn individual attention and water and fertilize each one exactly when it was needed? What if you knew exactly what to plant, when to plant it, when to harvest it? What if you could do agriculture perfectly on a per-grape basis, each grape getting individual attention? What would be possible then?

And then, the seeds we are using aren't anything to write home about, either. Although we have been genetically modifying them for a few thousand years (keeping any useful mutations that pop up and growing from those the next season), they are still bound by their limited genetic potential.

What does that mean? I mentioned Gregor Mendel, known as the father of genetics. A fascinating character and an extremely patient experimenter, Mendel was a German friar and scientist who figured out that plants (and presumably animals) had inheritable characteristics. Between 1856 and 1863, he bred 29,000 pea plants. He noticed that when he bred a tall one with a short one, sometimes he got tall offspring and sometimes a short offspring. He then noticed that when he bred short ones with short ones, he always got short ones. Hmmm. Then he noticed when he bred tall pea plants with another tall plant, he occasionally got a short offspring, but usually tall ones. Hmmm again. From all of this, he developed the idea of dominant and recessive genes (although they weren't yet called that) and the mechanism for how traits are inherited.

In any case, he found something else interesting. If he kept breeding ever-taller peas with each other, he could increase the size of the offspring with each generation, but only to a point. Eventually, the pea was as large as its genetic potential allowed it to be. The same worked for ever smaller and smaller pea plants. That range between the smallest pea plant and the largest is the full spectrum of what that plant can be. (We see this same principle with different breeds of dogs. Across all the varied breeds, the genetic potential for dog size evidently is Chihuahua to mastiff.)

All the seeds we have today have these inherent limits built into them that we still haven't figured out how to change. So we basically have inefficient seeds that grow into plants that do an inefficient job making food for us. We apply inefficient agricultural techniques to grow and harvest them, and then we inefficiently distribute them.

One guy from Iowa came along with some garbage bags and saved a billion lives. How much more should we be able to with the Internet, computers, and other technology? I say we can improve things not by 20 or so percent, but by twenty times or more.

The End of the Farmer

Burn down your cities and leave our farms, and your cities will spring up again as if by magic; but destroy our farms and the grass will grow in the streets of every city in the country.
—William Jennings Bryan

Food issues are complex and deeply emotional. After centuries of argument about how to feed our planet, the terms of the debate have become loaded with baggage. To describe ending hunger in the future, I have only these tarnished terms of the present at my disposal. And yet the future I envision is no more like what we have today than a state-of-the-art Volvo factory is like a nineteenth-century London sweatshop. They are alike in name only, in that they are both factories—but they are completely different.

So if I use language that in other hands has been politicized or co-opted, I use it with a completely different intent. When I use a term like factory farm, I am envisioning not what these things are now but what they will be. I ask the reader to resist the urge to pigeonhole me until the end of the section.

Remember the Warren Bennis quote I used earlier about the factory of the future having only one man and one dog? The farm of the future will have neither. It will be a massive, completely automated, robotic facility.

Why do I say this? Because the most efficient farms in the world are those that operate at vast scale. All the work is done by machines already. Only the decision making is left to the farmer—but in the near future, the decision making will be done better by computers. Sensors can constantly monitor moisture levels in the soil, the size and color of the plants, air quality, nutrient levels in the soil, amount of sunlight, and hundreds of other variables. Computers can even monitor markets to know when to harvest and where to transport goods. Computers can determine when to plant seed and even what to plant. The farm of the future will rotate crops automatically and decide which fields to leave fallow.

If the farm of the future plugs into the national grid, it will become part of the national food strategy and can be optimized for financial yield for the owners. The system will see that just the right amounts of black-eyed peas, potatoes, and corn are grown.

The farm of today already has tractors that use GPS to make perfectly parallel rows with great precision. How long will it be before the driver controls them remotely from his office? And then how much longer until they are completely automatic?

By one estimate in 1820, 70 percent of Americans farmed. By 1860, it was down to 60 percent; by 1920, 40 percent; by 1940, 20 percent; and by 1960, 6 percent. As I write this, it is down to 2 percent. By what logic would anyone assume it will not go to zero? There were more people farming in the United States in 1820 than there are today. How can this be? Mechanization and automation—both of which are about to get a lot better.

I know this sounds awful to a lot of people. It sounds mechanical, sterile, and just a little bit un-American. But the food would not only be produced with maximum efficiency; it would be extremely fresh and very healthy. Our ability to measure the nutritional value of each piece of food will rise, our knowledge of what makes food healthy will expand, and consumers will demand and receive vastly more information about their food. Right now, food with low nutritional value is grown because we don't have an easy way to look at a carrot and know the exact nutritional makeup of that carrot along with every trace chemical on its surface. In the future, that will be easy.

The farm of the future is not in a laboratory, staffed by robots with syringes injecting who-knows-what hormone into a turnip. Instead, it is a large, open-air farm with a robot assigned to make each turnip be all that it can be. Every turnip treated like a king, with the accumulated knowledge of humanity at its disposal. If the turnip is dry, it is watered, each drop carefully metered out. If the turnip is hot, it gets shaded. If a fly lands on it, the fly is shooed off. Can you imagine a better life for a turnip?

The farm of the future will be an exportable technology, able to function around the world. Food can be grown locally in any region in a highly efficient manner. Because of its reliability, agriculture will become more like an exact science.

I consider this all good. That may be surprising based on the fact that, in my personal life, I go to great lengths to avoid food from factories (see box at right). How do I reconcile my personal choices with my statement that the farm of the future is a good thing?

First, this future farm I describe is nothing like what I go out of my way to avoid today. Recall my comparison of a nineteenth-century London factory to a factory that makes Volvos today. The future I describe does not raise animals in the inhumane way we do today and does not produce the kind of food we grow today, which is optimized for volume and not nutrition.

Second, some people will still want their food grown the old-fashioned way, just like how I buy heritage meats and heirloom seeds. The farm of tomorrow is not designed to provide them food; it is trying to feed the most people the best food using the fewest natural resources in the least expensive and most reliable way possible. These farms will provide food security to the world with a fraction of the resources we use today.

Third, the day will come when the farm of the future will make a healthier, less expensive, more ecologically friendly, fresher, and better-tasting product. The mass-food industry of today cannot make this claim. At present, they win hands down on "less expensive" and put in a decent showing on a couple more factors. But when the farm of tomorrow delivers on this holistic promise, I think all people will embrace it. A century ago, cars were made one at a time by a half dozen people working together. Then Henry Ford came along, followed by a host of others, and cars got better and better while getting less and less expensive. No one today would want a car built the old way. It would cost a million dollars and not even be as good as a Chevy.

I foresee a day when, on a Sunday afternoon, a family might drive (or actually be driven by their car) out to a farm to see where food comes from. The proverbial "Little Timmy" will find it hard to believe that food isn't

A TRAITOR TO THE CAUSE?

I have eaten food pretty much my whole life. You can't do something that long and not have some strong opinions on the matter.

I grew up on a farm. Until I was ten years old, my family lived in rural East Texas and raised cattle, chickens, and turkeys. Additionally, we had a five-acre garden where we grew everything you can grow in East Texas. Every morning before I went to school I had chores to do, which began with mixing up the formula and feeding the calves. We did our own canning, especially pickles, and I picked berries every summer so my mom could make jelly. My fingertips are still stained a bit blue.

Today, I have a vegetable garden in my backyard. My daughter, the family gardener, only plants heirloom produce from non-hybrid seeds. We like these varieties and their tie to history. Every week, I buy my milk from a small local dairy on the day it comes forth from the cow. It is often still warm. This dairyman also makes some of the milk into cheese and we use a lot of that as well. I buy my eggs from a farmer whose chickens roam free. I buy my pecans from someone who picks and shells them himself. And I go to any farmers market I happen across. In the month of December, I make slow-rise homemade bread every morning, kneading the dough by hand.

I abhor the conditions under which we commercially raise farm animals today. In addition to the conditions being inhumane, we are losing the diversity of species that used to grace our dinner tables, which I believe is a terrible mistake. I am a huge fan of heritage meats. If you are not familiar with this whole issue, look into it; it is fascinating and, I think, important.

Additionally, I am quite interested in the history of food. I have an extensive library of very old recipe books, including several "autographs"—original, handwritten, unpublished, personal cookbooks—that date back to the early 1700s. My favorite cookbook, *Apicius*, is a 1,500-year-old collection of recipes from ancient Rome.

I write this to establish my *bona fides* as someone who truly cares about good food. One would suspect that, given all the above, I should be the last guy to write in favor of GMO, factory farms, manufacturing meat, and the end of the farmer. But I do not believe these technological leaps forward are a threat to good food. In fact, they will make food even greater.

manufactured like electronics but grown like an animal. Maybe. Maybe it actually will be manufactured. Let's briefly discuss that possibility.

Long term, we will be better off manufacturing our food as opposed to growing it. I know I am probably going to get disagreement from almost everyone on this point, but if it is any comfort, you probably won't live to see the farm of the future or its replacement by manufactured food. (Well, you will probably live to see manufactured meat, but, like my mom used to tell me at the dinner table as I stared down at some unknown new food, "You don't have to eat it all, but you should at least taste it.")

If the goal of food is to provide us sustenance, then raising plants and animals is a really inefficient way to do it. It is terribly wasteful in terms of the amount of calories invested relative to how many we get back. Plus, raising plants and animals takes a long time and is a lot of work to boot.

Food also serves two other purposes. Eating it gives us enjoyment when it is good. And it facilitates social interaction and connection. Both of these are hugely important parts of life, and I know of no one who would trade them away for a pill they swallow in the morning that gives them all their nutrition for the day. But what if manufactured food was tastier? What if a manufactured steak was as good as the best steak you have ever had? And cheaper. And greener (in the environmental way, not the color way). And healthier. Then what?

Fiona Harvey, environment correspondent for *The Guardian* in the United Kingdom, wrote this about the prospect of manufacturing meat:

> The researchers believe their work suggests artificial meat could help feed the growing world population while reducing the impact on the environment. According to the analysis by scientists from Oxford University and Amsterdam University, lab-grown tissue would reduce greenhouse gases by up to 96 percent in comparison to raising animals. The process would require between seven percent and 45 percent less energy than the same volume of conventionally produced meat such as pork, beef, or lamb, and could be

engineered to use only one percent of the land and four percent of the water associated with conventional meat.[8]

In his book *Our Molecular Future*, Douglas Mulhall raises questions about this possibility:

> In the more distant future, what happens to agriculture and agro-industry when each of us can conveniently grow our own food, or, ultimately, manufacture it? Are life sciences companies going to own the software that manufactures food, then make it available at an artificially high price? Such a strategy might backfire if intelligent machines are designing food fabrication software so quickly that patent legislation can't keep up.
>
> How will government agencies such as the Food and Drug Administration deal with synthesized food? Who regulates the right of individuals to alter food formulas for their desktop fabricators? If someone wants to add an amino acid to his synthetic steak one evening, does he need FDA approval?

I am certain this idea is going to take some time to get used to. But hey, today we eat things labeled "cheese-food" that have never been within a mile of a cow. Do you really know what is in a hotdog, or are you sure you want to? At times, it may be best to just enjoy the meal and not ask too many questions.

Genomics

Mapping the human genome has been compared with putting a man on the moon, but I believe it is more than that. This is the

---

8. From "Artificial meat could slice emissions, say scientists" by Fiona Harvey from *The Guardian* website, June 20, 2011. Copyright © 2011 **Guardian News and Media Limited**. Reproduced by permission.

outstanding achievement not only of our lifetime,
but in terms of human history.
—T. Michael Dexter

Rather than lump genomics and genetically modified organisms (GMO) into the upcoming chapter where I list technologies that will transform agriculture, I chose to address them here because a topic so controversial and misunderstood warrants extra time to sort through.

I am a big believer in the potential of genetically modified (GM) plants not only to end hunger but to dramatically improve the environment, decrease healthcare costs, lower the cost of food, expand where we can grow food, raise its quality, and make it taste better. That said, my "end hunger" case doesn't hang on the viability of GM crops. If I am ultimately proven wrong and the world rejects GM foods, we will still end hunger.

Let me start with a few caveats.

First, the technology can be abused and used irresponsibly, like pretty much every other technology in the world. Thus we need to develop processes that provide some degree of security without also hampering innovation.

Second, the real promise of GM crops will not necessarily come about from the food industry. Think of it this way. Food can be optimized according to three factors, broadly speaking: taste, price, and nutrition. Fast-food chains optimize for two of them: taste and price, at the expense of nutrition. Other businesses in the food industry—say those pricey health foods you see at fancy grocery stores—optimize for taste and nutrition at the expense of price. And we all know about those that optimize for cost and nutrition but the resulting food tastes awful; I have consumed enough wheatgrass to attest to this. You can't have everything. (The fast-food industry makes a product I regard as excellent for occasional indulgences. A double-double at In-N-Out is one of life's better pleasures, in my opinion. The problem comes only when the indulgence is more than occasional.)

Similarly, seed makers are judged by the crops the seeds grow into—specifically, the yield and how long it takes to get it. Bonus points are given for resiliency, low water requirements, and appearance. Since one cannot have everything, seed makers invariably will make trade-offs that might be different than what I would make. I don't think we can rely on the profit motive to make the best seeds possible. It will undoubtedly make the most profitable seeds possible but not necessarily the healthiest.

Caveats satisfied, let's dive in.

Have you ever eaten GMO foods? In a recent survey, only a quarter of Americans answered that question with a "yes." Yet in reality, virtually everyone has. The majority of processed food sold in the United States contains GMO. Presently, labeling of GMO content isn't a requirement—and since labeling is a complex and controversial issue that has no bearing on my thesis, I will pass it by. The point is this: GMO crops are everywhere.

Furthermore, "genetically modified" is itself a tricky term. Susan McCouch, a rice specialist who teaches at Cornell, told the *New Yorker*, "If you look even briefly at the history of plant breeding, then you know that every crop we eat today is genetically modified. Every one. Human beings have imposed selection on them all. So don't ask me what is natural and what is not. Because I have no idea."

Freeman Dyson makes basically the same point in *The Sun, the Genome, and the Internet* when he writes, "Traditional farming has always been based on genetic engineering. Every major crop plant and farm animal has been genetically engineered by selective breeding until it barely resembles the wild species from which it originated. Genetic engineering as the basis of the world economy is nothing new."

Genetic modification of plants and animals has been going on for a long time in the form of selective breeding. An example of that is a breed of cat called "Scottish Fold." In 1961 in Perthshire, Scotland, a white barn cat named Susie was found at a farm. Susie's ears had an unusual fold in the middle so they basically pointed downward. Susie had kittens, and two of them had folded ears as well. A neighboring farmer and cat-lover, William Ross, perhaps hearing a distinct "ka-ching" in his head, got one of the kittens and teamed up with a geneticist and began a careful breeding program. Over the next three years, forty-two folded-ear cats were born, and with them a new breed. The fold in the ears was caused by a heritable, dominant, mutated gene. The gene mutated accidentally, but once noticed, breeders bred for it. This is a form of genetic modification. Although the original muta-tion was not caused by human activity, human activity preserved and per-petuated it. All manner of breeds of dogs, cats, cows, and horses are bred in similar ways. Plants are as well.

Another method of genetic modification, called mutagenesis, dates to the early part of the twentieth century. It is based on the premise that naturally occurring mutations are too infrequent, so we should just start zapping seeds with radiation, plant them, and see if anything good happens. Mutagenesis was invented in the 1920s by Lewis J. Stadler of the University of Missouri who pointed X-rays at some barley seeds and noticed that the resulting plants were all different colors and had a variety of mutations. Soon everyone was zapping seeds and planting them and, lo and behold, it actually worked! In a 2007 article on the topic, the *New York Times* reported:

> The process leaves no residual radiation or other obvious marks of human intervention. It simply creates offspring that exhibit new characteristics.
>
> Though poorly known, radiation breeding has produced thousands of useful mutants and a sizable fraction of the world's crops . . . including varieties of rice, wheat, barley, pears, peas, cotton, peppermint, sunflowers, peanuts, grape-fruit, sesame, bananas, cassava and sorghum. The mutant wheat is used for bread and pasta and the mutant barley for beer and fine whiskey.
>
> The mutations can improve yield, quality, taste, size and resistance to disease and can help plants adapt to diverse climates and conditions.[9]

Thus we had genetic modifications in plants that could have occurred in nature but probably wouldn't have. If the first order of genetic modification is deliberately keeping desirable mutations, then this is the second order: creating conditions for such genetic modifications to occur more rapidly. Humans became the catalyst for the genetic modification, having no idea what was going to happen, and most of the time nothing good did: The mutations either had no effect or no positive effect. But sometimes it was like lightning in a bottle, and magic happened. Half the rice grown in California is a descendant of Calrose 76, created when gamma rays mutated some regular rice and the resulting mutant produced more grain and less spoilage. In Europe, scientists pointed their gamma ray gun at some barley and produced Golden Promise, a mutant with improved malting that is brewed into premium beer.

Today, genetic modification efforts are much more directed. We know exactly what we are shooting for. We dive into the DNA of seed and cut out something we don't like, such as a gene that slurps water greedily or attracts beetles or limits growth. Consider this the third order of GMO. This change *could* have occurred in nature; given enough monkeys and typewriters, it *would* eventually occur in nature.

At this point, things get harder. We don't fault, at the first order, Native Americans or Norman Borlaug for cross-breeding better corn or wheat. In the second order, we are a bit uncomfortable with the whole "zapping and hoping" thing, but it is hard to describe why, because all of it could happen in nature; we are just speeding things up a bit. Now we are at the third order: splicing genes within a species. This should feel better, because we are pretty sure we know what will happen, but people get a bit unsettled here (where the term Frankenfood invariably comes up). But again, this could happen in nature, so it is hard to see how we can object to this.

Finally, we get to the fourth order of GMO: being able to splice genes from one species into another species, a process known as transgenesis. This couldn't happen in nature (or, more precisely, could in theory, but is extremely unlikely). This is the part that makes some people even more nervous. Yet even given its unnaturalness, transgenesis is profoundly good. We fear it, frankly, because we do not understand it. If I said I took the sound system from my home stereo and put it in my car, you wouldn't freak out and call it a Frankencar and fear it would mutate and destroy other cars. While that's not a strict analogy, my point is that nothing is intrinsically bad about the concept of transgenesis. Let's look at a real-life example.

A commercial application of transgenesis is the GloFish, a trademarked brand of genetically modified, fluorescent zebrafish. The GloFish was developed in Singapore in 1999 when Dr. Zhiyuan Gong took a gene called green fluorescent protein (GFP) from a bright green fluorescent jellyfish and inserted it into the embryo of the drab zebrafish. The goal of this was to develop a fish that could detect pollution; it would glow in the presence of certain toxins. As a boon to the environment, how cool is that? But it also was suspected that people would like a glowing fish for a pet, and hundreds of thousands of them have subsequently been sold. They are popular all over the United States, except in California, where they are illegal to own.

Where transgenesis offers the most amazing possibilities is in GM foods because it allows plants to exceed their maximum genetic potential. For an example of this, consider the case of vitamin A deficiency (VAD). It affects more than one hundred million people in a hundred countries, kills more than a million people a year, and blinds another half million for good measure. UNICEF has said a program that gives children two large doses a year of vitamin A could all but eliminate VAD, although more frequent, smaller doses would be better.

VAD occurs mostly in Africa and Southeast Asia where rice is the staple food. Rice doesn't naturally have vitamin A. Enter transgenics.

In 2005, rice became the first crop plant whose complete genome had been compiled. Since rice is relied upon by so much of the world's poor, efforts here really can save lives. By one count, rice is the principle source of calories for about half the planet. But prior to this accomplishment, back in 1992, an effort was begun to insert a gene from a daffodil and a gene from a soil bacteria into rice, allowing it to produce vitamin A. The resulting rice was yellow-orange in color and was named "Golden Rice."

In 2005, a biotech firm called Syngenta produced a similar rice it called "Golden Rice 2." It has more than twenty times the vitamin A of the original, and efforts are now under way to add vitamin E, iron, and zinc, and to improve protein quality through genetic modification. Who could be against children not going blind?

Can you guess how many lives these two varieties of rice have already saved? Go ahead—guess.

The answer: none. It is not presently available for human consumption. In Africa, most genetically engineered crops that could grow well there are not welcome. In much of Europe, because of deep fear and suspicion of GMO crops, their importation is forbidden. And so Africans fear that by allowing the crops into Africa, they will hurt their ability to export food to Europe down the road.

This is especially unfortunate because a major crop in Africa, grain sorghum, has a somewhat indigestible protein that our bodies have a hard time metabolizing. This is exactly the kind of problem geneticists can sink their teeth into, so to speak, to make the protein in this grain digestible. GMO could make this a crop that Africa could easily use to feed itself, gain food independence, and maybe even export.

In late 2009, the entire genome of corn was decoded. This may not sound so impressive until you realize that while humans have 20,000 genes, corn has 32,000. To sequence corn's genome took four years and cost US$30 million. The corn genome data is free for anyone to download at maizesequence.org, in case you are bored some Sunday afternoon and want to see how to make corn.

Having the entire genome means we can begin making super corn, better, stronger, and faster growing. Why wouldn't we? Nature is constantly modifying the genetics of plants, capriciously, randomly, like a drunken sailor on shore leave. Why wouldn't we make corn better? In any case, it seems better to me than irradiating corn, planting it, and hoping to hit a jackpot.

The decoding of the corn genome will perhaps help in energy production. In 2008 DuPont identified a gene in corn that could increase the yield of oil by more than 40 percent, essentially making a chubby version of corn.

But biofuels are already so yesterday. American ethanol policies do not "kill" the poor, but they do drive up corn prices. There is a distinction. Me ordering a second helping of corn on the cob while dining at the Black-Eyed

Pea also increases demand for corn, but for doing so, I shouldn't stand trial for murder. In any case, there are other ways to use genetic modification to get energy. Consider what *Newsweek* said of Craig Venter:

> No one would accuse Craig Venter of harboring humble ambitions. In 2000 he decoded the human genome faster than anyone else—and he did it more cheaply than a well-funded government team. More recently he's set a new goal for himself: to replace the petrochemical industry. In a Maryland lab, he's manipulating chromosomes in the hopes of creating an energy bug—a bacterium that will ingest CO_2, sunlight and water, and spew out liquid fuel that can be pumped into American SUVs.[10]

Venter's plan is to use bacteria to brew fuel, much like we brew beer today. This fuel, he believes, will be vastly better than anything we currently produce.

Environmentalists should be the first people on board the genetic modification bandwagon. They should be advocating that genetically modified crops be created not because it would result in better looking strawberries, but because GM crops don't require fertilizer or pesticides. Wouldn't that be something: Plants that would convert nitrogen from the atmosphere directly into ammonia they could use or plants that gave off the odor of other plants that pests avoid?

While they are at it, environmentalists should push hard to develop crops that don't deplete soil as much or that taste good raw. Or are packed with vitamins. Or that taste like meat, taking pastureland off the grid. Or that need less water and land and thus free up more natural resources. Scientists at USC San Diego, working with universities in Finland, Estonia, and the United Kingdom, have figured out the mechanism whereby a certain plant gene controls the amount of ozone entering the plant's leaves by opening and closing tiny pores known as stomata. Why does this matter? Because, in

---

10. From "A Bug to Save the Planet" by Fareed Zakaria from *Newsweek*, June 7, 2008. Copyright © 2008 by The Newsweek/Daily Beast Company, LLC. Reproduced by permission.

theory, this knowledge could be used to make drought-resistant crops, opening up vast new parts of the world to farming.

If global warming is your issue, then push to make plants that remove CO_2 from the environment better than anything nature has produced so far. Don't limit it just to plants. If you worry about gas emissions from cows contributing to climate change, lobby for a cow that doesn't have gas.

This is not science fiction. In 2006, a pig was genetically engineered to produce healthy omega-3 fatty acids. Imagine that—healthy bacon. As far as scientific advancements go, that would be right up there with the proverbial sliced bread. (If that can be achieved, to my readers under age twelve, I hold out the possibility of Brussels sprouts that taste like chocolate.)

For environmentalist organizations like Greenpeace to be against GMO in all its forms under all conditions does nothing at all to serve them or the constituencies they purport to represent. By taking this "Absolutely no GMOs" stance they completely remove themselves from the debate and as such have no voice in the discussion about what direction to take GM: what are safe testing practices, what factors will we optimize for, and the whole host of questions that face us on this, the eve of a momentous leap forward.

I believe it to be within our grasp to make plants that grow in any environment and produce healthy food with fewer resources. Are there risks? In theory, yes. In practice, yes. But they are very remote. Weigh that against the certainty that nearly a billion people are hungry right now and I don't know why we would decline to acquire this knowledge. We can empower people to feed themselves. We can make better food that uses fewer resources.

The possibilities of GMO go far beyond prettier corn or cheaper strawberries. How about flowers that bloom in different colors when they are on top of land mines? Or how about bacteria that can process toxic wastes and oil spills into harmless biodegradable materials?

The Internet will greatly speed the research and, hopefully, the safety of GM foods. The massive amounts of information in these decoded genomes can only be processed by computers. Collaboration, communication, access to information, and the other advantages that the Internet brings will all come to bear here.

We can't naturally fly, so we make airplanes. We can't run sixty miles in an hour, so we make cars. We can't remember all that we hear, so we make pens and paper. Why don't we make seeds better than they are now?

I understand all the concerns. The issues are difficult because fundamentally none of us knows the ultimate effects. We hardly understand the process, which itself seems unbelievable. So I am not saying objections and caution are not warranted. Instead I offer the words of playwright John Patrick Shanley: "Everything really great possible in this lifetime requires a little more courage than we currently have. A deep breath and a leap."

Information and Agriculture

The greatest advances of civilization, whether in architecture or painting, in science and literature, in industry or agriculture, have never come from centralized government.
—Milton Friedman

As we have reasoned, when the Internet and related technologies help bring an end to poverty, the end of poverty will largely solve the problem of hunger. But the end of hunger also will be hastened by a host of Internet technologies that will dramatically change agriculture.

Cheap sensors, precision farming, and the Digital Echo of a radish. As noted previously, in the future much of what you do will leave a Digital Echo, a record of its occurrence, down to the very minutia of your life. Part of this will be enabled by very cheap sensors embedded in the things you use. This same technology will allow farming to be much, much more efficient.

Remember my earlier statement that a farmer treats a thousand acres of corn as a single entity because it is not cost effective to deal with each corn stalk separately? That is also the case because humans couldn't do a very good job at a stalk-by-stalk approach. Our eyes are capable of seeing only a narrow spectrum of light. We cannot determine the chemical composition of soil simply by touching it. We cannot perceive millimeter-sized changes. We are really good on the reasoning part, but as far as our sensory inputs go, we are massively outclassed by cheap sensors.

According to the *New York Times*, an Israeli company, Phytech, has produced a system that "uses sensors placed on fruit trees or other crops to provide information to farmers. One sensor monitors tiny changes in stem diameter, while another tracks size and growth of fruit. Avi Lulu, the company's chief executive, said the system would reduce irrigation costs while increasing yields. 'We are not irrigating what we think the plants need; we're irrigating what the plants really need,' he said."

This is all part of what is now known as precision agriculture. As futurist.com describes it, precision agriculture "involves the integration of satellite observations, on-the-ground instruments, and sophisticated farm machinery to apply the appropriate amounts of seed, water, fertilizer, and so on, literally meter by meter, so that maximum efficiency in food production is realized. This will become more feasible as technological advances are made in the next 10 years, and lead, it is assumed, to better food production."

The ultimate goal, I submit, is not to optimize just meter by meter but what I call "grape by grape," down to each individual piece of flora and fauna. If this sounds absurd, at present it is—but in the future, the price of technologies to do this will fall to nearly zero.

Precision agriculture involves collecting massive amounts of data, more than any human can process, and applying various algorithms, self-teaching in nature, to achieve optimum outcomes.

In the future, each plant will be on the Internet. Everything that happens to it will be recorded. The plant will have a Digital Echo. Different techniques could be applied to different plants side by side to constantly be refining agricultural processes. When a promising new finding emerges, that information will be shared with other farms and those techniques will be tested there. Thus the system will have measured inputs and measured outputs, and, therefore, controlled studies can happen constantly. Farming will be done on such a scale that thousands of experiments can be happening at any one time, putting a tiny fraction of the produce at risk.

Cheap sensors, cloud computing, self-teaching algorithms with feedback loops, and sufficient cycles to test a large number of techniques. That's all you need to optimize agriculture.

The price of such hardware is in free fall. The speed and quality of those

AGRICULTURAL (AND ASPARAGUS) INNOVATIONS

The city slickers among us might think the greatest innovation in agriculture is the move from a four-pronged pitchfork to the clearly superior three-pronged version. But in addition to the ways the Internet will revolutionize agriculture, other innovative solutions and advances are not related to information.

Bio-Agtive Emissions Technology redirects tractor exhaust into the ground as fertilizer instead of into the air as a pollutant. And advances in drip irrigation, which itself isn't exactly new but is becoming far more widespread and ever more efficient, allows crops to be grown with massively less water.

Sunscreens for plants protects them from ultraviolet and infrared radiation. In the not-too-distant future, tiny robots will detect pests on produce and emit a signal to shoo them away. And fascinating new ways to transport foods will keep them significantly fresher.

But my favorite has to be the asparagus harvester. The inventor describes how he got the idea:

> A selective asparagus harvester. That is the answer my father gave to me when I asked him if he could think of anything for me to invent. That was back in 1972. Since I've been working on it for over 30 years, I'm not sure you list it along with "new farming inventions"; maybe it is an old farming invention. . . . Asparagus spears grow randomly across a raised bed about 30 inches wide—at least that is the way it's grown in the San Joaquin Valley. The spears can grow up to 6 inches or more a day when the temperature is hot. The machine would have to determine if a spear was tall enough to be harvested, and then cut the spear off slightly below the ground and pick it up.

Prices start at $125,000. This machine sounds so cool, it makes me want to start growing asparagus.

algorithms will get ever better. I know it sounds all futuristic and expensive now, but what if this technology falls to just a few dollars per acre? How would it not find its way to the poorest regions of the earth?

Information and markets. As mentioned earlier, farmers suffer when they do not have reliable markets for their goods. Typically, a small farmer in a remote area will have some surplus. At some point a buyer will come to town, offer a low price, and the farmer will be compelled to sell because the risk of not selling is too high; he may not get another offer and the crop might rot for poor storage. This has been a common situation throughout areas with high degrees of poverty and is certainly the case in Ethiopia.

That is, before Eleni Zaude Gabre-Madhin came along. Eleni is CEO of the Ethiopian Commodity Exchange, which works like this: Farmers in Ethiopia bring their crops to any of two hundred market centers around the country. There they can see the world commodity prices for their produce in real time. Their produce is checked in to the warehouse and each farmer is issued a certificate corresponding to the amount of produce he brought. He can sell the certificate, use it as collateral, or hold it for the future.

The Ethiopian Commodity Exchange therefore serves many purposes. It can sell produce abroad for better rates, give farmers predictability in pricing and flexibility on when to sell, and act as a storehouse against lean times in the future. If the harvest is huge and the price of food is low, the farmer is insulated from this; he can put his produce on deposit and sell it later, or sell it for a higher price in the global market where prices may not have fallen.

This is made possible by technology and the Internet, which is used to connect buyers and sellers worldwide and bring information (world commodity prices) to the far reaches of the globe. These are the kinds of innovative solutions that technology and the Internet can enable. These are the kinds of solutions that will change the world.

The United Nations World Food Programme was so inspired by this success that pilot programs for an exchange were launched in twenty-one countries. The principle here is to agree to buy a certain amount of a commodity at a certain price from farmers in these countries. The farmers, with these contracts in hand, can plant aggressively knowing they have a ready buyer at a fixed price. Information plus sophisticated markets make this possible.

Mobile phones and local communication. In *The Rational Optimist*, author Matt Ridley cites a report from economist Robert Jensen regarding January 14, 1997, a typical day for a fisherman in India:

> [E]leven fishermen landed good catches in at the village of Badagara only to find that there were no buyers left: the local market was sated and the price of the perishable sardines was zero. Just 10 miles away in both directions along the coast, at Chombala and Quilandi, that morning there were 27 willing buyers ready to leave the markets empty-handed because they could find no sardines to buy, even at the inflated price of nearly 10 rupees per kilogram they were offering.

And then, Ridley leaps continents to Kenya and notes this: "Despairing of state-controlled landlines, one-quarter of the population acquired a mobile phone after 2000. Kenyan farmers call different markets to find the best prices before setting out with their produce, and are better off for it."

The access to information that mobile phones are bringing virtually everywhere on the planet is helping people raise their standard of living and will do so even more dramatically in the years to come.

Idle computer time employed to solve the world's problems. UC Berkeley created an open-source grid-computing platform called Boinc. You can install Boinc software on your computer, choose a project you want your computer to work on when you are away from it, and maybe do your bit to change the world. Current projects include IBM's World Community Grid, which describes itself as conducting "Humanitarian research on disease, natural disasters and hunger."

Peace and democracy. As Nobel laureate Amartya Sen has noted, democracies don't have famines. Especially democracies with free presses. If politicians are demonstrably good at one thing, it is getting elected, and people who are starving don't normally re-elect their representatives. A leader can only afford to let her people go hungry when she doesn't answer to them. Democracy, per se, isn't necessarily the requirement, but a form of government in which the politicians are directly answerable to the population for

their quality of life is. The world is quickly moving to participatory government. According to the Center for Systemic Peace's tally, the world went
from just twenty democracies in 1946 to ninety-two in 2009. Dictatorships
are toppling, and the Internet is helping that along.

Grassroots efforts to assist people in need. The Internet is allowing
more innovative methods for socially conscious individuals to directly help
people in need, instead of indirectly contributing through a telethon or a
payroll deduction for the United Way. One of these is micro-lending, which
directly connects the lender with the borrower and which the Internet has
made appealingly easy and personal. Although micro-loan operations all are
a little different, let me explain how one called Kiva works. With the help
of local agencies around the world that have experience in micro-loans, a
would-be borrower—say, a fish seller in the Philippines—uploads a picture
and an explanation of what she wants the loan for. If you decide to participate in the loan, you can kick in $25 or more. Once the amount the fish
seller requested is reached, the loan is funded and funds are transferred to
her. At some point, the loan is repaid to the local agency and your money
comes back to you. You can either withdraw it, reloan it, or donate it to
Kiva. Since its founding in 2005, Kiva has loaned out nearly a quarter of a
billion dollars and is repaid almost 99 percent of the time.

Micro-lending is not new; the idea of small loans to the entrepreneurial
poor is centuries old. But micro-lending via the Internet is different. It's a
manifestation of that online "We Share" attitude I mentioned earlier: people
helping strangers in distant places—in personal, one-on-one exchanges—
even though they have no way to profit from the effort.

Food as a Human Right

If you are among the brigands and stay silent,
then you yourself are a brigand.
–Hungarian proverb

All that we have explored in this section—rising incomes, advances in nutrition and genomics, innovations in agricultural technologies—will eventually end hunger. But in the meantime, hunger will stay with us even in the world of plenty. Why is this? Because, as mentioned earlier, your claim to food is a financial one, so if you have no money, you starve to death. The old adage is true: There really is no such thing as a free lunch.

There are those who would elevate the right to food as being a fundamental human right. I agree with them. As an American, I believe in the precepts of the Declaration of Independence, which Thomas Jefferson fashioned to be a statement of the basis on which America justified its Revolution. Among its best-known words are these:

> We hold these truths to be self-evident, that all men are created equal, that they are endowed by their Creator with certain unalienable Rights, that among these are Life, Liberty and the pursuit of Happiness. — That to secure these rights, Governments are instituted among Men, deriving their just powers from the consent of the governed.

The word "unalienable" (or "inalienable"—they are interchangeable) means, "unable to be taken away from or given away by the possessor." Think about that. You cannot give away your right to live. You cannot sell to someone the right to kill you or hold you prisoner. The right is inseparable from its possessor.

To think of the right to life as somehow different than a right to food is hard for me. It is akin to saying you have a right to life but not a right to a heart. I do not say this to advance any political doctrine. I am not saying governments are supposed to feed the world or that food should be free. I am simply saying that if life is a fundamental right, then its most essential requirements—food, water, and air—seem to be as well. At the very least, if the essential requirements of life are not present, the right to life doesn't mean much.

Napoleon Bonaparte made a comment along these lines when he stated, "Man is entitled by birthright to a share of the earth's produce sufficient to fill the needs of his existence."

Remember the remarkable Norman Borlaug? He seems to have agreed as well. It was his view that "the attainment of human rights in the fullest sense cannot be achieved so long as hundreds of millions of poverty-stricken people lack the basic necessities for life." Rights do not mean much, he reasoned, to those with an "empty stomach, shirtless back, roofless dwellings . . . unemployment and poverty, no education or medical attention."

How do we respond to this? What would we say to Borlaug if we met him in a cornfield and ended up discussing the world's problems over a beer somewhere?

Some might say, "Hunger is awful. Dreadful. *You* should do something about it." That is, agree in principle but decline any personal accountability.

Some might say something I consider even worse: "It is inexcusable that some go hungry while you have so much. I am going to take some of what you have and give it to someone else. If you have a problem with that, take it up with the man with the gun."

It would be a mistake to assume some sort of collectivist or communistic solution to hunger in the world. The record of the failure of such approaches is among the least ambiguous lessons history teaches us. The profit motive, in one form or another, remains the best exhorter of humanity.

No more vivid example of this is how what was supposed to be the most egalitarian system in the world, Communist China under Mao, caused the worst famine in the history of the world. During the period 1958 to 1961, an initiative called "The Great Leap Forward" was intended to increase the production of grain and other agricultural products. China pulled out all the stops, dividing its farmland into about twenty-five thousand collective farms with an average of five thousand households each. Instead of earning money, members of the collectives earned work points (which, of course, everyone prefers to money). The result was disastrous; collectivism, combined with bad weather conditions, resulted in a dramatic decrease in output.

During this three-year period, conveniently named by the Chinese "The Three Years of Natural Disasters," no one really knows how many people died; estimates range from fifteen million to a high of more than forty-five million. And the great tragedy is: During these three years, China exported more than twelve million tons of grain along with a literal cornucopia of other agricultural products.

According to Yang Jisheng, who wrote the definitive book on The Great

Famine, "In Xinyang, people starved at the doors of the grain warehouses. As they died, they shouted, 'Communist Party, Chairman Mao, save us.' If the granaries of Henan and Hebei had been opened, no one need have died. As people were dying in large numbers around them, officials did not think to save them. Their only concern was how to fulfill the delivery of grain."

Yang also quotes Mao as saying in a 1959 meeting, "When there is not enough to eat, people starve to death. It is better to let half of the people die so that the other half can eat their fill."

Consider, also, the case in Cambodia under Pol Pot and the Khmer Rouge. During his reign, fully a fifth of the population of Cambodia died. Pol Pot ordered the killing of anyone who wore glasses, presuming them to be intellectuals; anyone from the prior power structure, including police; anyone who was educated, or a monk, or an artist; and any Muslim whom, when ordered to, refused on religious grounds to eat pork.

And if that were not enough, he killed by starvation in the name of a program called—I kid you not—"The Super Great Leap Forward." Inspired by the Chinese effort, he, too, tried to increase the agricultural production of his country by emptying the cities and sending everyone to work on the farms under brutal conditions. Of those not part of the agrarian communist experiment, the Khmer Rouge declared, "To keep you is no benefit, to destroy you is no loss."

In Richard Ebeling's *Black Book of Communism* is an essay in which Jean-Louis Margolin writes, "The hunger that crushed so many Cambodians . . . was used deliberately by the regime in the service of its interests. The hungrier people were . . . the less likely they were to run away. If people were permanently obsessed with food, all individual thought, all capacity to argue, even people's sex drive, would disappear. The games that were played with the food supply made forced evacuations easier, promoted acceptance of the collective canteens, and also weakened interpersonal relationships, including between parents and their children. . . . Hunger dehumanized, causing one person to turn on another and to forget everything except his own survival. . . . Everyone, by contrast, would kiss the hand that fed them, regardless of how bloody it was."[11]

---

11. From "Cambodia: The Country of Disconcerting Crimes" by Jean-Louis Margolin from *The Black Book of Communism: Crimes, Terror, Repression*. Copyright © 1999 by the President and Fellows of Harvard College.

Before his death, Pol Pot conceded that his regime certainly killed people, but "to say that millions died is too much."

Eventually, I believe, food will be free. Everywhere you go in the United States are water fountains. Water isn't free; someone is paying a bill to purify the water that comes through that fountain. But the cost is so negligible that no one thinks much of it. I don't recall ever being in a department store, drinking from the water fountain, and having the staff look at me disapprovingly because I was running up the water bill. I believe we will see the day when food is like that.

Until then, what do we say? That we are content with a billion hungry people? I am not. And as long as those billion can only claim a right to food based on their ability to pay for it, the world will have hungry people.

In his 1944 State of the Union address, President Franklin Roosevelt observed,

> This Republic had its beginning, and grew to its present strength, under the protection of certain inalienable political rights—among them, the right of free speech, free press, free worship, trial by jury, freedom from unreasonable searches and seizures. They were our rights to life and liberty.

And then he added this:

> We have come to a clear realization of the fact that true individual freedom cannot exist without economic security and independence. 'Necessitous men are not free men.' People who are hungry and out of a job are the stuff of which dictatorships are made. In our day these economic truths have become accepted as self-evident. We have accepted, so to speak, a second Bill of Rights under which a new basis of security and prosperity can be established for all—regardless of station, race, or creed.

Roosevelt went on to outline what he believed would be in this Second Bill of Rights: food, medicine, shelter, and so on. In using the phrase,

"Necessitous men are not free men," Roosevelt was actually quoting from a decision in a well-known 1762 English legal case. The full quote runs: "Necessitous men are not, truly speaking, free men, but, to answer a present exigency, will submit to any terms that the crafty may impose upon them."

It would be tempting to characterize Roosevelt's remarks as socialistic. In support of this perspective, similarities have been drawn between the basket of economic rights proposed by Roosevelt and those guaranteed in the constitution of the Soviet Union at the time. But this is a misreading of both Roosevelt and history. The Communist system eschewed political liberties in favor of economic ones. The individual had no liberties, or at least very few, but in exchange was, in theory, entitled to certain economic rights. That setup didn't turn out so well.

Roosevelt, it seems to me, is arguing for an expansion, not a shifting, of the rights to which all Americans are entitled. He is raising the value of citizenship, not cheapening it. While Jefferson's "all men are created equal" statement was not meant by him to include slaves, we have broadened the application of the principle and should continue to do so. Roosevelt is saying that freedom itself cannot exist apart from some amount of economic liberty. All those who have swallowed their pride and endured an injustice out of fear of losing their job, or have compromised their values for the same reason, or have worked for a morally dubious company out of fear of being unemployed, know this to be true. Roosevelt is saying if a nation can guarantee some basic amount of economic security as a means to promote freedom, it should consider doing so.

To elevate food to the status of a human right does not require government to administer it—far from it. In the United States, you could do it via the tax code, with government only acting as an income redistribution agent but not as a food distributor. At this writing, the most recent U.S. Department of Agriculture statistics counted 14.5 percent of U.S. households struggling to put food on the table at some point in the year. But what if everyone in the nation, rich and poor, were to be mailed a $2,000 food card annually, redeemable at the grocery store for any of several hundred nutritious foods? To the conservatives, call it a tax rebate; to the liberals, an entitlement. Everyone would be happy. You will have ended hunger in the United States.

But, of course, I am not most worried about the United States. I hope that someday the whole world has only this nation's level of problems. In the United States, a number of institutions and programs do a pretty good job of keeping extreme, constant hunger at bay. For instance, de Tocqueville's voluntary associations still thrive, and anyone willing to make her way to a church or food pantry saying she is hungry will seldom leave empty handed. Food in the United States is so inexpensive as a percentage of national income that it literally is a throwaway item. In fact, according to the National Resource Defense Council, 40 percent of all food in the U.S. ends up in the trash. The average family of four wastes a thousand pounds of food a year, costing them $2,275. One could feed a third of the world's hungry with what Americans throw away.

As far as other countries go, while we may have no legal right to coerce nations that deny food to those who cannot pay for it, we can tie our friendship and goodwill to how those governments treat their weakest citizens. Do we not do the same in our personal lives? If you knew someone who was a good business partner, was fun to hang out with, but let one of his children starve to death so that he could enjoy a higher standard of living, what would be your opinion of this person? Would you be proud to call him a friend? Why would we conduct ourselves any differently in world affairs? Is our nation so poor or so weak that we must resort to the ultimate in pragmatism and befriend nations in the name of commerce or prosperity or military security while turning a blind eye to the suffering of their people? What good is our high economic standing in the world if we do not use it for good purposes?

What would we have the centuries to come to say about us: That we were so eager to maximize our position of power and wealth that we turned a blind eye to injustice? Or, instead, that we used our influence to promote the interests of the weak, the downtrodden, and the hungry, and that we led the world by our example?

The question answers itself. If we pursue that course, we will rightfully earn the admiration of the ages.

Beyond Hungry to Healthy

I just hate health food.
–Julia Child

As people grow wealthier (as the whole world will), they typically spend more money on food, though it is less as a percentage of overall income. They also become more interested in the food they eat. People who buy organic food, for instance, are not doing it simply because they have more money. But since they have more money, they choose to spend it on what they perceive as healthier food that is more responsibly and sustainably made.

As the world grows richer, people will care more about how their food is made, how the animals are treated, whether the laborer who picked the food is paid a living wage. We might pay a premium to support a family farm. We know all this is true because we see signs of it already.

Consider the marketing behind fast-food chain Chipotle, which puts its ingredients and business practices front and center in almost all its advertising. On its website, a section called "Food with Integrity" explains what that means:

> It means serving the very best sustainably raised food possible with an eye to great taste, great nutrition and great value. It means that we support and sustain family farmers who respect the land and the animals in their care. It means that whenever possible we use meat from animals raised without the use of antibiotics or added hormones. And it means that we source organic and local produce when practical. And that we use dairy from cows raised without the use of synthetic hormones. Food with Integrity is a journey that started more than a decade ago and one that will never end.

Similarly, on the Ben & Jerry's Ice Cream website, a section called "Caring Dairy" explains the company's philosophy:

We spend a lot of time thinking about milk and cream, including where ours comes from and how it's produced. For over 20 years, the 500 family farmers of the St. Albans Cooperative Creamery in Vermont have been our partners and primary suppliers of milk and cream. For all of those years, we've asked our farmers not to treat their cows with rBGH, a genetically engineered growth hormone used to increase milk production. It's clear to us that rBGH is a step in the wrong direction towards a synthetic, factory-produced food supply. Today, through a unique partnership we call "Caring Dairy," we're also working together to help our family farmers adopt leading-edge sustainable practices. We think Caring Dairy is a boon to cows, a boost for farmers, and beneficial for the planet—all of which helps to bolster Vermont's identity as a beautiful rural state dotted with real, working family farms.

The priority must be, of course, to address the needs of the hungry, who could only wish to have a chicken to eat, let alone to have the "high-class problem" of whether the chicken had a dignified life and death. But over time, as incomes around the world rise, people will migrate more and more to products associated with social practices that match their own ideals.

How the Internet and Technology Will End Hunger

For I was hungry and you gave me food.
I was thirsty and you gave me drink.
—Jesus Christ, speaking of those who will be blessed in heaven

I hope that at this point, you share my optimism about the end of hunger. It will come about through sensors, genetic engineering, better information, better communication, and precision farming. We will radically improve the primitive, inefficient process that agriculture is today. We will learn to grow more crops in more places, and make great breakthroughs relating to our seeds and our systems. With information, we will distribute better. With satellite images, we will plan better. With communications, we will grow more efficient.

By studying our collective Digital Echoes, we will unlock the mysteries of nutrition (and many a bar bet will be settled when this happens). As we understand our own genome better, we will know better how to eat in a way that is custom tailored for us. As technology improves, all these processes and systems will improve and also fall in price. Ever-increasing wealth will be generated by ever-faster technological advances. The cost of food will fall to nearly zero as the number of farmers in the world falls to zero and food becomes as cheap as clean water.

All this will happen eventually, I believe, even if global hunger policy were not to change one iota. But I also believe that hunger will end when we *decide* to end it, not only at the point when we *are able* to end it. We could decide today to end it—by, well, simply deciding to. We just don't want to badly enough. That is a hard truth, but a truth nonetheless.

When access to food is a human right and the leading nations of the world decide to tie their friendship and goodwill to that principle, that is when hunger will be ended.

In this case, sooner is so much better than later. Deciding to end hunger today saves the lives of millions, and we have the technology to do it. Why would we settle for anything less?

THE END OF WAR

- War

- Civilization

- Must We End War?

- Is It Possible to End War?

- The Difficulties of Ending War

- How the Internet and Technology Will End War

War

*I believe that the entire effort of modern society should be
concentrated on the endeavor to outlaw war as a method of
the solution of problems between nations.*
—General Douglas MacArthur

Throughout this book, I've maintained the way to know the future is by studying the past. Now, I'm faced with explaining why the past was full of war but somehow the future will not be.

As I did in foregoing sections on ignorance, disease, poverty, and hunger, I am essentially doing what logicians call constructing a proof: laying out a series of premises that build to a conclusion. But in making the case that war can and will be ended, I have my work cut out for me. Do not expect this to be a uniformly reassuring journey; it may be more of a roller-coaster ride with some rather bleak descents.

The chapter on civilization describes humanity's progress through the years and the importance of it. Then the next chapter asks flatly whether we *must* end war—whether that is genuinely an imperative if progress is to continue. I contend that it is.

The next chapter addresses the *possibility* of ending war. Maybe you will agree it to be possible, but after reading this chapter, you will likely think it is improbable. Something akin to getting a date with Miss America: Sure, in theory, possible—but realistically, it ain't gonna happen. This chapter will be a low point, a succession of arguments as to why war has been a constant and may always be.

Just when things look dark, well, they actually get worse. The following chapter catalogs the difficulties inherent in trying to end war, which in the past brought misery and destruction and in the future could bring annihilation. It's a pretty hopeless place to take a reader.

"But wait! Is that a distant bugle I hear?" Out of the blue, the cavalry comes to the rescue. All right then, not the cavalry, but a marshaling of arguments and observations that will show how the end of war is inevitable, or nearly so.

This chapter offers no silver bullet, no "aha" insight that will instantly persuade you. It's more like silver buckshot: a whole volley of meaningful, contributory uses of the Internet and associated technologies that will, acting together, bring about the end of war once and for all. I outline forty-five different ways this will happen—surely enough that even if you don't agree with them all, you will still have plenty of reason to be optimistic.

An old joke is about the city slicker who finds himself lost in the country. He pulls up next to a farmer and asks the farmer how to get to a certain place. The farmer replies, "You can't get there from here."

I know our world seems far from ending war. My goal is to convince you we can get there from here.

Civilization

Let us dedicate ourselves to what the Greeks wrote
so many years ago: to tame the savageness of man
and make gentle the life of this world.
—Robert Kennedy

Consider the following stories from history:

- Jordanes, a Goth, wrote the following about the Huns in 551: "They are beings who are cruel to their children on the very day they are born. For they cut the cheeks of the males with a sword, so that before they receive the nourishment of milk they must learn to endure wounds." The implication is that any time they nursed, they felt pain as well, to learn at an early age that there is no pleasure to be had in life without pain.

- On July 29, 1014, Byzantine emperor Basil II defeated the Bulgarian army in the Battle of Kleidion. The Byzantine army captured fifteen thousand prisoners. They were tied into one hundred fifty lines of one hundred men each. In each line of a hundred men, every man had his eyes put out, except for the leader of the line, who had only one eye put out so he could lead his line back to Bulgaria. The Bulgarian king Samuel was so stricken by the sight of his mighty army staggering back home that he suffered a stroke and died two days later. It should be noted that the Byzantines were among the most civilized people in all the world at that time.

- The Third Servile War occurred in the Roman Republic from 73 BC to 71 BC. It was a rebellion of slaves led by a gladiator named Spartacus. Eventually Spartacus and many of his followers were killed and six thousand of his fellow rebelling slaves were crucified, a slow and agonizing form of death. They were lined up as far as the eye could see on the Appian Way, the main road through Rome, as a warning to other slaves who might consider rebellion.

- In the 1600s in Paris, a form of popular entertainment was known as "cat burning." I will spare my readers a description of this other than to say it is exactly what it sounds like. It was enjoyed by the entire population from the poor to the rich to the monarchy.

- In 106, the Roman Emperor Trajan celebrated his defeat over the Dacians by ordering 123 consecutive days of gladiatorial games in the Roman Collosseum. In that time, eleven thousand wild animals were killed for the amusement of the crowd, and ten thousand gladiators hacked away at each other to thunderous applause.

I offer these stories not to demonstrate that people can be cruel. I offer them because they have something interesting in common. They are not tales of aberrant individuals but of societal norms. This is how people lived their lives in the past and if asked about it, they would have defended it.

The disturbing thing to realize is we would have been those people had we been born in those times. I know of no theory of theology, biology, or ethics that claims otherwise.

The ancient world was a cruel place. The only thing that separates us from that world is this thing called civilization. I want to spend some time talking about civilization, but first I want to recount the progress that we have made through civilization. This is not a defense of our present age; we will come to our own report card soon enough. Rather, it is an acknowledgement of progress made.

Slavery. We have ended the legal protection of slavery virtually everywhere on the planet. Although slavery still exists and the low price of slaves speaks to the low value of a human life, the legal institution of slavery is gone. No longer can a person own another person and have the power of the state backing him up. The magnitude of this accomplishment is difficult to overstate. Slavery has been a historic norm, and the idea that a conquered person, for example, could become the property of the conqueror seems to have been quite obvious to our ancestors. Yet in most parts of the world, emancipation came peacefully as the civilizing effects of culture transformed society.

Women. In most parts of the world, women are no longer legally regarded as chattel. Once again, this change was not imposed on people through coercion but came (and still comes) gradually through civilization. While unacceptable inequalities still exist around the world for women, the tide of history is flowing inexorably in favor of equal rights for women.

Race. In many places, we have ended the legal discrimination of people based on race. In the West, we have also ended legal discrimination against people on the basis of creed, national origin, and other "protected classes." We have stigmatized racism; and while it unquestionably still exists between many races, racism is becoming less and less relevant.

Self-rule. We have seen the end of hereditary monarchy. Until very recently, our world was ruled by kings. As recently as 1900, most of the world was governed this way. Monarchy is not inherently bad, and there have been fine kings and queens in history. But I consider it significant, and an earmark of civilization, that we are replacing this form of government with republics and democracies. We are replacing monarchy with self-rule.

Pain as entertainment. We have ended pain as entertainment—or at least, involuntary participation in pain as entertainment. Boxing matches still occur, but the boxers participate voluntarily. We no longer have public executions as a form of entertainment. We no longer force prisoners to kill each other for our amusement. In many parts of the world, we have even outlawed the use of animals fighting as entertainment, such as cockfighting and dogfighting.

Eugenics. There was a period when intellectuals believed and spoke openly of the idea that the "breeding" of the "unfit" should be limited. Some even went so far as to oppose charity for the poor and weak because they claimed it assisted the "least fit" in reproducing. Luckily, this uncivilized viewpoint has been stigmatized and is no longer the official policy of any nation, although it is doubtful that it is entirely gone.

The end of "Off with his head." People in power used to be able to order executions as capriciously as the queen did in *Alice in Wonderland*. And they frequently did. Not just rulers, either. During World War II, when General Patton got sacked for slapping a soldier whom he regarded as cowardly, the Germans couldn't believe it: Their officers could have soldiers shot without trial! Every day fewer places exist where a single person has the legal right to end the life of another.

Human rights. In the past, when the power of the state was absolute in many parts of the world, it was harder to argue that every person on the planet had rights no monarch or state could violate. We call these rights "human rights" because they apply to every single person on the planet by virtue of simply being alive. Even acknowledging that human rights exist is a great advance of civilization. And that advance continues, as the group of rights so acknowledged keeps expanding.

Widespread acknowledgement of human dignity. The concept of human dignity asserts that some things simply should not be done to a human, no matter the circumstances. This, too, is becoming widely accepted. Additionally, disfiguring mutilations used to be common punishments for crime, but today that concept is vanishing.

Political crimes in much of the world. The idea that a person can be a political prisoner, jailed for his beliefs about government, politics, or politicians, is ancient but happily fading.

Torture as punishment. I am not saying we have ended torture. But we have significantly reduced the use of torture as punishment. The very fact that we have debated in recent years whether we can use torture to get information that will save lives is a sign of the effects of civilization. While torture as punishment does occur, it is stigmatized.

Due process. Civilization invented habeas corpus and sees it as a fundamental legal right around the world. It is no longer legal for people to be secretly arrested, not charged, and left to rot in jail. We have come to expect due process for all. Trials are expected to be open and public. Rules of evidence are widely known and honored. The right to representation is spreading around the world. A formal appeals process and trial by jury are commonplace. Juries of one's peers have replaced trials by ordeal all over the world.

Courts of law, not courts of justice. The basic difference between a democracy and a republic is that democracies are the rule of the majority and republics are the rule of the law. Democracies are thereby prone to the majority abusing the rights of the minority. Republics consist of codified laws that apply to everyone, regardless of public sentiment. The United States is a republic, as even the Pledge of Allegiance says. We use democracy as a method of selecting representatives, but our form of government is republicanism.

The distinction between courts of law and courts of justice is somewhat like the difference between a republic and a democracy. Though the name sounds appealing, in practice a court of justice often has been frightful, meting out the kind of one-sided "justice" associated with lynch mobs and vigilantism. In contrast, courts of law apply the law to everyone. Courts of law are now the norm in the world, with laws being democratically established and widely published.

War crimes and crimes against humanity. It used to be the only crime in war was losing and if you committed that one, you were put to death. Now we identify certain acts as war crimes, although they are sometimes poorly defined and arbitrarily enforced. In general, we have come to agree that war must be waged with certain constraints, often with an eye toward limiting harm inflicted on civilians and prisoners. We have created the Geneva Conventions, a set of treaties that govern the treatment of non-combatants and prisoners. Here is an excerpt from one of them:

> Protected persons are entitled, in all circumstances, to respect for their persons, their honour, their family rights, their religious convictions and practices, and their manners and customs. They shall, at all times, be humanely treated, and shall be protected, especially against all acts of violence or threats thereof and against insults and public curiosity. Women shall be especially protected against any attack on their honour, in particular against rape, enforced prostitution, or any form of indecent assault. Without prejudice to the provisions relating to their state of health, age and sex, all protected persons shall be treated with the same consideration by the Party to the conflict in whose power they are, without any adverse distinction based, in particular, on race, religion or political opinion.

Animals. We have not only outlawed cruelty to animals, but increasingly, people care about the living conditions of even the animals they eat. At a farmers' market I recently visited, one vendor boasted that all his chickens "retained their dignity throughout their life." (I don't personally see how a chicken, in any situation, can be said to have dignity. After all, it is a chicken. But I get his point.)

Violent crime. As clichéd as it is to complain about rising rates of crime, the statistics tell a different story. Manuel Eisner, of the Institute of Criminology at the University of Cambridge, assembled a "History of Homicide Database" in which he meticulously logged all estimates of the murder rate in different countries throughout the last thousand years. In terms of murders per one hundred thousand inhabitants, England fell from roughly twenty-three in the 1300s to about one today. The Netherlands and Belgium fell from forty-seven in 1300s to about one today. Scandinavia was at forty-six in the 1400s and has fallen to one today. Germany and Switzerland fell from thirty-seven in the 1300s to about one today.

Murder isn't the only form of violent crime that is falling. Eisner points out that homicide rates correlate well to levels of robbery, assault, and sexual violence across multiple countries and there is reason to believe it was so in the past as well.

Non-violent resistance as a tool to political ends. Although non-violent resistance as a means of bringing about societal change has been around for at least two millennia, recently it has gone mainstream. More and more, those wishing to change the status quo adopt this as their primary tactic. They do this for a variety of reasons, not the least of which is that it often works. As Scottish historian Thomas Carlyle once observed, "Man seldom, or rather never for a length of time and deliberately, rebels against anything that does not deserve rebelling against." Gradually, civilization seems to be learning this.

What else has been achieved in our march toward civilization? We have eliminated debtors' prisons, developed the idea of "women and children first," stigmatized child labor, made accommodations for conscientious objectors, widely adopted freedom of speech and the press and freedom of assembly, and a hundred more. Here's how Harvard University psychologist Steven Pinker described it in his 2007 article, "A History of Violence:"

> Conventional history has long shown that, in many ways, we have been getting kinder and gentler. Cruelty as entertainment, human sacrifice to indulge superstition, slavery as a labor-saving device, conquest as the mission statement of government, genocide as a means of acquiring real estate, torture and mutilation as routine punishment, the death penalty for misdemeanors and differences of opinion, assassination as the mechanism of political succession, rape as the spoils of war, pogroms as outlets for frustration, homicide as the major form of conflict resolution—all were unexceptionable features of life for most of human history. But,

today, they are rare to nonexistent in the West, far less common elsewhere than they used to be, concealed when they
do occur, and widely condemned when they are brought
to light.[12]

The civilizing process is not flawless, and we may disagree on the ways it
has manifested itself. Maybe you think the British ban on fox hunting with
dogs is ridiculous. Maybe you think prisoners have it too easy serving time
while their victims struggle to piece their lives back together. Still, I would
argue these changes are the results of an overall increase in empathy and
that, more often than not, increasing empathy promotes civilization and
is splendid.

Even our aspirations have become more civilized. Ask people in what way
they hope the world will become better and you will certainly get replies
about reducing poverty, disease, and hunger. Just as likely, you will also hear
hopes for equal opportunity, justice for all, and increases in individual liberty. It is true that there is much disagreement over how to achieve these
ideals, but the fact remains most of us want a just society for all.

Yes, you can still see a cockfight in the United States. That is not the
point. The point is that it is now illegal in every state, with Louisiana being
the last to outlaw it in 2008. Yes, pro football player Michael Vick raised
dogs for dogfighting. That is not the important point. The point is that he
went to jail for it.

We have created documents that enshrine our values as a method of
articulating and preserving them. In the English language, these include
the Magna Carta, the English Bill of Rights, the Mayflower Compact, the
Massachusetts Body of Liberties, and the United States Constitution. These
documents, products themselves of civilization, try to provide legal protections for the most elemental features of civilization.

But for all that we codify and advance civilization, we must understand
that civilization can be lost. While it is not fragile, we must not take it for
granted. As historians Will and Ariel Durant noted in their book *The Lessons*

---

of History, "Civilization is not inherited; it has to be learned and earned by each generation anew; if the transmission should be interrupted for one century, civilization would die, and we should be savages again."

No matter your view of history and cosmology, civilization is very young. It is not surprising that we are taking awhile to get it right.

The most difficult work is in the past. Our forebears bore that burden. They made civilization in times of adversity and want, not in the relative luxury and stability we enjoy today. It is through this civilizing process that I find hope we will end war. War is the ultimate barbarism, the primitive belief that fighting determines who is right—but of course it doesn't. Maybe this is dawning on us. Then war can become obsolete, as foreign to us as slavery and public hangings. I think it can. We will see how this might come to pass—but first, let's ask whether it *must.*

Must We End War?

There are only two things we should fight for. One is the defense of our homes and the other is the Bill of Rights. War for any other reason is simply a racket.
—General Smedley Butler, USMC

The chapter title poses a valid question. After all, we have had war almost constantly throughout history and yet have still managed to progress. Maybe war does serve some purpose. Maybe we need it as a release valve that lets off societal pressure . . .

Yeah, I'm not buying that.

I am not a pacifist. I do believe some ideals are worth fighting for and worth killing for—but not many. I feel we have set the bar way too low and in doing so have fundamentally cheapened life, everyone's life. By declaring a broad range of things worth killing and dying for, we say that each of those is more precious to us than human life.

Of course, the people making that judgment call and the people doing the actual dying usually are not one and the same, and therein lies the problem.

President Dwight Eisenhower, lifelong military man and five-star general, had much to say on the waging of war, little of which was in favor of the practice. Early in his presidency, in a 1953 address that would become known as his "Cross of Iron" speech, he declared, "Every gun that is made, every warship launched, every rocket fired, signifies in the final sense a theft from those who hunger and are not fed, those who are cold and are not clothed. This world in arms is not spending money alone. It is spending the sweat of its laborers, the genius of its scientists, the houses of its children . . . This is not a way of life. . . . Under the cloud of war, it is humanity hanging itself on a cross of iron."

After speaking about the economic costs of war, the burden it places on the economy, and the toll this takes on the people, Eisenhower closed by describing the peace proposals he was offering Russia and China. Their aim, he said, was nothing less than "the lifting, from the backs and from the hearts of men, of their burden of arms and of fears, so that they may find before them a golden age of freedom and of peace."

As we contemplate whether we absolutely *must* end war, we should consider how life lived on a war footing affects our most basic rights and freedoms. Eisenhower understood that. So did de Tocqueville, touring nineteenth-century America, when he wrote, "All those who seek to destroy the liberties of a democratic nation ought to know that war is the surest and shortest means to accomplish it." And so did journalist Brooks Atkinson, who distilled the insight down to this: "After each war, there is a little less democracy left to save."

As Eisenhower's presidency neared an end, he spoke of war again, but less in terms of economic costs. Nearly two terms of fighting the Cold War led him to conclude, as he put it, "War in our time has become an anachronism. Whatever the case in the past, war in the future can serve no useful purpose. A war which became general, as any limited action might, would only result in the virtual destruction of mankind."

"The virtual destruction of mankind." That's a bold statement, coming from a sitting president and former general.

If it was true then, then it is even more true now. The ability of humanity to destroy is now exponentially higher. As Denzel Washington's character observed in the movie *Crimson Tide*, "In the nuclear world, the true enemy is war itself."

Just as technology magnifies our productive labor, it magnifies our destructive capacity as well. Albert Einstein reflected this when he famously said, "I know not with what weapons World War III will be fought, but World War IV will be fought with sticks and stones." And J. Robert Oppenheimer— who directed the project that created the atomic bomb—said flatly that that weapon "made the prospect of future war unendurable. It has led us up those last few steps to the mountain pass; and beyond there is a different country."

So there it is. In the past, humanity has been able to sustain both wars and progress. But in the future this will not be the case. We know it is easier to destroy than to create. We know technology magnifies that. A full-scale, no-holds-barred, nuclear-missiles-raining-down kind of world war would profoundly change the course of human history for all time. And given that regional conflicts tend to escalate and expand, as long as those conflicts exist, the very real threat of an unthinkable world war remains. So realistically, we know that we either *must* end war, or face the prospect that war will end us.

If we conclude that we must end war, the next question is: Is that even possible?

Is It Possible to End War?

As far as I am concerned, war itself is immoral.
–General Omar Bradley, U.S. Five-Star General

Is it possible to end war?

Many would answer this question with a resounding "no," and would cite both history and human nature to support their response.

But it is obvious to me that we can end war. Obvious? Yes, obvious. It is certainly possible to conceive of a single day without war. There have been such days in the past, albeit rarely, when the entire world has been at peace. If there can be a day without war, then there can be two days without it. Then there can be a week, a month, a year, a decade, and a century without war.

This is not semantics. It is an acknowledgement that war is completely a choice and our choice can be "no."

During the Vietnam era, a slogan (or question, or *kōan*) went, "Suppose they gave a war and nobody came?" It was a way for that generation to ask, "Why is there war? Why don't we just decide to stop?" Those asking it didn't offer a means for the world to escape from war. It was a rhetorical question and, to those posing it, simply a wish—just another way to say, "Why can't we all just get along?"

Well, there are a lot of reasons we don't get along. That's the problem.

I am not posing a naïve, rhetorical question. This is not a section about hope, ideals, wishes, or the brotherhood of all mankind. I will not advise getting in touch with our feelings or even group hugs. I will not propose that we should "give peace a chance." The word *kumbaya* appears in this book only once, and you just saw it.

My aim is to show you how war will end and convince you that the end of war is inevitable. This is not me fighting against the tide of history but being swept along with it. The flow of history will naturally end war.

War occurs for a very simple reason: To some nations at some time, war is preferable to peace. (Yes, I know that statement should earn the "Screamingly Obvious Statement of the Year Award," but bear with me.) If it can be demonstrated that in the future, peace will always be preferable to all nations, then war will end.

I realize this is a bold objective, living as we do in a world where one nation, Mozambique, has a national flag that features an AK-47. But I am making a case I believe I can defend and will begin by defining my terms. I define war as armed conflict occurring between nation-states or, in the case of civil wars, between factions within nation-states. (This definition does not encompass acts of terrorism such as the Oklahoma City Bombing or 9/11, which I will address later).

In our individual countries, sets of laws are created by the citizenry and are designed to protect life, liberty, and property. These laws provide recourse in the event that one citizen infringes on the rights of another. We have a police force and a court system to apply the laws equally to all. By this means, we largely keep the peace.

At the world level is no equivalent. No such system of laws controls relations among nations, no significant world police force exists, and the world court system is very weak.

The way to end war is not to set up some big world government or eliminate nation-states, which will always retain the right to take unilateral military action to defend themselves. Other mechanisms will encourage nations to cooperate and will provide disincentives to unpopular unilateral action, but the surrendering of sovereignty is neither likely nor, in aggregate, a good idea.

Why do I say world government is not a good idea and nation-states are? Nation-states allow groups of people to create governments that reflect their common values. This promotes freedom and self-rule. People in a small town in Alabama, a small city in Algeria, and a large city in Argentina all desire different forms of governments with different services. The government must reflect the different values these groups have. Accountability should reside at as low a level as possible, so that if government officials mess up, they answer to constituents in their locality. Faceless government in a distant land is no one's idea of paradise.

For these reasons and a hundred more, government should be the smallest unit that is economically and politically viable. I won't speculate on what that size is, but it certainly is not "the whole world."

Nations can retain sovereignty in plenty of ways, peaceably coexist, and get economic benefits without merging into some large country. Through the adoption of standardized treaties, they can enter into economic agreements, adopt the same weights and measures, and agree to honor the intellectual property of others. They can standardize in a thousand more ways to a world economy, while maintaining their values, traditions, and distinctions. In these ways, they can be part of a larger world economy without sacrificing much autonomy.

I wish the fifty United States of America were more heterogeneous in the sense that you could have different states specializing in different things. You could have the libertarian state, the green state, the clothing-optional state, the state with free public housing for all, the state where puns are outlawed, the state with a two-drink minimum, the fiercely pro-business state—even

THE DREAM OF ENDING WAR

When the Berlin Wall fell in 1989, I was an undergraduate at Rice University. The atmosphere on campus was electric! We sensed we were witnessing something spectacular happening in the affairs of the world. When the Soviet Union dissolved only two years later, not with a bang but with a whimper, we were slack-jawed with surprise.

I had not heard anyone predict even the possibility of these two events before they came upon us, in what seemed the blink of an eye. Everything we understood about the world and politics changed. For decades we had viewed everything as a monumental clash between ideologically and diametrically opposed systems: Communism and Capitalism. And that debate ended overnight.

No one I knew of had ever seriously considered the possibility that without any conflict, treaty, war, or even a coin toss, the Soviet Union would simply vote itself into nonexistence in 1991. And while a few remaining countries didn't get the memo from the Politburo that the Revolution was cancelled due to lack of funds, for all intents and purposes, the defining political struggle of the day had ended.

Francis Fukuyama wrote a famous essay entitled "The End of History?" which became the catchphrase of the day. It was followed by the catchphrase the "Peace Dividend," which was the money we would save by slashing military expenditures in an age where history had ended, war had ended, and our thousand-ship navy and hulking military apparatus were simply an obsolete relic of the past.

Of course, politics being what it is, the Peace Dividend was spent a dozen times over by as many special interests who felt they were the most deserving of such an unexpected largess. And life went on for a decade. The economy boomed and history obediently stayed ended until one Tuesday morning in September 2001 in New York City when it resumed again.

So, when I tell you we will see the end of war, if you are over thirty-five years of age, you have every reason to roll your eyes and tell me you have seen this movie before and aren't up for the sequel. I get that. Anyone projecting an end to the historical constant of war had better be ready to overcome no small amount of justified skepticism. It is an old dream. After all, World War I was called The War to End War. But just because it is an old dream, doesn't mean it is an impossible one.

a state that guarantees free speech but requires that you sing your speech like a show tune. As long as these states were to share a currency, a military, provide for interstate trade, and have a single foreign policy, they could retain the economic advantages of being a large nation while maximizing individual liberty and self-determination.

But I digress . . .

As good as nation-states are, they do have a tendency to wage war. As American diplomat Ralph Johnson Bunche aptly observed, "There are no warlike people, just warlike leaders."

Parents whose children are in the military generally aren't the ones hawkishly pushing for war. Anyone who has a child knows the love and concern parents feel for their offspring. To raise a child to adulthood requires your heart, energy, time, and wealth. Then someone else decides to send that child, at eighteen, to another land to kill people and to die? Someone else decides to empty the cities and send all the young people to go fight in the war?

That is exactly what happens, again and again, with predictable results: dead bodies by the millions, each someone's child, and millions more mutilated. The word "carnage," after all, means meat—and the carnage of war is the treating of the whole of humanity like a giant slaughterhouse, and population like animals. "What is absurd and monstrous about war," the author Aldous Huxley noted, "is that men who have no personal quarrel should be trained to murder one another in cold blood."

To what end? When the leaders of nations decide war is the best choice, they should know better. They are elected or appointed to protect the rights of the citizens, yet they become the agents of their death.

Ending war does not mean compromising values. It means deciding disputes by a method other than slaughter. A coin toss is more reliable and a hundred times less agonizing than deciding disputes based on who can inflict the most damage to the other guy, who can kill whom the best. So why do we choose the latter? Who really believes that whoever can prevail in war must be right?

Is war inevitable? No. The demise of war, now that is inevitable. And not a moment too soon. But not, to be sure, without obstacles.

The Difficulties of Ending War

People who are anxious to bring on war don't know what they
are bargaining for; they don't see all the horrors that
must accompany such an event.
—General Stonewall Jackson

If my claim that the Internet and related technologies will bring an end to
war seems dubious at first glance, subsequent glances may leave you even
more doubtful. Let's go through a half-dozen reasons this goal will be difficult to achieve.

First, war has been a historical constant. In the 1968 book *The Lessons
of History*, Will and Ariel Durant calculated that, "In the last 3,421 years of
recorded history only 268 have seen no war."

Second, in the past, technological improvements did not decrease human
beings' propensity to wage war; they only made people better at killing. By
far, the world's bloodiest century was the twentieth century, which saw one
hundred million people die from war. The increasing lethal capability of
weapons does not seem to have been a deterrent to war in the past. As we get
better at killing, we don't seem less likely to.

Third, vast amounts of money are spent every year by virtually every
nation on the planet to defend itself in war as well as to wage offensive war.
History has disappointingly few examples of weapons made by governments
and never used.

Fourth, an entire industry exists that is financially vested in war. In his
farewell address in 1961, President Eisenhower warned:

> Until the latest of our world conflicts, the United States had
> no armaments industry. American makers of plowshares
> could, with time and as required, make swords as well. But
> now we can no longer risk emergency improvisation of
> national defense; we have been compelled to create a per-
> manent armaments industry of vast proportions. Added to
> this, three and a half million men and women are directly

engaged in the defense establishment. We annually spend on military security more than the net income of all United States corporations.

This conjunction of an immense military establishment and a large arms industry is new in the American experience. The total influence—economic, political, even spiritual— is felt in every city, every State house, every office of the Federal government. We recognize the imperative need for this development. Yet we must not fail to comprehend its grave implications. Our toil, resources, and livelihood are all involved; so is the very structure of our society.

In the councils of government, we must guard against the acquisition of unwarranted influence, whether sought or unsought, by the military-industrial complex. The potential for the disastrous rise of misplaced power exists and will persist.

Fifty years after Eisenhower's warning, the armament industry is the largest industry on the planet.

Fifth, the people who declare war are not the people who fight it. Consider this absolutely astonishing quote by Hermann Goering, head of Nazi Germany's air force during WWII:

Why, of course, the people don't want war. Why would some poor slob on a farm want to risk his life in a war when the best that he can get out of it is to come back to his farm in one piece? Naturally, the common people don't want war; neither in Russia nor in England nor in America, nor for that matter in Germany. That is understood. But, after all, it is the leaders of the country who determine the policy and it is always a simple matter to drag the people along, whether it is a democracy or a fascist dictatorship or a Parliament or a Communist dictatorship. . . . [T]he people can always be brought to the bidding of the leaders. That is easy. All you have to do is tell them they are being attacked and denounce

the pacifists for lack of patriotism and exposing the country
to danger. It works the same way in any country.

I am not saying all politicians are like this: The Nazis were pretty much
the worst guys ever. But this politics of war have in fact worked this way
repeated, across place and time. As Frederick the Great observed almost two
centuries earlier, "If my soldiers were to begin to think, not one of them
would remain in the army."

Finally, and most disturbing, we must seriously entertain the idea that
we don't want an end to war. Writing in *Esquire* magazine in 1935, Edward
Roberts offered this grim litany:

> Peace Conferences, Disarmament Conferences, pacts and
> compacts, Leagues of Nations, Locarnos to the west of us
> and Locarnos to the east of us, blather from pulpits and
> platforms, from newspapers and Hollywood, and in the
> whole slushy twaddle not an ounce of honesty to a ton of
> hypocrisy, not a minimum of reality to a gallon of senti-
> mentality, not one voice in the saccharine wilderness to pro-
> claim: We cannot end war until we eradicate the love of war
> from the heart of man.

Five decades later, in an essay called "Why Men Love War," screenwriter
and Vietnam War veteran William Broyles Jr. argued that war "is, for men,
at some terrible level the closest thing to what childbirth is for women: the
initiation into the power of life and death."

We do seem strangely drawn to war. We raise children to play with war
toys. We love war movies. Even in civilized corporate offices, professionals
in business attire say their work tasks place them "down in the trenches"
or that a certain "campaign" requires "guerrilla" marketing. Corporations
are run by "officers," comprised of multiple "divisions," and set revenue
"targets." We live in a chillingly martial world, and it would seem we like
it that way.

How the Internet and Technology
Will End War

My first wish is to see this plague of mankind, war,
banished from the earth.
—George Washington

Just as there is no single cause of war, there will be no single way that war will end. In this chapter, I offer forty-three developments, dynamics, and new realities I believe will work together to bring about an end to war. When I first made this list, it had well over one hundred entries. Lest I try the patience of my readers, I will offer, in no particular order, forty-three that seem most worthy. Technically speaking, I have included a few that are not dependent on the Internet per se, but in which the Internet and technology plays some role.

We will begin with the economic factors I believe will help end war, eleven in all.

1. Economic accomplishments replacing military ones for men. As recently as the early twentieth century, relatively few careers existed in which young men of drive and ambition could distinguish themselves and leave a mark on the world. Because military accomplishments were one way to do that, the military attracted the most ambitious young men eager to prove themselves—and "proving themselves" meant battle.

Trivia question: How old was Colonel William Travis when he died leading the Texans at the Alamo? In the 1960 version of the film, he was played by a thirty-one-year-old Laurence Harvey. In the 2004 incarnation of the film, he was played by thirty-one-year-old Patrick Wilson. I think these aged and distinguished actors were employed because Colonel Travis was actually twenty-six when he died, and a modern audience might have found that unbelievable.

During the Revolutionary War, George Washington made the Frenchman known as Lafayette a general in the Continental Army at age nineteen and promoted Alexander Hamilton to lieutenant colonel at age twenty.

George Armstrong Custer, of "Custer's Last Stand" fame, became a major general at twenty-four. The most decorated soldier in U.S. history, Audie Murphy, was only seventeen when he enlisted in the army to help win World War II, with documents his sister helped him forge. This tradition goes back centuries: Alexander the Great was twenty when he became king and would die a dozen years later having conquered what he regarded as the whole world.

Small wonder that war was unending: Victory in battle was a path to success, while military service was highly regarded in all classes and was somewhat a prerequisite for a career in politics. While military service was less important to securing work in commerce, that was not a particularly noteworthy occupation.

How things have changed! Now the brightest start businesses. Now the "war stories" are about how Mark Zuckerberg was nineteen when he started Facebook, Bill Gates was nineteen when he started Microsoft, and Larry Page and Sergey Brin were in their early twenties when they started Google.

In the past, impetuous young men would drop out of college and run off to join the army. Now they drop out of college and run off to start corporations.

Much has been written about how boys are typically more competitive than girls, even at early ages. Young boys compete with other boys in sports and races and tug-of-wars and, well, in everything, because that is simply how they are wired. This need for competition existed in the past the same as it does in the present. Upon reaching adulthood, men continue competing. Thus the ablest men of days past migrated to war because it was the most dramatic form of contest, the ultimate way to test their mettle against other men. In the modern age, we have simply transferred the competition to a new arena: the business world.

Military heroes of the last several centuries, such as the aforementioned Lafayette and Hamilton and Travis, were not bloodthirsty. They did not revel in carnage. Had they been born today, they would have started companies, not become mercenaries reading *Soldier of Fortune* magazine. They didn't enter war to satisfy a desire to kill and maim but to be victorious in the way their society rewarded. Had Gates and Zuckerberg been born two centuries earlier, they might well have considered military careers.

This is not to say that Hamilton would have been a great CEO, nor Zuckerberg an outstanding general. What I am saying is that they both would have been drawn, like a moth to a flame, to the arena in which they could, for better or worse, potentially make a name and reputation for themselves.

Today's new battlefield, the battlefield of the market, is much better. Success is now defined by creating, not destroying.

2. The rising prosperity of wealthy nations and the emergence of more wealthy nations. Prosperity breeds peace. Or, put another way, the threat of the loss of prosperity breeds peace. The wealthier a nation gets, the more it stands to lose in war, and the less marginal utility it gains in conquest. If you have no food and are starving, you might invade your neighbor and take his food. If you have everything you have ever wanted, you have less to gain and more to lose by invading your neighbor.

In his 1999 book *The Lexus and the Olive Tree*, journalist Thomas Friedman offered this "Golden Arches Theory of Conflict Prevention":

> No two countries that both had McDonald's had fought a
> war against each other since each got its McDonald's. . . .
> When a country reached the level of economic development
> where it had a middle class big enough to support a McDonald's network, it became a McDonald's country. And people
> in McDonald's countries didn't like to fight wars anymore,
> they preferred to wait in line for burgers.

Some have questioned whether Friedman's thesis is 100 percent true, mentioning NATO air strikes against Yugoslavia as a potential exception. To me, it demonstrates the strength of his thesis, that people must search for exceptions. Thus the fact that there are 130 or so countries with McDonald's, and that the number keeps growing, should be good for peace.

In 2005 in his book *The World is Flat*, Friedman updates the theory and renames it the Dell Theory of Conflict Prevention which stipulates:

> No two countries that are both part of a major global supply
> chain, like Dell's, will ever fight a war against each other as

long as they are both part of the same global supply chain.
Because people embedded in major global supply chains
don't want to fight old-time wars anymore. They want to
make just-in-time deliveries of goods and services—and
enjoy the rising standards of living that come with that.

Similarly, the rising number of nations that are part of a major global
supply chain should bode well for peace.

3. The increasing destructiveness of war. Because it is cheaper to destroy
than create, advances in technology increase our ability to destroy. It is not
just that the price of weapons falls and that their destructive ability increases.
It is this combined with the fact that their targets, too, are worth more; the
cost of rebuilding a modern city today dwarfs the cost of rebuilding that city
fifty years ago. In the *Encyclopedia of Earthquakes and Volcanoes*, the authors
repeat an estimate of a cost of one trillion U.S. dollars to rebuild Tokyo if
it were hit by a major earthquake. One can only assume it would be substantially more if it were to be leveled with a nuclear device. This has to be a
serious deterrent to Japan (as an example).

This means that belligerents in war, who must always calculate both what
they might win in a war and what injury they might sustain, now face the
prospect of "winning" a worthless flattened territory and, in the process,
incurring financial damage of unimaginable degrees. Taken together, this
makes the financial consequences of large-scale war untenable. These trends
will continue into the foreseeable future. Imagine if every nation of the
world were as prosperous as Japan or Germany or the United States, which
will happen. Why risk it all and wage war?

During the Cold War, the peace was maintained based on a doctrine
called Mutually Assured Destruction, or MAD. The reasoning behind MAD
was that if we can annihilate the Soviets or the Chinese and they in turn can
annihilate us, then none of us will start a war. Preserving this mutual vulner-
ability was official U.S. policy.

I find MAD a disturbing strategy and see problems with it. It relies on the
enemy embracing several dubious beliefs: We will launch if they launch, they

cannot survive a first strike, they cannot secretly launch. It further assumes that non-state groups don't get nuclear weapons, that nuclear weapon facilities don't accidently launch, and that false-positive launch signals aren't generated. But at the time the doctrine was in force, MAD was effective (or at least, not proven ineffective). It was the basis for the movie *War Games,* in which the military's computer finally figures out it can't win in a nuclear launch scenario and says of such a war, "Strange game. The only winning move is not to play."

MAD is now back, but in economic form. I propose that peace will be maintained in the future by something I will call Mutually Assured Poverty, or MAP. MAP maintains that no matter who wins, when there is war, all parties are ultimately impoverished. This will become ever more unacceptable both to populations and politicians.

In the past, war could increase your financial position, both as a nation (through spoils) and a soldier (through plunder). Now neither is true. It is hard to see how all-out war turns a profit for anyone in any scenario. This unquestionably is good.

4. Rising prosperity of the poorest nations. The seventeenth-century Spanish writer Baltasar Gracián once offered this advice: "Never contend with a man who has nothing to lose." Impoverished nations and people have everything to gain and nothing to lose by engaging in war. Poverty leads to desperation, which in turn is a fertile ground for despots and autocrats who exploit the people for their own glory and megalomania. Think of how the worldwide depression of the 1930s helped fuel the rise of fascism in German, Italy, Spain, and a dozen other countries around the world. Poverty in sub-Saharan Africa is a contributing factor in any number of conflicts there.

As the poorest nations become wealthier, they, too, will grow less and less inclined toward war. Since the poorest nations will improve their financial conditions indefinitely, this is a long-term trend toward peace.

We are seeing hints of this already. More and more nations are developing a middle class that is interested in consumption, not war. According to a recent World Bank report:

information sector, the business owners have their financial interests firmly in the peace camp. They have no economic advantage in going to war. It is nothing but downside for them. The military doesn't buy their haircuts, website design, or piano lessons.

This is not to say that businesses are so materialistic they will favor a war to get a government contract. I don't believe that. What I am saying is that as more factors align toward peace, peace becomes ever more the better economic option.

Public opinion is ever more in the peace camp because the vast majority of the economy doesn't benefit financially in times of war. A very small slice of the economy does—that slice President Eisenhower termed the "military-industrial complex." However, I would argue the military-industrial complex doesn't want war either.

What?

I assume that virtually everyone working in defense industries believes they are serving their country and protecting freedom. But let's adopt the cynic's view for a moment and assume people in these corporations are chiefly concerned about their financial benefit, not about human suffering, when it comes to war. In that hypothetical situation, what would the defense contractor want?

He would want profit with certainty.

Imagine you are a defense contractor on top of the world. After a lot of work on your part, the U.S. government has standardized your widget, the C2000. You would argue that no other widget on the market can beat the C2000, no nation can ever gain widget superiority if the government just buys the C2000—and so they do. You get the contract. Yay! You can almost hear the champagne corks popping. Finally, you are making money hand over fist manufacturing the C2000.

Now, there is talk of war. Are you for it? Or against it?

If the nation stays at peace, you will still sell the C2000. Your contract goes on for years. You are already on top of the world, remember? Everything is great! Your massive effort to promote the adoption of the C2000 succeeded. If peace happens, all is well.

If the nation goes to war, the military would need more C2000s, right? That's certainly good for you; more C2000s means more profit. But now we have introduced uncertainty. The enemy has a widget too, the D2001. Might it be better? Who knows? Plus, if there is war, there are more competitors. More innovation. More new ideas. More . . . gasp . . . widget makers. (Not to mention the fact that, if the stuff all hits the fan, widget factories like yours would almost certainly be marked with bull's-eyes on the enemy's aerial bombing maps.)

Is this situation really preferable from a business standpoint? What would you choose? I, for one, would vote for peace.

Even if you don't accept this, try to accept that war is financially disadvantageous to 99 percent of the business owners in the country and that this is new and meaningful. It is yet another major disincentive to war—and we are only six items into our list! Does war stand a chance? I think not.

7. Increased world trade. Founding Father Thomas Paine frequently remarked how trade promotes peace. "In all my publications, where the matter would admit, I have been an advocate for commerce, because I am a friend to its effects," he once wrote. "It is a pacific system, operating to cordialize mankind, by rendering nations, as well as individuals, useful to each other."

Modern-day folk agree. Economics professors Solomon W. Polachek (State University of New York at Binghamton) and Carlos Seiglie (Rutgers University) wrote a paper entitled "Trade, Peace and Democracy: An Analysis of Dyadic Dispute." They compared historical data measuring conflict with data that measures trade. And they found "the overwhelming evidence indicates that trade reduces conflict regardless of the proxies used to capture the gains from trade and conflict." Further, by examining data on political interactions, they found "that trading nations cooperate more and fight less. A doubling of trade leads to a 20 percent diminution of belligerence."

To summarize: The world is witnessing increased trade among more trading partners. When partners trade more, they fight less. This promotes peace and deters war.

8. Intertwined world economy. As we just noted, when nations buy each other's goods, that promotes peace. But in addition, when nations trade, the underlying economies themselves grow ever more intertwined. Supply chains are spread across the world. If you manufacture something in Topeka, the parts to make it might come from Mexico or Honduras or Taiwan, and the parts used in those countries were probably sourced from other countries in turn. If you have a software company, you might employ programmers in India. If you are a masseuse, your massage oils might come from Indonesia.

This is simply another form of trade, so some might accuse me of double counting some of my forty-three reasons war will end. But the point really is different. In point #7, war would cost you your foreign customers. In this point, #8, it would cost you your domestic ones as well, because your ability to conduct business now relies on the intertwined world economy. Anything that creates a more intertwined world without compromising autonomy, self-rule, and self-determination is good for peace. The more I have a personal vested interest in your success, the better.

9. Intertwined worldwide financial systems. Centuries ago, North America saw a shortage of small coins, so large ones were cut into bits to circulate as small change. Because of this, "two bits" is still slang for twenty-five cents in the United States. In the modern age, money is once again represented by bits, but a different kind altogether: Money went from gold to paper and is now digital. Now we have an interlocked banking system that moves money around the world at light speed. Electronic transfers mean the money of a government, business, or individual might be anywhere at any time. My bank account has a "sweep" feature where every night the money is taken out of my account and loaned out for a few hours to banks halfway around the world where it is daytime. At the end of their day, the loan is repaid with a slight bit of interest. Arrangements like this are commonplace, although largely hidden from view.

In addition to that, many Americans own stock in other countries through their retirement savings. They might even own foreign currencies the same way. Huge numbers of foreigners own American stocks and debt instruments. The performance of non-U.S. stock markets are now routinely reported on American media, and not just the Tokyo and London exchanges. Large movements in any large foreign market are newsworthy.

When the Chinese revalue the yuan or the euro falls against the U.S. dollar, it is news that affects more and more people.

All this together means that our economic fates are more intertwined than ever. War at any scale would have disastrous implications for the economy based on this factor alone. Given that this financial infrastructure would be a legitimate military target in the event of conflict, the potential costs of war are incalculably high.

10. Increasing value stored in intangibles. It used to be that if you conquered another nation, your soldiers became looters and the military got to haul off everything of value in the country.

If you visit Rome and make your way to the Forum, nearby you will see the Arch of Titus. Erected almost 2,000 years ago, it features a carved panel showing the spoils of war being brought back from the conquest of Jerusalem. The arch not only celebrates this military victory, it points out that it was profitable.

Now, however, more and more wealth is tied up in intangibles such as intellectual property, patents, brands, media, and contracts. Try hauling those off.

In his book *Sonic Boom*, Gregg Easterbrook describes this shift well:

> As the transition toward knowledge-based economics makes ideas more valuable than physical resources, the incentive for war to seize resources declines. In the past, nations invaded other nations to seize the value of land or resources. Today it is more cost-effective to buy what you covet than to seize it, and so military spending and military adventurism are declining.

More wealth is digital, to be sure, but immeasurably more wealth is tied up in the intricacies of society itself. Think of a large city anywhere. Is the value of the city just the value of the buildings, cars, furniture, and other physical items in the city? No, no more than the value of your car is the value of the transmission plus the tires plus the seats. The value of the city is also in its ability to create wealth, foster commerce, and contribute to innovation. Its greatest value cannot be hauled off.

11. Asymmetry in warfare. In warfare, asymmetry is where something very small can do a huge amount of damage. The attacks on September 11, 2001, are the most obvious example of this, with catastrophic harm inflicted by nineteen men with box cutters and plane tickets.

Asymmetry is a mixed bag as far as the future goes. It is bad in that it allows a few to harm the many. Asymmetry will become more pronounced in the future, and we will either endure it, sacrifice individual liberty to prevent it, or come up with a new solution presently hidden from us.

That said, it also has its plus side. In the affairs of nations, large and powerful ones long have imposed their wills on the small and weak ones. If the weak nation will not willingly do the bidding of the strong one, then it is made to. And thus history books are written.

Asymmetry upsets this applecart. The weak can now do substantial harm to the strong. They cannot destroy the strong, but they can inflict significant damage.

The relationship between large and small nations has been like that between the playground bully and the small kid. In one sense, it's a peaceful world: The bully insists on the lunch money of the small kid, who has no recourse but to capitulate. The benefits of asymmetry happen when the small kid gets a Taser. The bully will now be more inclined to leave the kid alone. When might no longer makes right for the strong, they think twice about preying on the weak.

Roughly a quarter of the way through our list of factors that will end war, we have reached the end of the economic ones. To summarize: In a world of plenty, war would bring economic ruin and uncertain results, and would benefit virtually no one. We will avoid war because it is unprofitable; and while that is not a moral reason, any reason that brings peace is fine by me.

Thomas Jefferson once reflected that in the past, war sometimes had been avoided "from a due sense of the miseries, and the demoralization it produces, and of the superior blessings of a state of peace and friendship with all mankind." As true as that was in Jefferson's time, our age has amplified all of it: both the miseries war can produce and the blessings peace can produce.

* * *

Now, let's move on to the political factors that will cause war to cease.

12. The end of monarchies. Monarchies—the most prevalent form of government in human history—are disproportionately warlike for a number of reasons.

First, the king doesn't answer to people and therefore is not required to take their well-being into account when deciding whether to wage war. Second, monarchs themselves often have only a financial risk in war. In the event of a loss, they may be forced to pay tribute to the victor or give up territory, but they seldom suffer physical harm, as Charles V of France noted when he rhetorically asked, "Name me an emperor who was ever struck by a cannonball."

Third, in the past, kings regarded warfare as a form of competition in which they could test their mettle against other monarchs, in much the same fashion as the aforementioned ambitious men who longed for battle. (Of course, when a king proves himself through battle, he is not risking his life but the lives of thousands of his subjects. To him, it is a chess game, not personal combat.)

Fourth, monarchs have regarded war as a legitimate means to expand their tax base, which historically they used to enlarge their armies, which were then used to wage war to expand their tax base, which they then used to enlarge their armies, ad infinitum.

Today, monarchies have vanished from much of the world, except as tabloid fodder and tourist attractions. Notable examples exist, but the flow of history in this regard has rendered its verdict. Monarchies with any real, significant power are just waiting out the clock.

13. The end of dictators. While kings claimed they ruled by a divine right, dictators claimed their right to rule through might. For many of the same reasons as monarchies, dictatorships are inherently warlike.

Like kings, dictators have little regard for their subjects. They view individual liberty as a threat, new political ideas as subversion, and political opposition as treason. The way they secure their positions is through the ruthless application of violence. Because this is the only power they know, it is the only power they respect. Weakness in neighbors is regarded as an opportunity for conquest or, at least, coercion. They wage war because it is the only language they speak. Even a dictator's own citizenry is often viewed by the dictator as the enemy, each citizen a potential claimant and usurper. Anything but slavish adoration from the population results in retribution.

Dictators, in short, are the scourge of the earth. Or, they were the scourge of the earth. The number of dictatorships is falling. As I write this, the three most recent examples are the end of the twenty-three-year reign of Zine El Abidine Ben Ali in Tunisia, the thirty-year reign of Hosni Mubarak in Egypt, and the forty-two-year reign of Moammar Gadhafi in Libya. By the time you read these words, others may well have been toppled.

14. The rise of democracy as the most common form of national government. Not only are we eliminating historically warlike forms of government, we are replacing them with peaceful ones, namely democracy. As Gregg Easterbrook notes in *Sonic Boom*, "A generation ago, according to United Nations figures, only one third of the world's nations held true multiparty elections; today 80 percent do, and the proportion continues to rise. Many nations have in recent years converted from despotism or autocracy to at least some halting form of democracy, while there is scant movement in the opposite direction." Ted Turner echoes this. He said he believes the world is experiencing a "new dawn of an age of enlightenment, where war is becoming a thing of the past. Democracy and free enterprise are winning out all over the world. . . . Things are really looking up."

From the 1970s to the present day, the "Democratic Peace Theory" has been debated. The theory is that democracies do not go to war with other democracies. If you think about it, it is hard to come up with an exception. In World War II, the United States went to war with Germany, Italy, and Japan, a trio of undemocratic countries. Recent U.S. military activities are also aimed at non-democratic regimes such as Iraq, Libya, and Afghanistan. Wrinkles develop over who exactly is a democracy and what exactly constitutes war. But all in all, the theory seems to hold.

What underlying mechanisms would make the Democratic Peace Theory "work"? Some say it is because democracies are richer than other countries and thus have more to lose in war. Others say that democracy itself is a system of compromise and opposing viewpoints, so politicians trained in that system will conduct world affairs in the same fashion—that is, treating potentially belligerent nations as they would treat members of an opposing political party and seeking to negotiate, not destroy. Still others say that democratic leaders answer to populations that generally oppose war and conduct themselves so as to win reelection; or that democracies see other democracies as allies and non-democracies as threats, so they only wage war against the latter.

No matter why the theory works, it is good for the world that it does. The world is rushing toward democracy at a pace that can fairly be described as "breakneck" when viewed across the span of history. It is unprecedented for so many nations to change their form of government so quickly and peacefully.

15. The decline of military alliances and the rise of economic ones.
Some chapters back, I discussed the assassination of Archduke Franz Ferdinand, heir to the Austro-Hungarian throne, by Gavrilo Princip, a Serbian nationalist. This led to Austria-Hungary declaring war on Serbia on July 28, 1914. That should have been the end of it, right? One country angry at another one.

Alas, no. Russia, obligated by treaty to defend Serbia, mobilized its army. Germany, an ally of Austria-Hungary, was obligated by treaty to defend it. Germany viewed the Russian mobilization as an act of war and therefore declared war on Russia. France, bound by treaty to Russia, declared war on Germany and Austria-Hungary. Great Britain, bound by treaty to France, declared war on Germany and Austria-Hungary.

Between Austria-Hungary declaring war on Serbia and all the treaty partners entering the fray, how many days passed? Seven. It took one week for a localized event to escalate to world war.

With Britain in the war, its colonies and dominions joined in as well. This included Canada, Australia, New Zealand, and South Africa. By the end of the month, Japan, bound by treaty with Great Britain, declared war on Germany. The Japanese soldiers who battled the German soldiers must have wondered why they were fighting. In fact, virtually everyone should have wondered why he was fighting soldiers from places he couldn't find on a map.

It all happened because of military pacts in which an attack on one party was viewed as an attack on all. Back in the 1600s, French mathematician Blaise Pascal complained, "Can anything be more ridiculous than that a man has a right to kill me . . . because his ruler has quarrel with mine, although I have none with him?" Yet by the time of World War I, things were much worse: The whole world had to go to war because a Serbian shot an Austrian.

This is not the dynamic of our world today. Military alliances do not rigidly control world politics, in part because military competition has been replaced by economic competition. Economic alliances hold benefit for countries that military alliances don't: They remove barriers, more than erecting them, and an alliance with one nation doesn't preclude striking the same agreement with others. In other words, even if Country X and Country Y sign a free-trade agreement, either (or both) can still pursue such an agreement with Country Z as well. In military alliances, however, it is much likelier that when nations choose their friends, they create enemies where there were none before.

What about alliances like NATO, the security alliance of North American and European nations created by a 1949 treaty—how does it fit this thesis of mine? If NATO didn't exist today, no one would propose creating it. It is a relic of a different age. Almost three-quarters of all defense spending occurs within NATO countries, meaning the alliance is largely the only military show in town. Unless one can somehow imagine NATO countries going to war with each other, such as Belgium invading the United Kingdom, it is hard to see how "world wars" could escalate outside of NATO member countries. If NATO is responsible for the bulk of the world's military spending and NATO no longer has the stomach for full-on war with modern states, then large-scale war seems less likely.

We could go on here and talk about other military powers and alliances, but the simple fact is that large countries are less willing to risk war in defense of small ones. This has come about as we have left a polarized world behind us and the importance of military alliances has fallen.

16. The increased economic viability of smaller countries. After World War I, as the Ottoman Empire collapsed, several new countries emerged. These countries, particularly in the Balkans, were often small and tended toward war. The term Balkanization was thus created to refer to the division of an area into smaller and smaller hostile forces.

And yet over the last century, we also have seen colonies gain their independence and become nations, and nations peaceably divide. Fifteen new nations formed as the Soviet Union dissolved; Czechoslovakia split into the Czech Republic and Slovakia, and Sudan into North Sudan and South Sudan.

So while conventional wisdom once held that a greater number of small political units will result in more war, I am not sure this is the case in the modern world. Today's independence movements arise when a group of people within a nation wish to politically separate in order to form a state that better represents their shared values. This is exactly the sort of thinking that makes nation-states useful. People can come together and choose a form of government suitable to them. These newly formed states are not inherently hostile toward their neighbors; nor are they arbitrary states created in the past for political reasons by drawing straight lines on a globe. Those countries consisted of a citizenry bound by neither culture nor tradition, and that caused problems.

In the modern age, the size a country must be to be viable is quite small. The fact that small nations can adopt standard treaties, laws, currencies, and international practices of larger countries means that a small economic unit can be viable. Tiny countries willing to engage in free trade with their neighbors can prosper. Consider Liechtenstein, whose 35,000 residents live in about sixty square miles in Europe in the Alps. It has one of the highest per-capita incomes in the world, almost no crime, and no public or foreign debt. It has no military and is strictly neutral. It is a completely viable state, with a ski museum and a McDonald's. It stays small by avoiding bureaucracy, being represented by Switzerland in embassies around the world, and using Swiss currency and visas. It has no border guards, only a sign identifying when one has entered Liechtenstein.

I am not saying the world would be better if every country was the size of Liechtenstein. I am saying that for small nations to be economically and politically viable is good news for peace. It means that when groups within countries are discontent and prone to civil war or rebellion, a new opportunity is now on the table. Thus the largely Islamic northern Sudan and the largely Christian southern Sudan were able to decide to part company and form two separate nations. Even if these new states turn out not to be peaceful, their size probably will mean the conflict is limited, and the decline in military alliances means the conflict is less likely to entangle others and escalate.

17. Formalized agreements on conventions, measurements, borders, and international conduct. Consider the Treaty of Paris, 1783, that ended the American Revolution and resulted in Great Britain recognizing the United States. In the treaty, language describing the border between the United States and Canada, still part of Great Britain, included this:

> From the northwest angle of Nova Scotia, viz., that angle which is formed by a line drawn due north from the source of St. Croix River to the highlands; along the said highlands which divide those rivers that empty themselves into the river St. Lawrence . . .

The tricky part is the bit about the highlands, or mountains. There are no mountains between the Atlantic Ocean and the St. Lawrence river. Hmmmm. What to do . . .

Once this became known, the question was submitted for arbitration to the king of the Netherlands, who ruled the St. John River to be the border. This was fine with Great Britain but not with Maine. They expected the king to choose one border or another, not create his own compromise border. Tensions mounted all through the 1830s as militias were raised on both sides in what later came to be known as the Aroostook War, even though there was never actually a war or casualties. The border issue was finally resolved by the Webster-Ashburton treaty of 1842.

While this story had a happy ending in that bloodshed was avoided, thousands of similar disputes haven't ended so well. When countries do not agree on borders, laws, property rights, copyright, access to waterways, legal representation, and a thousand other issues, wars break out. What may have been an innocent mistake often is interpreted as a deliberate transgression.

Slowly but steadily, as part of the growth of civilization, countries are signing treaties and reaching agreements that spell out in detail the common set of rules those nations will abide by. As the number of touch points with other countries rises, so must our shared understanding of acceptable conduct. Is it okay to dump nuclear waste in the ocean? If someone writes a book in one country, does another country enforce the copyright within its borders? What about extradition, if a citizen of one country visits another and breaks the local law? How will food be labeled? These and literally thousands more issues are worked out in treaties and agreements between nations.

While diplomats create treaties, technologists help with their enforcement. A handheld GPS unit can settle any well-defined border issue. Satellite photos can uncover those who would transgress the rules. Ever more accurate sensors can track the contents of ocean water or assess food safety.

These treaties are good. They reduce uncertainty in international affairs, which can be dangerous and counter to free trade. Voluntary acceptance of shared practices is not a surrender of autonomy. It is a willing agreement to a set of values and procedures, and a standard of conduct. By making expectations explicit and public, these agreements reduce the number of sparks that can set off the powder keg of war.

18. Increasing rates of distrust of government. Governments are given the power to tax and wage war, two fearsome powers that can do grave harm to the world when placed in the wrong hands. With these powers should come enormous checks and balances on their use.

To greater and lesser degrees through history, citizens have trusted that their government officials will act in their best interests, not lie to them, and generally conduct themselves in an honorable fashion. However, we have come to realize those standards are not always met: Regardless of your nation, you probably have been bitterly disappointed at some point by the conduct of some government leader.

Would I like to feel I could trust my government to behave with integrity and always tell me the truth? Of course. But when my government proposes to wage war, it's less important that I trust them than that I ask hard, skeptical questions. The demise of war will be hastened when every impulse to war is regarded, at least initially, with a healthy measure of distrust.

19. Non-violence as a successful political tactic. As discussed in the chapter on civilization, non-violence as a tactic for societal change is growing. This can happen because empathy is growing and the price of mass communication is falling.

In the past, a weak group unjustly persecuted by a strong group had few options. The weak group could fight and lose, or comply with whatever the strong group demanded. Now there is a third way: The weak group can chronicle its persecution, draw attention to its plight, and essentially generate such public outcry and support that the persecutors grow tired of being condemned. It sounds like a crazy tactic, but it works, and it works increasingly well.

20. The rise of public opinion as the most powerful political force in the world.

What does the end of war have to do with smoking, drunk driving, and racism?

There was a time, not so long ago, when almost everyone smoked. Every part of every restaurant was a smoking section. Cigarettes were advertised on TV and in magazines and their packages carried no warnings. Movie stars smoked and it was so cool! James Dean is locked in our minds with a cigarette. All this seemed perfectly normal.

Then slowly, over time, things changed. A few airline flights went non-smoking. Restaurants established a "smoking section," then some bold ones banned smoking altogether. Next, entire cities banned smoking in all indoor public places; contending a private business's right to allow smoking was trumped by the dangers of exposing patrons to secondhand smoke. Now, in most places you can smoke in your car, in your home, and in remote places away from civilized people. Smokers have been both shamed and shunned, and their chief remaining right is the right to pay taxes of more than 100 percent on their cigarettes. Tobacco companies were well-funded opponents of smoking bans, while their proponents had little money and no profit motive for promoting them. Yet laws and culture changed dramatically.

Now, to drunk driving. In a fine Alfred Hitchcock movie called *Notorious*, the troubled character played by Ingrid Bergman gets very drunk at a party and asks Cary Grant to come for a drive. Slurring her words, she says, "I'm, I'm gonna drive. That's, that's understood." And drive she does! She swerves off the road and narrowly averts collisions. Seeing Cary Grant smiling at her, she asserts she will wipe the smile off his face by accelerating to 80 mph—and then does. Under Hollywood's production code at the time, movies could not include nudity, criminal activity, or offensive language, or depict illegal drug use, venereal disease, or childbirth. But having your starlet drive 80 mph whilst liquored up, well, that was fine.

MADD would not have been amused. Until the formation of Mothers Against Drunk Driving in 1980, the blood alcohol content level that constituted driving while intoxicated was 0.15, and in some places 0.20. Through the efforts of MADD and kindred groups, the legal definition was reduced to 0.10 and then 0.08 (or as low as 0.01 for drivers under twenty-one). We criminalized driving while intoxicated, increased the penalties, and broadened the definition, all with substantial public support—and all in a short amount of time. It was a huge shift in public opinion in which no group benefited financially; if anything, financial interests were aligned against this change, just as with tobacco.

Finally, racism. We all recognize the dramatic degree to which racism has been stigmatized. Many people alive today were adults when signs that said "Whites Only" were common. Now we have completely stigmatized racism, and a formerly common racial slur is one of the most unprintable words in the English language.

All these are profound shifts in public opinion. It isn't that one generation died out and another one emerged with new beliefs. These changes occurred in a single lifetime, which meant people changed their minds.

Why do I recount these stories? We need to stigmatize war in the same fashion. As Alfred Einstein once observed, "Nothing will end war unless the people themselves refuse to go to war."

It will be difficult. While the right thing to do is never to drive drunk, be a smoker, or be a racist, occasionally war is the right thing to do. The day after the Japanese bombed Pearl Harbor, civilization had to be defended.

But war is seldom the answer. We choose it much more often than we should. However, if it were stigmatized, and public opinion dramatically and pervasively changed, that would force policy change. Thanks to the burgeoning of technology and social media, public opinion is the most powerful political force in the world today. It can be a jumble of voices: politicians and corporations, celebrities, religious figures, and opinion leaders, a million conversations in a single room. But maybe as a civilization, we have to talk out loud to figure out where we stand, to make progress.

Some might argue this is not in and of itself a force for peace. After all, public opinion may just as easily be stirred up in favor of war as against it. I don't think this is likely, though. Given all the other points that tend to set the population against war in general, it will become increasingly difficult to sell wars to populations, especially when governments don't have any sort of monopoly on information and reporting.

President Eisenhower said it best: "I think that people want peace so much that one of these days, government had better get out of their way and let them have it."

* * *

Well, here we are, not quite halfway through our list of ways the Internet, technology, and civilization will come together to end war. Having covered the financial and political factors, let's look at thirteen ways communication and information will help bring about war's demise.

21. Better communication. Pause, just for a moment, and consider how profound a force for peace this is: to be able to communicate with anyone, anywhere, instantly. From the mobile revolution to satellite phones to FedEx to Skype, we can communicate effortlessly.

Poor communication leads to war. This is so widely recognized that in June 1963, the United States and the Soviet Union signed the "Memorandum of Understanding Regarding the Establishment of a Direct Communications Line" which led to the installation of the famous red hotline. This was done in large part because the two powers came so close to going to war over the Cuban Missile Crisis. It was used in 1967 for the first time during the six-day Egypt-Israel War, when Soviet and U.S. officials kept each other informed of their actions relating to this conflict, lest anything be misinterpreted by the other party.

President Kennedy, speaking at a 1962 press conference broadcast live across the ocean using the first communications satellite, refers to the Telstar satellite and its implications:

> This satellite must be high enough to carry messages from both sides of the world, which is, of course, a very central requirement for peace, and I think this understanding, which will inevitably come from the speedier communications, is bound to increase the well-being and security of all people—here and those across the oceans.

History is full of wars started over misunderstandings, wars that could easily have been averted, and battles fought after hostilities were to have been ended by treaty. Two examples: the Battle of New Orleans, fought after the treaty ending the War of 1812 was signed; and the Battle of Palmito Ranch, fought a month after the Civil War ended.

In the absence of efficient communication, potential belligerents are left to impute the worst possible motives to the unexplained actions of others. Better communication is a huge step toward peace.

22. E-mail. In addition to communications in general, I include e-mail as a stand-alone force for peace for a number of reasons. First, e-mail causes people to communicate more, so it increases overall understanding. Second, being both free and global, it shrinks the world and allows for international connections to increase. If violence erupts in, say, Turkey, all the millions of people around the world who know someone in Turkey e-mail those contacts and ask for information. This is a highly accessible form of distributed news reporting, and causes all those people to be more personally vested in the information and outcome. This is starkly different than if violence breaks out in a distant, unreal place where the only flow of information is from official sources. Third, e-mail makes so many people accessible that wouldn't be otherwise. Whereas phone numbers are often unlisted and guarded, e-mail addresses are frequently public. People who would not take time to write their congressman or a news outlet will easily e-mail them instead.

23. The World Wide Web. The World Wide Web will play an enormous role in ending war, on several levels.

First, the web promotes access to information, a huge force for peace. Think of what the web is packed with: books, reports, eyewitness accounts, press releases, manifestos, maps, opinions, analysis, transcripts, debates, histories, contracts, encyclopedias, and so much more.

Second, in addition to facts, the web has become the face of almost all organizations of the planet. Whether you are the NRA, the CIA, IBM, or the Asian Dawn, you are what you put on your home page. When everyone, and every nation, and every organization, and every movement all have a presence on the web, they can be understood in terms of it. It gives everyone a chance to make her case and be heard. It is the ultimate manifestation of the marketplace of ideas; the more people who proffer their ideas to the world, the better the outcome will be for us all. Plus it promotes empathy, the ability to see the other guy's viewpoint. That is never bad.

Third, the web acts as a feedback loop in that it allows all people to say what is on their minds. Very seldom is that, "I should go to war to force others to my will." Public opinion is a powerful force, and if it is generally a force for peace, then the web magnifies it.

The web is a force for truth, connectedness, understanding, and communication—all things whose absence can trigger war.

24. Twitter. I include Twitter in this list as a larger idea, not only as the literal Twitter.com. And yet, Twitter.com is pretty important. The idea is the power of short, instant messages broadcast to interested crowds. Twitter.com is unquestionably the most efficient way in the history of humanity to send a single idea, invitation, complaint, or observation to the world.

Despite being the most efficient method ever, it is still highly inefficient, and this inefficiency inspires hope. It is inefficient because I must know to follow people in order to receive their updates, and that knowing spreads haphazardly. I have no doubt there are all kinds of things in the Twitterverse that I want to know about, but I only find the ones that I first knew to look for.

Twitter already has saved lives, toppled dictatorships, and silenced its numerous critics whose basic argument was "because I don't understand this, it must be irrelevant." It is an altogether new concept that meets a need we didn't even know existed. Twitter is profound, and it unquestionably furthers peace because it promotes the interests of the many against the interests of the few. While the few may be for war, the many are almost always for peace.

25. Facebook. How can I not include Facebook as a force for peace? After all, it has connected hundreds of millions of people and shows no sign of stopping until everyone is connected. Before it is all over, the number of Facebook accounts will exceed the number of people on the planet. Everyone will be on Facebook, as will be every business, every idea, every brand, and all the people who were once members but have since passed away.

Already, we get a glimpse of what is to come. It is the "weak ties," our informal connections with other people, that are most influential because there are so many of them and their connections are so diverse. Our "strong ties"—family, close friends, and the like—we can always count on, but they are relatively few. Facebook expands your number of weak ties. More precisely, it catalogues and tracks them and then allows you to communicate with them easily.

Most Facebook users have people of other ethnicities and national origin as Facebook friends. They may not bump into them very often in what we call "everyday life" but do know them well enough to friend them. Thus one's Facebook friends may be more diverse in all sorts of ways than one's "actual" friends. Facebook has reduced the famous six degrees of separation down to even fewer.

We tend to regard information that comes to us through our friend network as more authentic and reliable than information we receive from traditional media. For instance, if you have a Facebook friend Abigail in Albania whom you only met once at a rock-paper-scissors competition years ago, you will generally regard Abigail's first-hand account as authoritative, even though you don't really know Abigail all that well.

Also, simply having a Facebook friend in Albania will tend to make you more interested in the events of Albania. And through this, peace is promoted. Seldom will one decide that war with a friend's nation is the only recourse.

This is not a particularly new idea, similar to the phenomenon of getting to know and care about "pen pals" in far-flung places by exchanging postal-mail letters. Organizations have encouraged "pen pals for peace" exchanges—but such efforts tend to be limited in scale, and if there is one thing Facebook has, it is scale.

26. FactCheck.org and Snopes.com. It is ever harder for politicians to trick people. Consider this, from Thomas Friedman's book *The Lexus and the Olive Tree*:

> There is a story that in the 1980s, the Soviets once ran a picture in *Pravda* illustrating bread lines in America. Upon closer examination, it turned out that the picture was of a group of people in Manhattan waiting in line for Zabar's Bakery and Delicatessen to open on a Saturday morning.

Friedman goes on to point out that almost anywhere in the world today, it would be impossible to get away with this fraud. Within minutes, your propagandist subterfuge would be revealed and your credibility (if you still had any) undermined.

I mention FactCheck and Snopes as two examples of the many enterprises on the Internet that subject every government utterance to scrutiny in something approximating real time. Governments in the past could lie with impunity. Publishing was expensive, and by the time news of the lie came out, days or weeks had passed. This is no longer the case.

The system we have is not perfect, but it is highly distributed and bottom up. This is unquestionably good. No one has the monopoly on truth. If there were one final source that everyone looked to and regarded as true, then that source might become corrupt or simply wrong. In the Internet age, everyone fact checks everyone else. And while there is a lot of noise, weak analysis, and incorrect information, the truth can be found. And truth is a force for peace.

27. Alternative sources of information. I realize in these pages I must seem very distrustful of government, but it is not really true. Government is a great achievement of civilization. It helps us bring about our social ideals. It is necessary to protect life, liberty, and property. However, practically speaking, it sometimes has a corrupting influence on those whom it empowers to act for the state. If this happens, the government becomes an agent that works against the very ideals it purports to protect. Frequently, this includes individual liberty and freedom of expression.

Practically speaking, governments often act as if their first duty is to protect the government, not the people. To those in power, this has a certain perverse logic: After all, without the government to protect the rights of the people, those rights would crumble. Thus, governments are very sensitive to criticism and to challenges to their authority.

To government officials, freedom of speech and assembly can be somewhat threatening. Free elections can be threatening as well, literally to their livelihoods. News and information that undermine their credibility or authority aren't so welcome either. Therefore, governments have a tendency to . . . let us be gracious . . . filter the news. (Were we ungracious, we might say they "lie through their jackal teeth to protect their worthless hides.")

Whatever level of graciousness you can summon at this moment, we can all be grateful for the presence of alternative sources of information. If you are in government and these alternative sources of news conform to your understanding of reality, you can be that much more confident you are on the side of right. But if these other news outlets contradict the official account, then all the better. In the sorting through of the facts from a multiplicity of new sources, truth can be determined.

More information leads to more peace, unless you want to argue that ignorance is more peaceful.

Even in autocratic regimes, truth has a way of seeping in—which means today's dwindling crop of dictators has a serious problem. They need the Internet, mobile phones, computers, and the other accoutrements of the modern age for the wealth they bring. But along with wealth, these technologies bring information and thereby sow the seeds of their undoing. Dictators may think they can control information access and technology. But by giving their citizens the means to converse, dictators have enabled them to converse subversively, to learn truths that official sources had hidden from them, and to check every statement of every ruler. And this is a force for peace.

28. More official information transparency. In his autobiography *Man of the House,* former U.S. House Speaker Tip O'Neill wrote about how the government funded the Manhattan Project to build the atomic bomb. Because the project had to remain top secret, government officials went to different federal entities and told them they were giving them extra money in their budgets but would need it back for a secret project. O'Neill observed that scrutiny of government had become so intense that officials never could have gotten away with that—and he was writing in the late 1980s. Fast-forward a couple of decades, and the Internet has done vastly more than O'Neill could have imagined to promote open information about government. *Everything* is up for scrutiny.

In O'Neill's day, getting a copy of the federal budget meant writing away and buying a hefty paper copy. You still can buy it from the government's bookstore; a recent one ran about two thousand pages and cost about $200.

Or, you can download it for free. And that's just the beginning of what's on U.S. government websites. There are Congressional records, hearings, court rulings, patent applications, declassified intelligence reports, and the copious regulations that government agencies churn out. There are meaty websites with vast amounts of information from the EPA, CIA, SEC, FCC, FDIC, National Labor Relations Board, Office of Government Ethics, U.S. Census Bureau, the Postal Rate Commission, and even the Advisory Council on Historic Preservation. There are sites like Challenge.gov where the government offers prizes for solutions to problems it faces, such as how to drop humanitarian aid into cities without it damaging anything or hurting anyone. The National Security Agency even has a website with a section called CryptoKids for "America's Future Codemakers & Codebreakers."

Other nations are becoming more transparent as well. Of course, this does not include many of the nations that are considered the most repressive in the world. But a sizable number are attempting this, and the direction the world is heading is obvious. In an article in *The Economic Times*, a British cabinet office minister said that the United Kingdom government "is determined to have the most ambitious open data agenda of any government in the world . . . in order to create public accountability and efficiency in our services and to drive economic and social growth."

Secrecy, while occasionally necessary, is less desirable than openness. Free and peaceful societies function best when government is transparent and open.

29. The mobile revolution. The International Telecommunication Union estimated that by the end of 2010, there were 5.3 billion mobile subscriptions around the world, and the number was up several hundred million from 2009.

According to Portio Research, 7.8 trillion SMS messages were sent in 2011, and it is expected that 2012's number will come in at ten trillion. That would average over three SMS messages per day per person on the planet.

Strategy Analytics estimates over half a billion users browsed the web on their mobile devices in 2009 and expects a billion to do so by 2015.

One can argue the mobile revolution doesn't promote peace in that it magnifies civil disobedience. I'll accept that. But if the argument is that people demonstrating for free elections or civil liberties or other forms of rights is bad, then that is simply siding with the tyrant against the people.

As you may have noticed, I am fond of quoting the Founding Fathers of the United States. They were men of ideas who were forced by circumstance to become soldiers. They were not, for the most part, military men.

Their revolution was not made up of a bunch of hotheads with torches and pitchforks. They were political theorists, and arguably some of the best the world has ever known, if the success of the United States, both in civil liberty and financial wealth, is any measure. Thus I find their thinking on such matters as tyrants and kings and liberty and democracy illuminating. So, I will quote from the Declaration of Independence again:

> But when a long train of abuses and usurpations, pursuing invariably the same object evinces a design to reduce them under absolute despotism, it is their right, it is their duty, to throw off such government, and to provide new guards for their future security.

Linger over that phrase: "It is their duty, to throw off such government." The mobile revolution empowers the populous, to the detriment of the rulers, and so it might be argued that it promotes violence and thus civil wars. But what the mobile revolution ultimately does is promote individual liberty, freedom of speech, and accountable government—all of which promote peace.

It is a roundabout argument to be sure, but essentially the mobile revolution allows people to band together and eventually bring down tyrants.

In free societies, the ballot box and free press serve this purpose. In places where the government interferes with such rights, the mobile revolution provides a Plan B. Organize from the bottom up, pass information from person to person, and protest without stopping. Repeat until things change. This was the strategy in Tehran, Tunisia, Cairo, Syria, Jordan, Morocco, Oman, Lebanon, and Kuwait. We have seen it most recently and most profoundly in the Arab Spring, where the motto we see again and again is *Ash-sha`b yurid isqat an-nizam*, or "The people want to bring down the regime."

Some argue, "Be careful what you ask for. These new governments may not be friends of liberty." But if that is the case, they will fall in due course. History has rendered its judgment on such matters. Autocrats can hold power indefinitely if they control the media, the military, business, the money, and information. When they can't, they are deposed. People want to be free. Is there any more fundamental truth? Free people establish governments to protect their rights. Those rights lead to prosperity and security, and wars serve no use. We don't have this world today because we have much scarcity, much poverty, poor infrastructure, bad information, and all the other contributing factors of war that history is discarding.

30. Tiny, cheap digital cameras on cell phones and everywhere. Maybe you don't think this deserves its own point. Sure, it isn't as big a force as Democratic Peace Theory or Mutually Assured Poverty. But it is worth noting.

Around the world, more than a billion mobile devices that both take and send photographs are currently in use, spread even to the poorest parts of the globe. We saw the results of this in the 2009 Iranian protests, when these devices captured and relayed powerful, real-time images of events. In point #29, we described how peace is served when mobile devices allow people to organize and communicate in a widely distributed fashion. I add this point because the images from this mobile revolution represent a force all their own.

The vast majority of new phones have cameras. In just a few years, virtually all phones will be camera phones. And while the cameras have been of poor quality in the past, now more people are relying solely on their cell phones as their cameras, and the quality is rising. (This trend is so pronounced that it is having a negative effect on the sale of cameras.)

All of this means examples of atrocities by the government or by the mob are increasingly likely to be documented and publicized. As Supreme Court Justice Louis Brandeis wrote a century ago, "Sunlight is said to be the best of disinfectants." By throwing light on barbaric and provocative actions, we may stop their spread before they can escalate to broader conflict. This is good.

31. "Internet in a suitcase" and the "shadow Internet." The Internet is still able to be "turned off" by despotic rulers. This happened in Egypt and

Libya and is sure to become a common tactic of dictators and autocrats. In response, efforts are under way around the world to create an Internet that cannot be turned off. Two interesting government programs are under way in the United States, according to a June 2011 article in the *New York Times*. "The Obama administration is leading a global effort to deploy 'shadow' Internet and mobile phone systems that dissidents can use to undermine repressive governments that seek to silence them by censoring or shutting down telecommunications networks. The effort includes secretive projects to create independent cellphone networks inside foreign countries," the paper reported.

The article also describes a second project where "a group of young entrepreneurs who look as if they could be in a garage band are fitting deceptively innocent-looking hardware into a prototype 'Internet in a suitcase.' Financed with a $2 million State Department grant, the suitcase could be secreted across a border and quickly set up to allow wireless communication over a wide area with a link to the global Internet."

Enabling people to communicate in a method with which their governments cannot interfere is a force for freedom and peace. While in the short term such systems might fan civil unrest and spark government reprisals, ultimately they would lead to more accountability by governments and more transparency. In the end, this means more peace.

32. The end of language barriers. I am not going to make many friends with this point, but here goes: At some point in the future, there will be only one language. It will be English, although not really the English we speak today. All other languages will pass from daily use. I know this is a controversial forecast, and to many people a very depressing one, but I think it is both inevitable and good.

Imagine if the reverse were true. Imagine if today everyone spoke one language and I said that in the future we will speak hundreds of different languages and not be able to understand each other. Would you regard this as good? I doubt it.

Everyone in the future will learn English because it will be the language of the Internet and thus the language of the world and commerce. To be successful in the world, for a while both English and one's native tongue will be requirements. But learning two languages comes at a cost. And if everyone you know speaks English and it is the language of the world, commerce, the Internet, and success, what will be the primary language you teach your children? English. Their "native language" will become their second language. Then it will slowly die out.

Long before English became the *lingua franca* of the Internet age, the world has wanted a common language. In the ancient world, it was Greek in the European arena. Then Latin became somewhat universal, from a Western viewpoint, as Rome's reach spread. French became the language of diplomacy and international affairs. But English seems to have taken hold, thanks to the Internet. More people speak some English than any other language. More people are learning English in China than there are people who speak it in the United States. It is already the official language in more than fifty countries spread across every continent. These nations will play a substantial role in shaping this new English, as they bring grammatical structure, idioms, and nuanced words from their native tongue. As the number of words in regular usage expands, other terms will fall into disuse, the language will slowly morph, and the earth will have a mother tongue, Germanic in origin, which derived its name from its earliest speakers, the Angles who called their homeland "Angeln."

"While English is not spoken as a native language by the largest number of people, it is the most worldwide in its distribution," according to anthropologist Dr. Dennis O'Neil. "It has become the second language of choice in most countries. About one-fourth to one-third of humanity now understand and speak it to some degree." The converse, O'Neil writes, is that "as many as one-half of the languages in the world are no longer spoken by children. This is a major step in the direction of language and cultural extinction. The languages that are becoming extinct are not doing so because they are 'primitive' or unable to allow adequate communication. They are dying because their speakers find it more useful to speak other languages."

Philologists and lovers of language everywhere will shake their fists at me for predicting and even preferring such a thing. But a preference for obscure tongues is a sentimentality, divorced from the reality that economic opportunities that come with speaking English, the world language, out-weigh the intangible benefits of linguistic diversity.

I don't think local customs and national characteristics will go away. Nations will maintain their own traditions, holidays, music, idioms, diets, and a thousand things that make them different from other nations. But language? Keeping that one comes at a large financial price: Learn proficiency at two languages or remain separate from the world economy.

Before you despair at this, consider how it will contribute to peace. Wars have often been the result of misunderstandings brought about by language. It is easy to be suspicious of the person who speaks in some strange tongue. During World War I in the United States, fourteen states outlawed speaking German. In Montana, where 10 percent of residents spoke German and another 10 percent were of German descent, ministers weren't allowed to preach in German to congregants who understood no English, and one town publicly burned German textbooks, the *Bozeman Daily Chronicle* reported.

I mention these reprehensible actions to illustrate how language can divide us. Honestly, if we all spoke the same language today, would you want to change that? In the future, we will need no translators, because we will understand each other. (If I am wrong in projecting that English will be *the* world language, it will unquestionably be spoken by a global majority in the future, and thus we will be that much better at understanding each other.)

If it is any comfort, languages won't truly be dead. Computers will be able to reproduce them at will and hobbyists will still study them. They will simply disappear from daily use. As difficult as it might be to "let go," this is good for peace.

33. More people coming online. It seems fitting to end this part of the list—ways that information and communication will help end war—by noting that every day, every moment, more and more people have access to the Internet.

In 2000, Africa had fewer than five million Internet users. Today, there are more than one hundred million. In Central and South America in 2000 were eighteen million Internet users; today, more than two hundred million.

In 2006, roughly a billion people had access to the Internet. As of the end of 2012, the Internet has more than two billion users. By 2020, it is estimated that five billion people will be online, representing two-thirds the population of the planet.

Every other metric is still climbing: data throughput, mobile phone usage, messages sent, websites created, amount of information online, data transfer speed, and CPU speed. Nothing is slowing down.

So whatever trends we have observed so far are only getting started. The Internet is still in its adolescence. It is only really about twenty years old. If it were a person, it still couldn't even order a beer to toast itself for all it has done in such a short time. Oddly, it could, however, join the military and go fight in a war overseas. Go figure.

* * *

We are more than three-quarters of the way through our forty-three steps toward world peace. The final ten cover a range of topics that don't fit neatly elsewhere.

34. Higher education levels. Educated people seem to pose more of a threat to autocrats. How do we know this? Because dictators have the intellectuals killed, not the farmers. In Russia, Joseph Stalin had thousands of writers, intellectuals, and scientists arrested and put into concentration camps. And of course the Nazis were ardent book burners themselves. During one of the book burnings, when tens of thousands of volumes were burned, Joseph Goebbels, German Minister of Public Enlightenment and Propaganda, advised the crowd that "the era of extreme Jewish intellectualism is now at an end. . . . The future German man will not just be a man of books, but a man of character. It is to this end that we want to educate you. . . . And thus you do well in this midnight hour to commit to the flames the evil spirit of the past."

In 1966, Mao Zedong closed the universities in China and sent their students and professors to the country to farm. In 1980 in Bolivia, General Luis García Meza Tejada seized power, suspended the constitution, restricted liberty, and closed the universities. In 1979, a revolution in Iran overthrew the monarchy and replaced it with an Islamic republic. In 1980, Iran closed the universities. When there was a coup in Burma, now Myanmar, in 1988, they closed the universities.

This list goes on, but I will spare you. Suffice it to say it is with good reason tyrants distrust the educated, not just because they ask questions, but because they challenge answers. Who needs that?

The world is becoming more educated at an amazing rate. In 1950, about 44 percent of the world was illiterate; by 1980, it was 30 percent; and as I write this, it is down to about 16 percent. On the other end of the education spectrum, college degrees are up: A recent Harvard University study reports that 6.7 percent of the world has a college degree, up from 5.9 percent in 2000.

As the Internet lowers the cost of education, makes it better, and promotes distance learning, illiteracy will drop further and college degrees will proliferate. As education rises, a thousand other things rise with it: income, health, political engagement, and an overall concern for world affairs. This all leads to more peaceful states.

35. A shift in power to the young. Traditional wisdom says that political clout flows to those with money. This is because, like technology, money also multiplies the labor of man. With money, you can buy machinery or hire workers to do your work.

Younger people have less wealth than older ones, on average. Older people, because they have the money, have tended to be more productive, and thus more powerful.

However, at present—and for the future as far as we can see—growth in technology outpaces growth in wealth. Because young people generally understand and utilize technology better than older people, we will see a shift in power and influence toward the young. Young people, enabled by technology, will multiply their labor, and thus they have more impact in whatever they do. Young people, who would be expected to do the dying if another war came, are generally more determined to keep the peace than their elders.

36. International and interracial marriage. In the past, political alliances were sealed by marriages among monarchs or nobles. The thought was that if the prince of Country A married the princess of Country B, the likelihood of those countries going to war was reduced for at least a couple of generations.

We see this process democratized and popularized in the world today. According to Pew Research Center data reported in *USA Today* in 2011, "Marriages between spouses of different races and ethnicities are more common than ever before. . . . A record 15 percent—about one out of every seven—of new marriages in 2008 landed in the 'Marrying Out' category."

This is a force for peace, as more and more people have family members in more than one culture and share the interests of more than one nationality. If your father is American and your mother Chinese, you will have a different understanding of differences between those countries, and, on balance, will be less amenable to war between those nations.

37. More exchange students, more studying abroad. American universities are thought by many to be among the best in the world. Being educated in the United States has long been a mark of distinction for the elites of other nations. But the notion of "elites" is broadening, as is the number of non-Americans who study in the United States. In 2010, almost 700,000 international students were studying in America's colleges and universities.

According to Allan Goodman, president and CEO of the Institute of International Education, "The United States continues to host more international students than any other country in the world. Active engagement between U.S. and international students in American classrooms provides students with valuable skills that will enable them to collaborate across cultures and borders to address shared global challenges in the years ahead."

But that is not all. Not only are we hosting more students, the number of Americans studying abroad is rising. *Newsweek* reports that "in 2006–07, more than 241,000 Americans studied abroad, up from less than 100,000 who did so a decade earlier." In addition, the magazine reported, the U.S. State Department estimates that more than five million Americans live overseas.

This is a deterrent to war and a force for peace because it increases understanding, empathy, and mutual self-interest.

38. Increased international travel. When you have visited a place, you will find it harder to advocate its destruction. And with every passing year, more people have visited more places. Here is a fact to get your head around: In 1980, about seven million Americans had a passport. How many do you think there are now—ten, twenty, fifty million?

In 2011, more than one hundred million Americans had passports. That is a huge change and a force for peace.

In addition, more than one billion of the world's seven billion people visited a country other than their own in 2011. This is a profound shift from a century or even a decade ago. More than 70 percent of the British have passports, as do 50 percent of Canadians and 25 percent of Japanese. Even China had 20 million passport holders in 2007—a minuscule proportion of its population but a substantial number in its own right.

This is a reassuring trend. More people using passports to travel internationally will increase understanding and help reduce touch points that could lead to war. I have never met someone who returned from another country saying, "Man, those guys are such jerks. We should totally go to war with them."

39. The growth of a common popular culture worldwide. Half a century ago, the United States had three channels on TV and everyone watched them. What happened on ABC last night would be common knowledge at the office, school, or hairdresser the next day. This gave people a shared set of cultural references. When *Seinfeld* was on TV and a new episode came out, it could introduce a meme—something as nonsensical but catchy as "Yada yada"—into the popular culture overnight. Today, the memes fly thick and fast from a soaring number of commercial, public, cable, and online broadcast channels.

The world is developing a shared popular culture with elements drawn from around the globe. The United States contributes much to this, including its movies, products such as iPhones, and websites such as Google,

YouTube, Twitter, Amazon, and eBay. Around the world, American celebrities are known and American video games are played. American English is taught in schools and American slang is practiced in bars everywhere. And, of course, American fast food is the food the world loves to say it hates.

I am not implying that the world popular culture is simply the U.S. popular culture. Far from it. Nations all around the world make their contributions. British music is known and loved around the world, as is its comedy and royalty. French wines and luxury brands are appreciated by connoisseurs (another French concept) everywhere. Italian exotic cars are the daydreams of much of the world. People around the world have Swiss watches on their arm, German luxury cars in their garages, and Japanese gadgets in their pockets.

This is a force for peace—to the extent that as we share the same set of cultural references, we understand each other better. It isn't just that we can communicate better but that we actually relate to each other better.

It's like the Coca-Cola commercial I remember from my youth. An American guy and a European girl are on a train, seemingly in Europe. They don't know each other and the guy, of course, wants to strike up conversation with the girl, but he doesn't know what language she speaks. So he starts by asking, "*Parlez-vous français?*" No reaction. "*Sprechen sie deutsche?*" Still nothing. Eventually he gives up and grabs a Coke. The girl says, in accented English, "Coca-Cola?" He smiles and gives her his Coke. Sparks fly.

If we can connect over our shared fondness for Apple, the Beatles, Armani, Porsche, Rolex, Burger King, or any of a thousand more products, we are that much less likely to decide to kill each other.

40. YouTube. One might have expected to find YouTube making its cameo in the earlier "communication" section, but I deliberately moved it here. I do not think the importance of YouTube lies in its role as a communication method nor as a fundamentally new means of distribution of media. Granted, it does those things and does them well, but its greatest contribution lies in the fact that it promotes empathy.

In an era when cameras were cumbersome and the number of channels on TV could be counted on one hand with enough fingers left over to snap, very little video of any kind was seen. Now video is everywhere—on my phone, in my cab in New York, and in the elevator as I zoom to the fourteenth floor. Whatever did we do without TV in elevators? How did we endure the monotony?

Against this backdrop, YouTube appears. We don't simply have more video screens; we now have an infinitude of broadcasters. The range of subject matter on YouTube is as incomprehensibly large as the range in quality.

Now, on a regular basis, videos appear that bring to life something that would otherwise be merely an ill-formed image in our minds. Instead of reading words on a page and trying to imagine a concept, we can see it, as the old expression goes, in Technicolor.

Because of this, our outrage and our sympathy and our revulsion are amplified—not artificially through deliberate manipulation, but through a more real and visceral experiencing of our world. Now, instead of just intellectually engaging with the news, we feel the government brutality, we experience the war, we are electrified by the demonstrations, and we are horrified at the suffering.

A single image can end a war. If you do not believe this, go to image.google.com and type "Nguyen Ngoc Loan execution" (without the quotation marks). And if an image can end a war, a video can change the world.

YouTube's contribution to world peace is not simply to add empathy to current events, although that would be enough. Because of YouTube, galvanizing events that might otherwise have been seen by only a few are available to anyone. If you've never seen a YouTube video that moved you, put down this book and watch just two (searchable by these keywords): "Randy Pausch Last Lecture" and "Steve Jobs' Stanford Commencement Address."

A single video a moment long can increase empathy and understanding. These are forces for peace.

41. A decline in nationalism. Let's talk a moment about patriotism and nationalism, words frequently used but seldom clearly defined. I am going to use definitions of my own in order to draw a contrast between two ideas that I consider very different—one peaceful and one not.

Patriotism, in my view, is an admiration for the values, institutions, and ideals of one's country. If you believe in the Bill of Rights, our system of checks and balances, republicanism, representative democracy, equal opportunity, rugged self-reliance, entrepreneurship, individual liberty, and any of the other thousand things "America" (or your own country) stands for, then you are a patriot. You love your country's ideals, goals, values, and aspirations.

Being a patriot and loving your country, you are quick to point out when it strays from its core beliefs. You view it as your duty to protest when people who do not hold to those values gain power. You might often repeat Edward Abbey's remark: "A patriot must always be ready to defend his country against his government."

Nationalism, in my use of the term, is being an uncritical fan of your country. Come what may, the nationalist will stick by his country. Nationalism is thus a form of tribalism. It is the same spirit that makes people fanatical about a certain sports team, regardless of the players or the score. The nationalists are the ones who say, "My country, right or wrong." They view dissent as a form of betrayal and ingratitude. They view the opposition by others to the actions of their country as treason, or at least, inexplicably self-destructive.

From the way I have written this, it is clear where my sympathies lie. But to be fair, I see certain admirable qualities in the nationalist: a kind of loyalty, not to an ideal, but to an organization; the unquestioning devotion and the complete lack of self-doubt. The problem is the nationalist is almost always taken advantage of by those in power—the one who yells the loudest at the political rally, the one the rulers count on to cheer their decrees regardless of substance. The patriot, by and large, cannot be co-opted by those in power. The patriot is the annoying protester everyone wishes would just shut up.

Nationalism is on the decline. Sadly, patriotism is as well. But the decline of nationalism is a force for peace.

42. The continuing advancement of civilization. I have listed plenty of pragmatic, self-interested reasons people will see war as less desirable and act to end it. But we do not have to rely solely on those. As civilization advances, we are becoming better people, and unquestionably more empathic.

This civilizing process seems to be picking up steam. The social reformer of the past is depicted as a dour spinster wielding an axe to break barrels of "Demon Rum." Nowadays, the social reformer is cool and hip. Ancient ideas and institutions that were norms in history for millennia, such as legal slavery and second-class status for women, are disappearing at an incredible pace.

43. Less tolerance for casualties in war. During the U.S. Civil War, in the Battle of Sharpsburg, there were 23,000 casualties in a single day: September 17, 1862. The population at that time was a tenth of what it is today. So if a battle today were similarly costly, the proportional number of casualties would be 230,000. In one day.

Can you imagine the public reaction to that today: A quarter of a million people killed or wounded in a single day?

In World War I, in the Battle of the Somme, were over a million casualties, and the action advanced the Allied line just seven miles, or about two deaths for every inch of ground. Another million people were lost in the Battle of Verdun. In World War II, even more battles had a million casualties each.

We seem to have lost our stomach for these kinds of losses. Mass communication means we no longer read a number like "a million dead"—we actually see them, see pictures of them. Every dead soldier has a face, a story, and a bereaved family. Their stories circulate around the web and their families make blog posts. This is the present reality in a world defined by the ease of communication. There are pros and cons to this, to be sure, but overall, this has increased our empathy. It has increased our desire for peace and our unwillingness to wage war.

* * *

So that ends my list. I hope that along the way you thought of a few I missed, a few trends or developments that lead toward peace. It is the inevitable flow of history.

In the future, nations still will have differences. But the critical question is, will they resort to war to resolve them? I believe that increasingly, they will not. In the end, violence will become obsolete. We will live out the realization that, as Bertrand Russell said, "War does not determine who is right, only who is left."

War as the remedy will fall out of favor for the many reasons I outline above. This is not a "wouldn't it be nice if we all got along" wish, but an understanding of the social, financial, and political realities of the future.

In the end, we shall be satisfied if we do not end war but are able to redefine it. People will always try to get other people to do what they want them to. The world is happiest when this process is one of persuasion, goodwill, reason, logic, and negotiation. It is the unhappiest when it is "Do what I tell you to do or we will inflict unspeakable horror on one another until one of us is destroyed." If we get to a point where it is "Do what I want you to do or you will be slightly less wealthy," we can be pretty happy there. We will have ended war with an honorable peace.

This is how our Founding Fathers intended our nation to behave: to try to achieve our foreign policy aims through negotiation and, if that failed, through economic sanctions. "I love peace," Thomas Jefferson once wrote, "and am anxious that we should give the world still another useful lesson, by showing to them other modes of punishing injuries than by war, which is as much a punishment to the punisher as to the sufferer."

IN CONCLUSION

• Do We Lose Our Humanity?

• What Could Possibly Go Wrong?

• Optimism, Revisited

Do We Lose Our Humanity?

To be or not to be, that is the question.
—Hamlet in William Shakespeare's Hamlet

At some point while reading this book, some part of the future I describe may have been unsettling to you. Whether it is the notion of manufacturing meat or having the computer tell you what you should order at the restaurant, you may have cringed and thought, "Man, that's kind of creepy."

I get it. We value our humanity, and insofar as life in the future seems different from our life today, it somehow seems less human. Right? I mean, we know how we live and thus, how humans live. Anything different doesn't seem as human to us and we instinctively recoil from it. Anything that looks too much like *The Matrix* movies or *The Terminator* movies is just, well, kind of creepy.

So let's address it head-on: In this world of the future, do we lose our humanity? My answer to that begins in the past, in the time of William Shakespeare.

Shakespeare was undoubtedly the greatest master the English language has ever known and, quite probably, will ever know. Nearly four hundred years after his death, Shakespeare's works are read and studied around the globe. Colleges offer degree programs in Shakespeare. His plays run in every major city in the English-speaking world, and Hollywood makes movies of them—good movies! Baz Luhrmann's hip version of *Romeo + Juliet* with Leonardo DiCaprio and Claire Danes. Kenneth Branagh's *Much Ado about Nothing* and Julie Taymor's *The Tempest* with Helen Mirren. And dozens— nay, hundreds—more (the *Guinness Book of World Records* says about 420).

Why is this? All kinds of artists have come and gone in the last four centuries, popular in their time but forgotten now. Writers, composers, painters, sculptors. We don't find ourselves endlessly returning to their work again and again.

Shakespeare remains so popular because he wrote about timeless human experiences: love and fear and envy, anger and revenge and jealousy, ambition and regret and guilt. All these things are the same today as they were in Shakespeare's time, and because of that, his stories are still very relevant to us. Under the terms of the definition I offered earlier, that makes Shakespeare the epitome of art—that is, something that continues to speak to future generations.

In Othello is a character named Iago, an evil man who never does anything illegal himself but is always planting ideas in other people's minds, to get them to do his dirty work. He convinces Othello that Desdemona, Othello's wife, is unfaithful to him. Othello ends up killing the virtuous Desdemona out of jealousy. We still have Iagos today—you may even know one—so this story resonates with us.

Macbeth is the story of a ruthless wife, Lady Macbeth, who persuades her husband to murder the king and take his throne. It is a tale of ambition and then of guilt. We get that. Who doesn't know a Lady Macbeth, a cunning person who pushes her spouse toward greatness?

King Lear is about a father who has three daughters—two who flatter him, but a third who speaks honestly and bluntly to him because she loves him. Infuriated, the king disowns the honest daughter and gives the kingdom to the two deceptive daughters. This seems like a page out of contemporary life as well.

Hold that thought, as we will return to it. But first we must go further back, from Shakespeare at the end of the sixteenth century to Plato around 370 BC.

In *The Phaedrus*, Plato describes a dialogue between his great teacher, Socrates, and Phaedrus. Socrates has some criticism for this new-fangled writing everyone is talking about: "Their trust in writing, produced by external characters which are no part of themselves, will discourage the use of their own memory within them. You have invented an elixir not of memory, but of reminding." His claim is that literacy will not improve the mind; if things are written down, the memory will suffer.

It is often said that ancient people had better memories than we have today, which makes a great deal of sense to me. If they had not, lengthy epics would never have survived oral transmission for centuries. When you have no books to turn to for reference, no Google to go to, no pen and paper in your pocket to jot down a note, you better be really good at remembering.

Simonides of Ceos was. As described in the writing of Cicero, Simonides, a Greek poet who lived around 600 BC, was hired by a nobleman named Scopas to write a poem in his honor. When the final work included extensive praise for the twin gods Castor and Pollux, Scopas complained. He told Simonides he was only going to pay him half the fee and if he wanted the other half, he should collect it from Castor and Pollux.

Later that evening when Simonides was at a banquet with Scopas, he got word that two young men were outside looking for him. He went to the door but didn't see anyone so went outside to look for them. While Simonides was outside, the roof of the house caved in and killed everyone. The implication was that Castor and Pollux, knowing of the imminent collapse of the roof, had come calling with the purpose of saving Simonides's life as their payment for the poem.

Although the bodies in the collapsed house were mangled beyond recognition, Cicero records that Simonides was able to close his eyes and recall where each banquet guest had been sitting. That's what interests me about this story (which may or may not be purely true): What Simonides did—recalling the names and locations of everyone at a large banquet—is described as entirely possible and an enviable, practical skill.

Two millennia later, it is fair to assume that humans are still capable of this kind of memory. But with rare exceptions, we simply don't train our brains to do this particular task.

If you went back in time and talked to these people, like Simonides, and you told them there would be a day in the future where you will have access to all the information in the world through books and the Internet but that the cost of this was a substantially lessened memory, I believe they would have said, "No, thank you. That seems creepy. My memory is a big part of who I am and I have no desire to trade any of it away."

Now, fast-forward a few centuries to the late 300s, where we can glimpse the life and times of a Christian bishop named Augustine of Hippo, thanks to an autobiography he wrote. Augustine describes a day when he saw his mentor, Ambrose, looking intently at an open book. After staring for two or three minutes, Ambrose turned a page and continued staring. When Augustine finally asked, "What are you doing?" Ambrose replied that he was reading.

Augustine said this could not be the case because he could neither hear Ambrose nor see his lips moving. Ambrose replied that he was looking at the words and reading them that way.

Augustine records that this idea blew his mind (or words to that effect). In a society where most knowledge was transmitted orally, where books were uncommon, the only way you learned things was by hearing them. The libraries that existed, such as the one at Alexandria, contained reading rooms because when you read a book, you read it aloud. You processed the information through your ears.

At times, we still do this today. Imagine you are putting together an office chair, sitting on the floor with an instruction sheet that has been translated through four different languages to something we shall generously call "English." When you reach a step you do not understand, do you not start reading out loud really slowly? You say, "Insert the left buckle into the V-shaped grommet . . ." In this way, you are processing aurally, which is much slower but more focused than silent reading. Processing aurally was familiar to Augustine while reading silently was revelatory, so noteworthy that he wrote it in his autobiography.

Now, try to guess how Augustine's contemporaries would respond if you told them, "The day is coming when you will look at a page and the ideas on that page will come up through your eyes and be written on your brain—and although you will not have heard them, you're still going to know them." I think they would have said, "That is kind of creepy. That is just so alien to me. I don't want that."

I see us today in a situation like those historical ones. In both those cases, a technology or technique came along that actually changed the way people think. In one case, the technology, writing, probably resulted in our memories getting worse, but we gained much more than we lost. In the second case, the technique of reading without vocalizing allowed for faster reading and a new, visual way to process verbal information—again, a net gain.

So in the present and future, when a technology comes along that represents such a change—that saves details of our activities with which to advise us later, or has us speaking to machines as if they were creatures—it will simply be more of the same. And it will come at no cost to our humanity.

Therefore, if we could go forward in time to an age where all the things I have written about have come to fruition, we would notice something very familiar: The people would still be reading Shakespeare.

What Could Possibly Go Wrong?

There are not enough Indians in the world to
defeat the Seventh Cavalry.
—George Armstrong Custer

I love old cars. I owe this passion to my high school friend Jason. He taught me everything I know about old cars and why they are cool. So it was natural that to earn extra money, Jason and I would buy cool, old cars we found in junkyards for a few hundred dollars apiece. We would then work feverishly on them for months before selling them for slightly less than we had paid. (At age sixteen, we weren't yet great businessmen. It turns out that, even when doing what you love, both passion and profit matter—but that particular piece of wisdom came later with age.)

We embarked on these car projects with grandiose visions, many as unrealistic as they were ingenious. Thus a typical plan—say, for getting a 1968 Olds 98 convertible from a field in the country to Jason's driveway—ended up involving hitchhiking, a rusty boat trailer, and car jacks perilously placed atop stacks of bricks. Yet at the time that we devised each plan, we were confident it would succeed. We would recite it to each other like a Homeric epic. As we approached the end of the flawless narrative, one of us would invariably ask sardonically (but never sarcastically), "What could possibly go wrong?"

The implied answer: everything.

Frequently everything *did* go wrong. I remember in autumn of '87 thinking it was perfectly reasonable to take the red 1964 Corvair convertible for a test drive, despite its lack of functioning brakes. Jason concurred and rode along. Oddly, it still seemed reasonable even as we coasted through three red lights to get home. The title of Ralph Nader's book was right: That car was *Unsafe at Any Speed*, at least with the master cylinder removed. It also seemed perfectly reasonable to take the 1962 Nash Metropolitan for a spin around the block, even though it didn't have brakes either. (In our defense, it was 2:00 a.m. on a Tuesday. If you don't believe me, check the police report.)

The problem for us was always that it is easier to get a car running than it is to fix the brakes. I don't think there is an extensible life-lesson here. This isn't a metaphor for anything else, like 401(k)s or raising children. It just happens to be the case with old cars.

From those adventures, though, I did learn (the hard way) to think ahead about what could possibly go wrong. It's a lesson well applied to the projections in this book.

Though the world foreseen in this book may seem far away to you, I believe it will be achieved—and once achieved, that it will grow in stability over time. Technology gets better. Algorithms get smarter, computers faster.

Everyone gets richer. Civilization advances. Life, as they say, is good. At that point, the iffy parts of human history are behind us and it is blue skies and clean sailing ahead.

But getting there . . . hmmmm. Well, that seems riddled with pitfalls.

My grandmother used to say, "There is many a slip between cup and lip." I don't think the axiom is literally true (except perhaps for the chronically clumsy), but I get the gist.

So let's take a moment and conduct a three-step evaluation. First, we will list the basics of my thesis about the future. Then we will list the things that might derail us on the way to that future. And finally, we will ask whether the whole proposition—the possibilities *and* the hazards—still seems too optimistic and, therefore, unrealistic.

Because the end of disease, war, and other global plagues is unprecedented in history, the burden of proof clearly is mine. So let's review my key points to see if they are compelling.

Technology brings about economic wealth through improved production, facilitation of trade, and promoting the division of labor. Technology multiplies the productive power of people, and technology makes things better, more efficient, and cheaper. So technology supports quality of life (from vaccines to Volvos) and generates wealth. Technology compounds over time.

1. We have achieved all that we have today in a very low-tech world. We are entering a point where technology will change at extreme speeds. Think of how a few thousand years of human civilization got us to a certain amount of computational power. In the next eighteen months, we will double that. Technological change is about to accelerate, giving us a century of progress in a single decade, and another century in a couple more years. Just as technology grows exponentially over time, so do its benefits.

2. Wealth and society encourage civilization, which is advantageous to everyone. Civilization, like technology, also compounds over time, as do its benefits. Civilization increases empathy, encourages beneficial competition, and promotes human rights and the rule of law.

Through all of this, we can end war by making it a worse choice than the status quo for everyone.

3. Disease is a problem of technology; thus, its solution will be technological. Famine is largely a technological problem as well, but it has a social aspect that civilization, technology, and wealth will mitigate. Scarcity, or what we term scarcity, is a technological problem as well.

4. The availability and propagation of cheap sensors, cheap storage, and cheap computational cycles will allow humanity to develop a collective memory of the activities and outcomes of everyone on the planet. Instead of relearning things over the course of centuries, people will be able to learn from the choices others have made. This will end ignorance.

5. The wealth created by technological advance will grow as fast as technology grows. That is to say, wealth creation is about to skyrocket. While this wealth will flow naturally to those who already have wealth, the unequivocal lesson of history is that some amount also will be redistributed to the poor. When there is extreme wealth, a relatively small amount of redistribution more than provides for everyone.

6. A world without hunger, disease, ignorance, poverty, and war is not a perfect world. The world will still face many challenges, which we will discuss shortly. But these five things exacerbate most other social problems, so their elimination will ease pressures on other problems while creating very few new ones. This is a giant leap forward for humanity.

As I review these points, none of them seem particularly like "stretches" to me. They all flow naturally from our daily and historical experience. Because the advances are highly distributed, they are thus highly likely. Moore's Law works because many thousands of people compete with each other to drive technology forward. It does not rely on one person.

The economy makes new machines that replace manual labor because many thousands of people are paid very well to do so. Thousands of people research alternative energy because a breakthrough will change the world and make fortunes. Thousands of people research diseases because they individually want to cure them.

Progress is widely distributed. As more nations become wealthier, they become more educated. Once they become more educated, they are better able to participate in the modern economy. More minds are thinking about more problems, coming up with better solutions. If the whole world had only ten thousand people, how many breakthroughs would you expect? Not many. But imagine the difference if the world had ten billion healthy, well-educated people! We are heading toward that, which makes progress ever more certain.

For centuries up until very recently, when the Catholic church was considering whether to raise someone to sainthood, they appointed a person whose job it was to dig up all the dirt on the candidate saint and make the case that the person should not be so elevated. It was a check on the system. The church's term for this person, the Devil's Advocate, is now an everyday expression.

What follows is my best attempt to serve as Devil's Advocate to my own vision—to think of arguments against this future I am describing. I can list a few that might eliminate it and a few more that might delay it.

First, catastrophe. Yes, a comet slamming into the planet or some galactic cataclysm could wipe us all out. We are a tiny dot of life suspended in a nearly infinite universe. Certainly this could happen, although the odds are remote.

Second, asymmetry. The ability of a few people to do a massive amount of damage rises as civilization becomes more complex and destructive power increases. We all saw what happened on 9/11, and it is likely similar acts will occur in the future. In spite of the massive benefits civilization offers to every person in every station of life, a crazy few will always see it very differently. Their ability to inflict carnage will rise in the future.

As troubling as this thought is, equally troubling would be the response of the country so attacked. There would no doubt be a tremendous restriction of civil liberties, a tremendous expansion in the size of government, and bloody military response.

Such an attack could escalate into a widespread conflict, although I doubt it. When a nation is attacked by a non-state, there is near-universal sympathy for the target, regardless of the grievance of the attacker, and few nations are willing to support groups that attack purely civilian targets.

Prosperity requires civil liberties, prosperity thrives under lower taxes, and prosperity shrivels as wars disrupt the free flow of labor and capital. So while such an attack and its aftermath would not derail our eventual arrival at the next golden age, it quite possibly would delay it.

Third, government. Anyone who loves civilization necessarily appreciates the role of government in protecting liberties. Without it, the strong merely prey on the weak. The government operating in its correct role is instrumental to civilization.

Although there is some disagreement on the exact amount and style of government that is best, the growing consensus is in favor of constitutional democracies, free markets, private property, and the welfare state. Love it or hate it, this seems to be where we are going.

Any given nation usually has a large amount of homogeneity. In the United States, where we have mostly Democrats and Republicans, life is largely the same no matter who is in charge. The fact that there is little material difference between these two parties should not be considered a shortcoming of the system; it merely reflects a large degree of consensus among citizens as to the kind of government they want. You may be a Democrat and disown your daughter if she marries a Republican, or you may be a Republican who has a brother who is a Democrat who drives you crazy, but this is only because we define ourselves by our differences. You never point out that you both believe in the Constitution, property rights, free speech, that murder should be illegal, that the government should build the roads, and virtually everything else. Instead, you have to find small things over which to argue, like whether the capital gains tax should be raised.

Having said all of that, government should certainly be watched with a suspicious eye, for it could conceivably delay or derail our ascent to the next golden age.

How? It can take growth for granted and thus overtax. It can overspend and rack up public debt and destroy the currency. It can lessen its enforcement of private property rights. And most damaging, it can wage war and thereby siphon off wealth, technology, and the lives of its citizens.

As a government grows in size, even if the growth is in social programs, it inevitably grows in its intrusion on civil liberty. The Roman orator Cicero, as far back as 44 BC, was warning that "the more laws, the less justice"—and it is a warning we should heed. Our republic has prospered because it fiercely protected life, liberty, and property, and must continue to do so.

Other than cataclysm, asymmetrical attack, or government gone wild, we have little to worry about.

Some will try to argue that "Big Oil" or "Big Pharma" or Big Something Else won't permit this progress, but I am dubious. If the idea is that those who have a huge financial interest in the status quo will keep change from happening, this viewpoint represents a misunderstanding of how innovation has derailed every status quo there has ever been. It can't explain how cars came to displace carriages (What about "Big Carriage"?) and planes displaced trains for vacation traveling. Or how AT&T got broken up. Or how IBM got flattened in the PC wars. Or how Google displaced Alta Vista.

All big companies fall. All big industries are replaced by better ones. "Big Candle" is not still around. "Big Whale Oil" couldn't stop the move to kerosene. Further, there is no "Big Pharma." There are Pfizer, Roche, GlaxoSmithKline, Novartis, Merck, and a dozen more, each of which would like nothing more than to put all the rest out of business, and each in turn living in fear that the rest will do something that puts them out of business. If you made an engine that ran on water, I guarantee you that while Texaco may not like it, Toyota sure the heck would love a patent on it. They could put all their competitors out of business.

This "Big" viewpoint is conspiratorial and I hate even to raise it because now that I've dismissed it, some will insist I must therefore be part of the conspiracy. Sadly, I am getting no Big Check for writing this.

I am not even especially worried about the growth of terrorism, which is based on an ideology that is anti-technology and would seek to derail the golden age. The benefits of civilization—from wealth to individual liberty and self-determination, from better health to safety and peace—all outweigh what its proponents can offer. As I see it, the grandchildren of those who would strap bombs on themselves today will not be rushing to imitate their elders.

I think the future I describe is pretty secure. So will everything be great? Not at all!

A term, "techno-utopian," is often applied to people who believe a technology will bring about a perfect world. I am not a techno-utopian. I think the range of problems that technology can solve is confined to technological problems.

Four of the problems I address in this book—ignorance, disease, famine, and poverty—are purely technical problems. And war is a by-product of several technical problems. We will end war by making peace more desirable.

So nothing is unreasonable or even unlikely about predicting that the technological problems of today will have technological solutions.

Many technological problems I don't address in this book, but I believe technology will provide solutions for those also. Among them are problems related to clean water, the environment, pollution, energy, weather, and transportation.

When confronted with any thorny societal problem, I apply the same basic thought process I used on the five topics of this book. I begin by asking, "Does this problem have to exist? Is there possibly a solution to it? Are we moving in the direction of the solution now? Does someone get paid for solving it?" If the answers to those questions are affirmative, then making assumptions about increasing rates of technological progress is very reasonable. Therefore a solution is almost certain to be found.

However, I don't think finding these solutions means an end to all our troubles. All these problems that technology will solve have made our underlying differences worse—but removing these problems will not eliminate those underlying differences.

In the end, many cases abound where the values of two individuals or groups are mutually exclusive and thus, there will always be human conflict. But a world without want and without disease, a world with opportunity for all, is a world where getting along—even when we don't see eye to eye—is going to be a good bit easier.

Optimism, Revisited

Optimism is the foundation of courage.
—Nicholas Murray Butler

This book began with the assertion that it is the optimists who get things done. I will end on that same topic.

There are those who insist that an optimistic outlook encourages Head-in-the-Sand Syndrome. They claim it tells people, "Everything is going to be all right," which causes people to go about their lives, business as usual, while the world goes to hell in a handbasket (whatever that phrase means).

That claim is simply not true.

It is pessimism that says, "We are doomed." It is pessimism that says, "Why bother?" Pessimism is numbing, demoralizing, depressing. Pessimism turns to cynicism, which turns to apathy, which turns to paralysis. Pessimism is all the reasons "this won't work." Pessimism hides in the closet, fearing the worst.

Pessimism, quite frankly, will get us all killed.

Optimism, on the other hand, says, "There is a way." Optimism says, "Let's get to work." Optimism is empowering, uplifting, inspiring. Optimism turns into enthusiasm, which turns into action. Optimism is "we will figure out as we go along." Optimism faces the world, hoping for the best.

Optimism, simply put, will save us all.

This book is a call to action, not complacency. It is based on the idea that what we believe about the future determines what we do in the present.

My goal is not to convince people that the world will be perfect in the future. Rather, I aim to show that the world will be what we make it to be. If we have the will and if we do the work, we can make the world greater than we have ever imagined.

As a historian, I know it has been the vanity of every age to think it represents a high point in history. I hope that, after reading this far, you appreciate that for our age, this is no idle boast. It is simply a realization. We live at a defining moment for humanity, as the compounding effects of technology and civilization reach an inflection point.

Everything is about to change. And it's about time.

You might be asking, "Then what? What happens after that?"

I think the technological leap beyond the next one will take us to the stars. After all, we live in a universe that looks like it has plenty of room for us to expand into. Today, all of our eggs are in a lone planetary basket, Earth. I look for the day when a billion planets are populated with a billion people each.

I think we will learn to conquer distance though a method of which we cannot yet conceive. Then we will launch terra-forming nanites into space that land on lifeless rocks and planets and transform them, at the atomic level, to be filled with carbon, hydrogen, oxygen, and everything else we might need. Atmospheres will form, then plants will be seeded, and then the colonists will arrive.

I think we will go forth and fill these billion worlds with generations that in kind will produce their own Dante, Columbus, Copernicus, Da Vinci, Newton, Shakespeare, Bach, Washington, Carver, Curie, Edison, Chaplin, Earhart, Tolkien, and ten thousand more masters in a thousand more arts.

So, far from reaching that point the pessimists foretold—where we have exhausted the meager resources of Earth and find ourselves dwindling away—something entirely different is happening. We are gaining speed, not winding down. We are blooming, not withering, as we leverage the greatest natural resource on the planet: the human mind.

I believe in the future I describe not out of a childish wish, but because it seems the obvious and natural progression of history. It is consistent with all we know of the past, which is progress and prosperity. As we stand on the cusp of this great new epoch, I wonder why it is that so many people can see nothing but bad in the world around them. At the time in history when our future has never looked brighter, it is baffling that some people are more pessimistic than ever.

How can this future I describe not be ours? For each of us, existence is a brief moment, a narrow window of life through which we contribute our bit to history. And yet, in our moment, we are allowed a glimpse of what is to come, a hint of human destiny. We have looked ahead and glimpsed the infinite progress that is to come, the never-ending blossoming of humanity and civilization that we help create and then bequeath to our descendants through our actions of today.

We were not born in that age that had no word for change. No, quite the opposite: We live in what can only be termed the Age of Change.

Like Moses, who was allowed to glimpse the Promised Land but not to enter it, not all of us will live to experience the fullness of this future, the ultimate manifestation of this golden age. But we will see it begin to take shape and will know that we were there the moment the world changed. And because it changed for the better, wondrously better, we can proudly claim our part in its forming.

ACKNOWLEDGMENTS

Writing a book is very humbling. If you haven't done it before, but are considering it, let me give you a bit of foreshadowing, a literary device I understand to be all the rage in intellectual circles.

You begin with an idea. You chew it over a bit in your head, and you think, "This might make a good article or movie or book. Or maybe just a long fortune cookie."

Then at some point, you decide to write a book. You sit down in front of your keyboard and start typing. I found it helpful to have Hemingway's advice to writers taped to a wall nearby: "There is nothing to writing. All you do is sit down at a typewriter and bleed."

After an extensive period of Hemingway-inspired bloodletting, you have a manuscript.

I will save you the rest of this story because it takes a hundred turns. Suffice it to say, at that point, when I thought I was almost done, I learned that the real work had hardly begun. It took the additional toil of many amazing and talented people to bring forth this book. If you happen to be Michelangelo or Bill Watterson, you can probably do it all yourself. But for us mortals, creative endeavors are usually an ensemble activity.

So here is my partial list of the many people who helped me bring this book from my hard drive to wherever you happen to be right now.

First, my wife of twenty years, Sharon. Sharon is always so supportive and has never once complained about all the hours my writing takes. She also provided a constant stream of thoughtful feedback and insights as the writing progressed.

Richard Rosenblatt, who unconditionally supported and encouraged me in this project.

Emily Serven, who at the time was Emily Johnson, for immeasurable help. She challenged my ideas, proofed my writing, dissected my logic, and provided unceasing support. Since she did rough edits for me, Emily was always the first person to read my writing and she provided much useful feedback at the earliest stages of my writing.

The amazing Patty Edmonds, my editor, who brought to bear all of her skill, wisdom, and talent onto my manuscript, and in doing so, made it so much better than it was, and much better than I could have ever made it.

The folks at Greenleaf: Justin Branch, Kris Pauls, Alan Grimes, and all the rest. Oh, and Ben Kirshner for introducing me to Clint Greenleaf.

Patricia Meyer, who has been my most unrelenting advocate. Leyla Farah who provided the encouragement early on to finish the book. Monica Landers, who is pretty much always right, for her sage advice.

All the people who read very early copies of the book and gave me feedback: Kevin Stambaugh, Jeff Hebert, Dave Panos, Steve Lanier, Drew MacPherson, Ellis Oglesby, David Yehaskel, Priscilla Jones, and Melanie Dunham.

And Marika Flatt, Tatum Sapinoro, and Megan Renart who worked hard to make the book a success.

And all of the other people who have given me feedback along the way: Jaclyn Sugg, Jennifer Johnson, Stephen Wolfram, Andy Sernovitz, Brian Dillon, Blake Messer, Mark Hall, Jason Horton, and Howard Love.

Thank you one and all.

INDEX

A

Abbey, Edward, 275
Adams, John, 2
Adwords, Google, 99
Africa, 179, 197
aging, 57–58, 91
agricultural economy, 148
agriculture industry, 170, 176,
    179–86, 186–91, 200–
    205. See also genetically
    modified organisms
aid strategies, international,
    176–77
Alaska Permanent Fund,
    144–45
Amalrik, Andrei, 12
Amazon.com, 43–44, 45–47,
    97
Ambient Corporation's Audeo
    device, 90
American Association for the
    Advancement of Science
    (AAAS), 171
American Dream and dreamers,
    2–3
American Experience, 2
American High (O'Neill), 62
Amish social order, 166
androids vs. robots, 119
answer engines, 42
Apollo 13 (movie), 4
art on the Internet, 25–26
asymmetry in warfare, 246,
    287–88
Atkinson, Brooks, 226
Augustine of Hippo, 282–83
Avery, Oswald, 80

B

Ben & Jerry's Ice Cream,
    212–13
Bennis, Warren, 117, 186
Berlin Wall, end of, 230
bionic eyes, 89
Birthday Balls, Roosevelt's,
    60, 61
Black Book of Communism
    (Ebeling), 208–9
blogs, 17, 24–25
Boinc (open-source grid-
    computing platform),
    204
books, invention of, 31–32
Borlaug, Norman, 181–84,
    186, 207
Brandeis, Louis, 265
Broyles, William, Jr., 234–35
Bryan, William Jennings, 163
business startups, 26
Byzantines, 217–18

C

Caesar, Julius, 142
Cambodia, 208–9
Carlyle, Thomas, 223
Center for Systemic Peace, 205
change, rate of, 5–6
charities and nonprofits, 161–
    62, 164
China, 91, 106, 171, 207–8,
    269
Chipotle, 212–13
civilization and civilizing
    process, 217–25, 275–
    77, 285–86

Cleveland, Grover, 163
collective memory, 37, 49, 76,
    286. See also Digital
    Echo
collectivism, 207, 209
Collins, Joseph, 170–71
commodity pricing, 203–4
"common man" stereotype,
    151, 153
communication
    and ending war, 257–58,
        277
    end of language barriers,
        267–69
    interactive information
        exchange, 98
    international agreements,
        252–54
    mobile phones, 204,
        264–66
communism, 207–9, 210
Community Public Health
    Nursing Practice, 60
competition, 236–37, 289
computer technology
    anthropomorphizing
        computers, 120
    correlation identification,
        42, 43–48
    cost decreases, 125–26,
        127
    efficiency of, 45–47
    modeling complex
        interactions in the
        body, 84
    open-source grid-
        computing
        platform, 204

processing speed, 19–22
See also data
consumer's perspective of war,
240–41
contact lenses with augmented
reality, 90
Cooperative Wheat Research
Production Program
(Mexico and Rockefeller
Foundation), 181–82
copyrights, 253
corn genome, 197–98
cotton gin, 110–11
cowpox, 65–67
credit cards, 96–97
Crockett, Davy, 162–63
crop yield volatility, 175–76
crowdsourcing, 78. See also
Digital Echo
culture, worldwide, 273–74
custom vitamin formula, 76

D

data
and agriculture, 200–205
analysis leading to end of
disease, 72–78
choosing questions to ask,
74–76
collecting, 40–41, 44,
46, 88
for correlation
identification, 42,
43–48
defining, 40
on markets, 203–4
and outliers, 76
pattern analysis, 78
turning into knowledge,
41–43, 50–52
See also Digital Echo;
genome
Declaration of Independence,
206, 209, 264–65
De Grey, Aubrey, 91
Dell Theory of Conflict
Prevention, 237–38
democracy, 205, 226, 248–49
Democratic Peace Theory,
248–49
depression, 72
DeSalle, Rob, 85
de Tocqueville, Alexis, 161–62,
164, 226
diabetes vaccine, 122

dictators, 248, 262–63, 270
Digital Echo
computerized utilization
of, 49–53
extreme logging, 77
and individual genomes,
82–83
overview, 34–37, 286
of plants and crops, 200,
201, 203
privacy protection and, 40,
52–53
sharing with others, 38–40
specific personal analysis,
77–78, 169–70
disease, 56–58, 68–72, 286
disease, end of
data analysis leading to,
72–78
and genome sequencing,
82–85
information and
collaboration,
86–88
overview, 56, 67–68, 91
polio, 59–63, 67–68
from pooling medical
and demographic
information,
39–40
smallpox, 63–67, 67–68
vaccines, 43, 61–63,
66–67, 68, 71, 85,
121–22
victory, defining, 58, 59
disorders and disabilities, 57,
58
division of labor and wealth,
99–101
DNA, 80–81
Drucker, Peter, 18
drunk driving, 255–56
Durant, Ariel, 224–25, 232
Durant, Will, 13–14, 138,
224–25, 232
Dyson, Freeman, 106, 193

E

Easterbrook, Gregg, 125, 245,
248–49
eBay, 97–98
Ebeling, Richard, 208–9
economics and economic
theories
degrees of utility, 95–99,

101, 128, 237
externalities, 112–13
increasing viability of
smaller countries,
251–52
military actions vs., 235–
37, 250–51
pricing theories, 103, 110,
114–15, 125–31
scarcity, 102–8, 142
subsidies, 113, 177–78
taxation, 112–13, 135,
136, 140–43,
144–45, 163
war benefits declining,
241–43
wealth redistribution, 135,
136–37, 138, 211,
286
welfare state, 135, 138,
140–42, 163–64,
165
world economy and
financial systems
intertwined,
244–45
education and ending war,
270–71, 272
efficiency, improvements in
in agriculture, 181–84,
186
computer technology,
45–47
nanites, 121–23
and outsourcing, 110–11,
124
robots, 119–21
and wealth creation, 101,
111
See also technology
Einstein, Albert, 227, 256
Eisenhower, Dwight, 226, 233,
241, 256
Eisner, Manuel, 222–23
electronic stores, 16–17,
43–47, 97, 98
Elizabethan Poor Law, 165
Ellsworth, Henry, 156
e-mail as force for peace, 258
empathy, 224
employment
agricultural jobs, 174, 187
freeing humans from
drudgery, 108–9,
114–21, 146–47,
152–154, 156, 287

and free trade, 110–11
laborsaving technology, 108–9
outsourcing, 109–11, 113, 114–17, 123–24
EndoBarrier tubing, 89
"End of History?" (Fukuyama), 230
energy, 103–7, 108, 198
Enough (Thurow and Kilman), 176, 176–78, 179
entrepreneurs and the Internet, 18–19
Ethiopian Commodity Exchange, 203
Etsy, 97
expropriation and wealth, 137

F

Facebook, 259–60
FactCheck.org, 260–61
famine, 160–61, 207–8
FAO (United Nations Food and Agriculture Organization), 171, 175
farm subsidies, 177–78
Ferdinand, Archduke Franz, 29–30, 250
fertilizer, 180
Feynman, Richard, 107
Flemming, Walther, 80
food
    as free to all, 209
    future prices of, 129
    as human right, 206–12, 214
    money as means for getting enough, 175, 206–7, 209
    nutrients in, 166–70, 184, 187, 212–13
    organic foods, 189
    See also hunger
food supply, 170–75, 187, 188, 190–91
France, 106, 109, 249
Francis, Thomas, 61, 62
Frederick the Great, 234
freedoms, 146, 262, 265, 288, 289
free enterprise system, 5, 96–97, 100, 131, 156, 249
free markets, 5, 18, 94, 177, 288
free trade, 109–11, 112–13

French Revolution, 137, 161
Friedman, Thomas, 121, 237–38, 260
Fukuyama, Francis, 230
Fund for American Studies, 240
fusion energy, 105–6
futurists, 10–12. See also predicting the future

G

Gabre-Madhin, Eleni Zaude, 203
gap between rich and poor, 144–45
gastrointestinal liner to treat obesity, 89
gecko-inspired bandages, 90
gene splicing, 195–96
genetically modified (GM) foods, 84–85, 192–93, 196–99
genetically modified organisms (GMOs)
    dining on, in United States, 193
    gene splicing, 195–96
    mutagenesis, 194–95
    opposition to, 198–99
    overview, 192–93, 200
    transgenesis, 180, 196–98
genetic factors and diseases, 82–83
genetic factors and nutrition, 167
Geneva Convention, 222
genome, 79–85, 197–98
global culture, 273–74
globalization, World Bank on, 240
global warming, 199
GloFish, 196
GNP and energy use, 104
Goebbels, Joseph, 269
Goering, Hermann, 233–34
"Golden Arches Theory of Conflict Prevention" (Friedman), 237–38
Gong, Zhiyuan, 196
Goodman, Allan, 271
Google, 24, 99
governments
    democracy, 205, 226, 248–49

dictators, 248, 262–63, 270
    increasing distrust of, 254, 261
    information from sources other than, 262–63
    and key ingredients to prosperity, 118
    monarchies, 247–48
    potential for problems, 288–91
    role of, 138–43, 162–63
    transparency of officials, 263–64
    world government vs. nation-states, 229
Gracchus, Gaius, 141–42
Great Britain, 249, 252
Great Depression, 10, 30, 164, 178
"Great Die-Off, The," 173
gross world product (GWP), 132

H

Harvey, Fiona, 190–91
Haynes effect, 48–53
Haynes, Jim, 48
heritage meats, 189
Herodotus, 69
Hillman, Jeffrey, 89
Hippocrates, 69
history
    of access to knowledge, 31–32, 49–50
    of agriculture, 180–81
    discontinuous nature of, 10–11, 12
    of disease, 68–72
    as guide to optimism, 12–14
    and human genome sequencing, 79–80
    of hunger, 160–66
    of jobs and machines, 148–49
    of polio, 59–63
    of smallpox, 63–67
    of wealth and poverty, 132–43, 144–45
    world wars from a wrong turn, 29–30, 250
"History of Violence, A" (Pinker), 223–24
hope vs. reason, 1

human genome. See genome
human nature
  belief in scarcity, 107–8
  creativity, 47–48, 150–51
  energized by following
      your passion, 154
  and history repeating
      itself, 13–14
  imperfect memory, 44–45
  importance of humanity,
      279–83
  opinions based on
      assumptions,
      168–69
  sensory input
      interpretation
      deficiency, 201
  The Spoiled Rich Kid
      Problem, 154
  and Star Trek vs. WALL-E
      path, 149–51
human potential, 116–17
human rights, 206–12, 214,
    288
hunger, 160–66, 175–79
hunger, end of
  agriculture industry,
      179–86
  end of the farmer, 186–91
  food as a human right,
      206–12, 214
  and food supply, 170–75
  genomics and GMOs,
      192–200
  nutrition and, 166–70,
      184, 212–13
Huns, the, 217
Huxley, Aldous, 231
hyperinflation of currency, 136

I

ignorance
  overview, 29–31
  wisdom vs., 32, 33, 34,
      40, 50–52, 54
ignorance, end of
  creativity, 47–48
  data and knowledge as,
      40–43
  Jim Haynes effect, 48–53
  overview, 53–54

sharing personal and
    intellectual
    information,
    37–40
  wise decisions, 43–48
  See also Internet;
      knowledge;
      technology
I Have A Dream Foundation,
    152
impaired function of the body,
    56–58
India, 134, 171, 182–83, 204
Industrial Revolution, 108,
    131, 148, 173, 180
infectious diseases, 56–57
information and government,
    262–64. See also data;
    governments
intangibles, value stored in,
    245–46
intellectual labor, sharing, 25,
    37–38
interactive information
    exchange, 98
internalizing externalities,
    112–13
international aid strategies,
    176–77
international conduct, 252–54
International Trade Centre
    (ITC), 171
Internet
  and commodity pricing,
      203–4
  defining, 14–15
  ending hunger, 214
  and entrepreneurs, 18–19
  and genetically modified
      foods, 200
  massive creative
      participation,
      23–25
  universal access to, 266–
      67, 269
  and variables influencing
      nutrition, 169–70
Internet Renaissance, 22–28
Internet uses
  art, 25–26
  blogs, 17, 24–25
  corollaries, 16–18, 44–45
  e-mail, 258

Facebook, 260–61
  grassroots efforts to help
      those in need, 205
  overview, 96–99
  reallocation of existing
      goods, 97, 101
  as repository of life
      experience, 34–37
  search engines, 32, 39, 42,
      45–47, 50–52
  source of wisdom, 34
  trade, 96–99
  Twitter, 17, 37, 259–60
  World Wide Web, 258
  YouTube, 25–26, 274
"Invitation to History"
    (Durant), 13–14
"I, Pencil" (Read), 100

J

Japan, 177, 178
Jefferson, Thomas, 246, 277
Jenner, Edward, 65–66, 86
Jensen, Robert, 204
Jim Haynes effect, 48–53
Jisheng, Yang, 207–8
Joplin, Janis, 108

K

Kennedy, John F., 3–4, 257–58
Kenya, 204
Kilman, Scott, 176, 177–78,
    179
Kiva (micro-loan operation),
    205
knowledge
  availability of, 87–88
  defining, 33, 34, 40
  disagreements about
      interpretations
      of, 41
  eliminating mistakes with,
      53–54
  history of access to,
      31–32, 49–50
  turning data into, 41–43
  See also data
Koontz, Dean, 97
Kurzweil, Ray, 20

L

labor, value of, 114–17
land ownership, 178–79
land reform, 136–37
Lang, Eugene M., 152
language barriers, end of, 267–69
Lappé, Frances Moore, 170–71
Lego factory, 119
Lessons of History, The (Durant and Durant), 224–25, 232
Letterman, David, 166
Lexus and the Olive Tree, The (Friedman), 121, 237–38, 261
libraries, 16, 31, 32, 133, 282
Liechtenstein, 251–52
Life of Solon (Plutarch), 135
life writing, 24
linear viewpoint of history, 10–11
literacy, 270–71
Lunsford, Andrea, 24
lymph node replacements, 89

M

MacDonald, Kyle, 94–95
machines
    building a wise machine, 33, 41
    for farm work, 186–88
    freeing humans from drudge jobs, 108–9, 114–21, 146–47, 152–54, 156, 287
    human beings vs., 53
    robots, 118–21, 123–24
    See also computer technology
MAD (Mutually Assured Destruction), 238–39
MADD (Mothers Against Drunk Driving), 255
Malthus, Thomas, 173
Man of the House (O'Neill), 262
manufactured food, 190–91
March of Dimes, 60–61
marginal tax rates, 136, 145

marginal utility, 95, 101, 128, 237
Margolin, Jean-Louis, 208–9
markets
    free markets, 5, 18, 94, 177, 288
    information and, 203–4
    profit motive, 207
marriage, international and interracial, 272
McCouch, Susan, 193

measures, 43, 89, 90
medical progress
    accelerating pace of, 71–72
    and Digital Echo, 88
    genetically modified (GM) foods, 84–85
    modeling complex interactions in the body, 84
    overview, 89–90
    vaccines and vaccinations, 43, 61–63, 66–67, 68, 71, 85, 121–22
    See also vaccines and vaccinations
Mendel, Gregor, 71, 184–85
mental illness, 57, 58, 72
Mercedes Benz for $50, 102, 126–27
meritocracy of online business, 99
Mexico, 181–82
microchips for internal measures, 89
micro-lending, 205
microscopes, 70, 79–80, 83
military-industrial complex, 233, 242–43
mobile phones, 204, 264–66
monarchies, 247–48
money
    and doctors in China, 91
    invention of, 95
    lack of, as reason for starvation, 175, 206–7, 209
    and prices or wages, 110, 114–15
    stable and valuable supply of, 138–39

and trade, 95, 96
    transferring, 96–97
Moore, Gordon, 19–20
Moore's Law, 20, 46, 181, 286
MSNBC.com, 84
Mulhall, Douglas, 121, 122, 191
Murrow, Edward R., 62
"musical chairs" children's game, 103
mutagenesis, 194–95
Mutually Assured Destruction (MAD), 238–39

N

nanotechnology, 121–23, 292
Napoleon I (Bonaparte), 206
National Academy of Science (NAS), 125
nationalism, 275
nationalization of industries, 137
nation-states, 229, 251–52
NATO, 250
negative utility, 95
"New leukemia treatment exceeds 'wildest expectations'" (MSNBC.com), 84
New York Times, 194–95, 201, 266
non-infectious diseases, 57
nonprofits and charities, 161–62, 164
non-violence as political tactic, 223, 254–55
Notorious (movie), 255
nutrition, 166–70, 184, 187, 212–13

O

obesity, gastrointestinal liner to treat, 89
Ó Gráda, Cormac, 173
O'Neil, Dennis, 267
O'Neill, Tip, 262
O'Neill, William, 62
online employment, 96
Open Directory Project, 38
open-source grid-computing platform, 204–5

Oppenheimer, J. Robert, 227
optimism, 5, 291–93. See
   also reasoning behind
   optimism
Oracle at Delphi, 33
O'Reilly, Bill, 143
organic foods, 189, 212
Our Molecular Future
   (Mulhall), 121, 122,
   191
outliers, understanding, 76
outsourcing, 110–11, 113,
   114–17, 123–24

P

Paine, Thomas, 243
Pakistan, 171, 183
"Paradox of Hunger in the
   Midst of Plenty, The"
   (Niagia), 171–72
Pascal, Blaise, 250
Pasteur, Louis, 71, 86
patriotism, 275
PayPal, 96–97
pay per click (PPC), 99
peace and democracy, 204–5
Peace Dividend, 230
personal information, sharing,
   38–40
pessimism, 291
Pew Research Center, 271
philanthropy, increases in, 27,
   205
Phytech (Israeli company), 201
pi, calculation of, 45
Pierce, John, 20
Pinker, Steven, 223–24
plants and solar energy, 184
Plato, 281
Plutarch, 135
Polachek, Solomon W., 243
polio, 59–63, 67–68
politics and political tactics
   for ending war, 247–57
   non-violence, 223,
      254–55
   power of technology, 271
   public opinion, 242,
      255–57, 259
Pol Pot, 208, 209
population die-off predictions,
   173

possibilities vs. focusing on
   problems, 4–5
poverty
   and conflict with the
      wealthy, 134–35
   defining, 94, 132–33
   and degrees of utility,
      95–99, 101, 128,
      237
   desperation of, 239–40
   and externalities, 112–13
   history of wealth and,
      132–43, 144–45
   Mutually Assured Poverty
      theory, 239
   scarcity aspect of, 102–8
   subsistence level, 160–61
   workhouses, 165
   See also wealth
poverty, end of
   falling prices, 125–31
   free trade, 109–11,
      112–13
   outsourcing, 109–11, 113,
      114–17, 123–24
   overview, 155–57
   technological
      displacement,
      108–9, 114–21,
      146–47, 153–54,
      156, 287
PPC (pay per click), 99
precision agriculture, 200–205
predicting the future
   overview, 6–7, 10–12,
      126–27, 285–87
   population die-off, 173
   potential for problems,
      287–91
pricing, theory of, 102, 110,
   114–15, 125–31
privacy protection and Digital
   Echo, 40, 52–53
private property laws, 117,
   135, 137
product information, 98
productivity, 115–17, 123–24,
   145. See also efficiency,
   improvements in;
   technology
property rights, 118, 134, 138
prosperity, 117–18, 124–25,
   237–38, 239–40. See
   also wealth

public opinion as a political
   force, 242, 254–56, 258
Pulcher, Clodius, 142

Q

questions, changing the world
   with, 7, 57–58, 74–78

R

racism, 256
radiation breeding, 194–95
Rational Optimist, The
   (Ridley), 172, 174, 204
Read, Leonard, 100
reallocation of existing goods,
   96, 101
reasoning behind optimism
   accelerating progress,
      19–22
   futurists' errors, 10–12
   history as guide, 12–14
   Internet Renaissance,
      23–28
   Internet technology and
      human ingenuity,
      14–19
   overview, 9–10, 27–28,
      285–87, 292–93
reason vs. hope, 1
redistribution of wealth, 135,
   136–37, 138, 211, 286.
   See also taxation
relative definition of poverty,
   133
Renaissance, 22–23, 26
rice, genetic modifications to,
   196–97
Ridley, Matt, 172–73, 204
"Rising Above the Gathering
   Storm" (NAS), 125
Roberts, Edward, 234
robots, 118–21, 123–24
Rockefeller Foundation,
   181–82
Rome, ancient, 141, 161, 218,
   245
Roosevelt, Franklin D., 60–61,
   209–10
Rosset, Peter, 170–71
rule of law, 117, 135, 137, 221,
   224, 228–29

S

Salk, Jonas, 61, 62, 86
savants, 57
scarcity, 102–8, 142, 145–46
Schell, Jesse, 36–37
Schmidt, Eric, 24, 41
science, 27, 43, 86, 87–88. See
    also technology
science fiction, 11
search engines, 32, 39, 42,
    45–47, 50–52
seed makers, 193
Seiglie, Carlos, 243
selective breeding, 193–94. See
    also genetically modified
    organisms
self-teaching/learning
    algorithms, 46, 51
Sen, Amartya, 204
sensors for agriculture, 201,
    203
shadow Internet, 266
Shakespeare, William, 280–81
Shanley, John Patrick, 200
Simonides of Ceos, 281–82
Simon, Julian Lincoln, 172
skin cancer, 73–74
slavery, 219
smallpox, 63–67, 67–68
smart contact lenses, 90
smart nails, 124
SmartSkin, 90
Smith, Adam, 100–101
smoking and tobacco, 255
Snopes.com, 260
socialism, 146, 210
societal costs of externalities,
    112–13
Sonic Boom (Easterbrook),
    125, 245, 248–49
Soviet Union, 11–12, 250
space race, 3–4
Spoiled Rich Kid Problem,
    The, 154
Stadler, Lewis J., 194–95
Stakman, Elvin, 181
Stanford Study of Writing,
    23–24
Star Trek path, 149–50
stores, 44–46, 136. See also
    electronic stores
subsidies and externalities, 113

subsidies, farm, 177–78
suggestion engines, 45–47,
    50–52
sunlight, energy from, 105, 184
Sun, the Genome, and the
    Internet, The (Dyson),
    106, 193
supply chains, global, 238, 244
Sutton, Walter, 80
symptoms and syndromes,
    57, 58

T

taxation, 112–13, 135, 136,
    140–42, 144–45, 163
technology
    ability to improve human
        life, 43, 285
    accelerating progress of,
        19–22, 26–27, 181
    and agriculture, 170,
        187–88, 201
    and communication,
        86–88
    and disease cures, 68
    ending hunger, 214
    and energy output, 104–7,
        108
    falling prices due to,
        125–31
    and gap between rich and
        poor, 144–45
    of GM crops, 192
    housing, 129–30
    laborsaving technology,
        108–9
    nanotechnology, 121–23,
        292
    overview, 15–16, 155–57
    and perceived scarcity, 108
    and political clout, 271
    prosperity from, 124–25
    robots, 118–21, 123–24
    smart contact lenses, 90
    smart nails, 124
    SmartSkin, 90
    super pan, 128
    and value of labor, 114–17
    and war weapons, 232
    and wealth, 101–2, 128,
        132, 145–46,
        285–86

See also computer
    technology;
    Internet
techno-utopia, 290
telegraph definition vs. Internet
    definition, 14–15
television, evolution of, 16
terrorism, 289–90
Third Servile War, 218
Thompson, Clive, 23–24
Thurow, Roger, 175–76,
    177–78, 179
Tocqueville, Alexis de, 161–62,
    164, 226
tooth decay, preventing, 89
Touré, Hamadoun, 87
trade, 27, 96–101, 109–13,
    243–44
"Trade, Peace and Democracy"
    (Polachek and Seiglie),
    244
traffic-speed-optimization
    engine, 39
transgenesis, 181, 196–98
transportation, 130
travel, international, 272–73
treaties, 250, 251, 252–53, 258
"Truth Is Out There Problem,
    The," 31–32
Turner, Ted, 248
Twitter, 17, 37, 259–60

U

Uldrich, Jack, 184
Ultimate Resource 2, The
    (Simon), 172
United Kingdom, 263
United Nations Food
    and Agriculture
    Organization (FAO),
    171, 175
United States
    Declaration of
        Independence,
        206, 209, 264–65
    economic security and
        independence,
        209–10
    energy consumption,
        103–4
    focusing on problems, 4–5
    food waste, 211

freedoms in, 145–46, 288, 289
and fusion development, 105
heterogeneity, lack of, 229, 231
historical optimism, 1–4
humanitarian reasons for friendship of, 211–12
informational websites, 263
international students in, 272
interpretation of the Constitution, 139
Peace Dividend, 230
poverty threshold, 133
and red hotline with Soviet Union, 257
Tocqueville on, 161–62
urban populations and land ownership, 178–79
U.S. Department of Agriculture, 211
utility, degrees of, 95–98, 101, 128, 237

V

vaccines and vaccinations, 43, 61–63, 66–67, 68, 71, 85, 121–22
variolation, 65–66
Venter, Craig, 198
vitamin A deficiency (VAD), 196–97
vitamin formula, custom, 76
voice from thoughts, 90
Volvo factory, 186, 188

W

WALL-E path, 150–51
war, end of
casualties and, 231, 277
communication and information factors, 257–70
difficulties of ending war, 232–35
dream of ending war, 230

economic factors, 235–47
overview, 216–17, 225, 235, 247, 270–78
political factors, 247–57
possibility of ending war, 227–32
reasons for ending war, 225–27
war vs. civilization, 217–25, 276–77
Washington, George, 70
wealth
consumption of, 143–46
creation of, 94, 124–25, 156–57
history of poverty and, 132–43, 144–45
housing, 129–30
prosperity, 117–18, 124–25, 237–38, 240
reallocation of, 96
redistribution of, 135, 136–37, 138, 211, 286
and technology, 101–2, 128, 132, 145–46, 285–86
and trade, 94–99
See also trade
Wealth of Nations, The (Smith), 100–101
websites
Ben & Jerry's Ice Cream, 213
Chipotle, 212–13
as force for peace, 258–59
I Have A Dream Foundation, 152
MSNBC.com, 84
and trade, 98
of U.S. government, 263
Wolfram Alpha, 42
Welcome to the Genome (DeSalle and Yudell), 84–85
welfare state, 135, 138, 140–42, 163–64, 165
Wellbutrin (bupropion hydrochloride), 72
"What I Have Learned" (O'Reilly), 143
Whitney, Eli, 110

"Why Men Love War" (Broyles), 234–35
Wikipedia, 38, 182, 183
"Will the Soviet Union Survive Until 1984?" (Amalrik), 12
wisdom, 32, 33, 34, 40, 50–52, 54
Wolfram Alpha website, 42
workhouses, 165
World Bank on globalization, 240
world government, 229
World Hunger (Lappé, Collins, and Rosset), 170–71
World Is Flat, The (Friedman), 238
world trade increase, 243–44
world wars from a wrong turn, 29–30, 250

Y

Yelp, 98
"You Don't Know What to Ask Problem, The," 32, 34
YouTube, 25–26, 274–75
Yudell, Michael, 84–85

Z

Zimbabwe, 136–37